Vivien Leigh

Manchester University Press

Vivien Leigh

Actress and icon

Edited by

KATE DORNEY AND
MAGGIE B. GALE

Manchester University Press

Published by Manchester University Press
Altrincham Street, Manchester M1 7JA

www.manchesteruniversitypress.co.uk

In association with the Victoria and Albert Museum

British Library Cataloguing-in-Publication Data
A catalogue record for this book is available from the British Library

ISBN   978 1 5261 2508 8   paperback

First published 2018

Typeset
by Toppan Best-set Premedia Limited
Printed in Great Britain
by TJ International Ltd, Padstow

Contents

List of illustrations

Plates

Figures

Every effort has been made to obtain permission to reproduce copyright material, and the publisher will be pleased to be informed of any errors and omissions for correction in future editions.

Notes on contributors

Kendra Bean is a historian and owner of the blog www.vivandlarry.com. Her writing on Vivien Leigh and classic film has been published by i-5 Publishing, the BFI, the National Portrait Gallery (London), Cohen Films and *Bright Lights Film Journal*. She is also the author of *Vivien Leigh: An Intimate Portrait* (Running Press, 2013) and is currently working on an illustrated biography of the actress Ava Gardner. Kendra lives with her partner Robbie and cat Lulu in London, where in addition to writing about old movies she is training to be a museum curator.

Lucy Bolton is Senior Lecturer in Film Studies at Queen Mary University of London. She is the author of *Film and Female Consciousness: Irigaray, Cinema and Thinking Women* (Palgrave Macmillan 2011, paperback 2015), and of many articles and book chapters on film philosophy and on stardom. She has recently co-edited a collection of essays called *Lasting Stars: Images that Fade and Personas the Endure* (Palgrave Macmillan, 2016), and guest edited a special issue of *Film, Fashion and Consumption* on the enduring cultural iconicity of Marilyn Monroe. Her current research is for a monograph on cinema and the philosophy of Iris Murdoch.

Susanna Brown is Curator of Photographs at the Victoria & Albert Museum, London. She studied at Wimbledon School of Art, Bristol University and the Courtauld Institute, and previously worked at the National Portrait Gallery, London. Susanna has a research interest in fashion photography, portraiture, and the changing status of photographs within museums. Her V&A publications include *Horst: Photographer of Style* (V&A, 2014); *Horst Highlights* (V&A, 2014) and *Queen Elizabeth II: Portraits by Cecil Beaton* (V&A, 2011), and she has contributed essays to *Cecil Beaton: Portraits* (Pera Museum, 2015); *Alexander McQueen* (V&A, 2014) and *Photography: The Whole Story* (Thames & Hudson, 2012). She curates international touring exhibitions, most recently *Selling Dreams: One Hundred Years of Fashion Photography* and *Horst: Photographer of Style*, as well as displays on the history of photography for the Museum's permanent photographs galleries. Susanna contributes to journals and magazines such as *The British Journal of Photography* and *Photography & Culture*, lectures at Newcastle University, London College of Communication and Sotheby's Institute, and has been an invited juror and reviewer at festivals including Fotofest, Houston, Brighton Photo Fringe and Hyères Festival International de Mode et de Photographie.

Kate Dorney is Senior Lecturer in Modern and Contemporary Performance at the University of Manchester. She was Senior Curator of Modern and Contemporary Performance for the Theatre and Performance Department of the Victoria and Albert Museum from 2005–2015. She is co-editor of the series *Women, Theatre and Performance*, for Manchester University Press with Maggie B. Gale and co-editor of *Studies in Theatre and Performance*, Routledge. She has published widely in the area of modern and contemporary theatre and performance curation and documentation. Recent publications include *Played in Britain: Modern Theatre in 100 Plays* (Bloomsbury, 2012); *The Changing Language of Modern English Drama 1945–2005* (Palgrave Macmillan, 2009) and *The Glory of the Garden: English Regional Theatre and the Arts Council 1980 to 2009*, co-edited with Ros Merkin (Cambridge Scholars Press, 2010).

Maggie B. Gale is Professor and Chair of Drama at the University of Manchester. She is a co-editor of *Contemporary Theatre Review*, and with Kate Dorney, of the series *Women, Theatre and Performance*, and with Maria Delgado and Peter Lichtenfels, of *Theatre: Theory – Practice – Performance* (both for Manchester University Press). She has written and co-edited numerous books including the *Routledge Drama Anthology: from Modernism to Contemporary Performance* (Routledge, 2016); *Plays and Performance Texts by Women 1880–1930* (Manchester University Press, 2012) and *Auto/Biography and Identity: Women, Theatre and Performance* (Manchester University Press, 2004); and with John Stokes *The Cambridge Companion to the Actress* (Cambridge University Press, 2007), and Clive Barker, *British Theatre Between the Wars 1918–1939* (Cambridge University Press, 2000/2007). Maggie is author of *West End Women: Women on the London Stage 1918–1962* (Routledge, 1996) and *J. B. Priestley: Routledge Modern and Contemporary Dramatists* (Routledge, 2008). She is currently a Leverhulme Major Research

Fellow completing a monograph, *A Social History of British Performance Cultures 1900–1939: Citizenship, Surveillance and the Body* (forthcoming Routledge, 2019).

Keith Lodwick is curator of Theatre and Screen Arts at the V&A's Department of Theatre & Performance and has contributed to numerous publications including *Diaghilev and the Golden Age of the Ballet Russes* (V&A, 2010), *Oliver Messel: In the Theatre of Design* (Rizzoli, 2011), *Hollywood Costume* (V&A, London, 2012), *Alexander McQueen: Savage Beauty* (V&A, 2015) and *Vivien Leigh: Actress and Icon* (Manchester University Press, 2018). He was the assistant curator for the V&A's major 2012 exhibition and international tour *Hollywood Costume*, which examined 100 years of costume design for film and is one of the most successful exhibitions in the museum's history. Keith is also the curator of the touring exhibition *Vivien Leigh: Public Faces, Private Lives*, drawn from the Vivien Leigh Archive, which the V&A acquired in 2013. Before joining the curatorial department of the V&A in 2007, Keith trained as a set and costume designer at Royal Central School of Speech and Drama, London. His theatre design work has been exhibited nationally and his stage adaptation and design for Angela Carter's *The Bloody Chamber* won a Herald Angel Award at the Edinburgh Festival (1997).

Arnaud Duprat de Montero is a lecturer at Université Rennes 2, and a former pupil of the CLCF (Conservatoire Libre du Cinéma Français). His research is centred on Luis Buñuel's final films and, in terms of actor studies, on Isabelle Adjani and the partnership between Carlos Saura and Geraldine Chaplin. He has published articles concerning Luis Buñuel, Jean-Claude Carrière, Raúl Ruiz, Pedro Almodóvar, Carlos Saura, Víctor Erice, Jaime Rosales, Isabelle Adjani, Geraldine Chaplin, Ava Gardner and Vivien Leigh. He collaborated in the 2012 Studiocanal release of the Blu-ray edition of *Cet obscur objet du désir* (Luis Buñuel, 1977) in France and Germany, and has published two books: *Le dernier Buñuel* (Presses Universitaires de Rennes, coll. 'Le Spectaculaire', 2011) and *Isabelle Adjani, un mythe de l'incarnation* (Le bord de l'eau, coll. 'Ciné-mythologies', 2013). He edited with Eva Tilly the book *Corps et territoire, arts et littérature à travers l'Europe et l'Amérique* (Presses Universitaires de Rennes, coll. 'Des sociétés', 2014).

Hollie Price is a Postdoctoral Research Fellow in the School of Advanced Study, University of London. As part of the AHRC-funded project, 'A Publishing and Communications History of the Ministry of Information (MoI)', she is researching the MoI's films and other visual outputs. She also teaches in the Film Studies department at Queen Mary, University of London, where she completed her PhD on the depiction of domestic life in British 1940s film in 2015. Her recent publications include 'A "Somewhat Homely" Stardom: Michael Denison, Dulcie Gray and Refurnishing Post-War Domestic Modernity', *Journal of British Cinema and Television* 12: 1 (January 2015) and 'Furnishing the Living Room in Film Noir: Disillusion and the Armchair' in *Spaces of the Cinematic Home: Behind the Screen Door*, ed. Eleanor Andrews, Stella Hockenhull and Fran Pheasant-Kelly (Routledge, 2015).

John Stokes is Emeritus Professor of Modern British Literature at King's College, London and Honorary Professor of English and Drama at the University of Nottingham. His publications include *The French Actress and her English Audience* (Cambridge University Press, 2005), and *The Cambridge Companion to the Actress* (Cambridge University Press, 2007), co-edited with Maggie B. Gale. He has recently co-edited, with Mark W. Turner, two volumes on Oscar Wilde for the Oxford English Texts edition of *The Complete Works of Oscar Wilde: Volumes VI and VII, Journalism* I & II (Oxford University Press, 2013).

Acknowledgements

We would like to thank former colleagues at the Victoria & Albert Museum, London, particularly Tom Windross, Keith Lodwick, Brian Peters and Claire Hudson for their support in setting up this project. We thank all the estates and copyright holders kind enough to grant permissions: Harvard Theatre Collections with special thanks to Dale Stinchcomb, The Kobal Collection, The National Portrait Gallery, the estate of Cecil Beaton, the Farrington family (the estate of Vivien Leigh), The British Library, the Victoria & Albert Museum, the University of Manchester and Matthew Frost at Manchester University Press for his enthusiasm for the project. Thanks to our anonymous readers and to our partners, Richard Lee and Jenny Hughes.

PART I

Re-reading Vivien Leigh

Vivien Leigh, actress and icon: introduction

Kate Dorney and Maggie B. Gale

This volume of essays has been generated as a response to the Victoria and Albert Museum's 2013 acquisition of twentieth-century actress Vivien Leigh's personal archive made up of, amongst other things: letters, scripts, photographs, personal documents, bills, speeches, appointment diaries, lists of luggage contents for tours and even lists of domestic items for repair. Among the tasks this introductory chapter undertakes is to outline the ways in which the archive has been constructed – which elements were put together by Leigh's mother and daughter, how the archive was and has since been arranged – and what the constructed nature of this evidence might tell us about the curation of Leigh's life and legacy.[1] Many of the essays in this volume have made use of materials from the archive, as well as drawing on other related collections such as the Laurence Olivier archive at the British Library and the Jack Merivale papers at the British Film Institute. These materials have been used in combination with contemporary approaches to theatre historiography, feminist biography and screen and celebrity studies with the specific aim of providing new readings of Leigh as an actress and public figure.

Vivien Leigh: Actress and Icon explores the frameworks within which Leigh's work has been analysed to date. We are interested in how she, and others, shaped and projected her public persona, and constructions of her personal and domestic life, as well as looking at the ways in which she approached the craft of acting for stage and screen. One of the few mid twentieth-century actresses who successfully and serially moved between stage and screen, picking up two Oscars and a Tony award on her way, Leigh's work deserves closer attention than it has hitherto received. Contributors draw on, and will hopefully add to, the growing body of work in feminist theatre historiography recovering and reconsidering the role of women in performance histories more generally. In doing so we are following Tracy C. Davis's suggestion that to create a feminist theatre historiography we must connect 'the woman to the work and the work with the world at large' (Davis, 1989: 66–69). Davis's chapter appeared a year after the last major biography of Leigh was published, a biography, like so many other treatments of Leigh, in which the focus on the work was somewhat lost among the discussions of her personal life. Celebrity always assumes its subjects are atypical in the world rather than formed by it, and extant accounts of Leigh are no exception. Our aim in this volume is to both interrogate and thicken those accounts.

Vivien Leigh: a brief biography

Born in India in 1913, the daughter of affluent British middle-class and somewhat distant parents, Vivien Leigh was deposited at a Catholic boarding school in Roehampton at the age of 7. She was visited on average once every year by her mother Gertrude, invariably accompanied by Tommy, their 'family friend' (John Lambert Thomson), rather than Leigh's father Ernest, who remained a distant figure in her life (Vickers, 1990 [1988]: 13).[2] After training briefly at RADA, married and a mother at 20, with less than half a dozen years of stage and film work under her belt, Leigh shot to fame as Scarlett O'Hara in David O. Selznick's 1939 *Gone With The Wind*, winning an Oscar and a generation of avid fans globally, but especially in the US and at home in the UK.[3]

As her career progressed, and despite her 'star' status as a film actress, she was more frequently noted for the supposed inadequacies of her talent as a stage performer in comparison to her second husband Laurence Olivier. While fans sometimes questioned her choice of roles – and wrote to her concerned that she was doing herself a disservice by taking on professional engagements with socially 'deviant' or uncomfortably sexual roles such as Blanche DuBois – they rarely critiqued her playing of such roles with the vitriol of some professional critics.[4] For the new *enfant terrible* of British theatre criticism in the 1950s, Kenneth Tynan – whose middle name of 'Peacock' rather suited his style of theatre criticism and the manner in which he inserted himself into the theatre clique he so disapproved of – Olivier was the theatrical genius, and Leigh the demanding, and largely incapable, beauty, riding on the wave of her husband's success and benefitting from his superior knowledge of stage technique. In reality, Leigh was the 'star' commodity in the deeply patriarchal, financially driven world of film, while Olivier struggled to win the same level of acclaim and global fan base from his film work until much later in his career. Leigh was also 'out of time' as an actress, moving into film not long after 'talkies' replaced silent movies and after a relatively short stage career. She battled with Selznick's studio over parts, refusing to leave England during the Second World War (1939–1945), and became embroiled in legal battles over her employment choices. Selznick wanted his own way and so did she: their mutually beneficial position, however, was usually to maintain a harmonious public profile.[5] Of her generation of actresses, she was unusual in her insistence on continuing and building her stage career after Hollywood success: she continued to move between stage and screen throughout her career, from her early 20s to her early 50s. While other actors such as Bette Davis and David Niven famously fell out with their studios over roles and being contracted out to other studios, Leigh usually won her battles over casting. Although she was sometimes disappointed not to be cast opposite Olivier on screen – for example in *Rebecca*, *Wuthering Heights* and *Henry V* – she rarely took on screen roles she thought unsuitable.[6] This meant, however, that for most of the 1940s she was embroiled in battles with the studios; as Charles Drazin points out, it was largely a contract that 'governed Vivien Leigh's career' (Drazin, 2011 [2002]: 262).

Professional marriage: a business affair

Her private and professional relationship with Olivier saw them dubbed as 'theatre royalty' and they certainly seem to have been as frequently photographed, interviewed and written about as the Queen and Prince Philip. The Oliviers had something to sell: films, stage performances, good causes, goods (through their advertising contracts), so living their lives in public was part of the deal. They were *professional* partners as well as domestic ones: a perspective on their relationship that is often lost in the retelling of the love affair that burned out. That narrative depicts them gradually falling out of love because of Leigh's health issues, which needed active consideration and prevented Olivier from focusing on his own career, and so he drifted away. They had become lovers in the mid to late 1930s, while still married to Jill Esmond and Leigh Holman respectively. Their colleagues all knew they were having an affair – Leigh had surprisingly followed Olivier and Esmond on a holiday to Capri as early as 1936.[7] During her year working on *Gone With The Wind* they sent each other cryptic, romantic telegrams using pseudonyms and writing short but ardent messages.[8] Their divorces and subsequent marriage were carefully staged, with studio intervention: divorce was still socially outlawed and only available to a minority, and adultery was frowned upon. Not long after their marriage and return to England, they were separated by war, hampered by Leigh's illness and beholden to the implications of both of their demanding ambitions for stage work.

Numerous biographers frame their relationship almost entirely in terms of Leigh being beholden to Olivier's professional superiority as an actor (see Jesse Lasky Jr and Pat Silver, 1978). Some of the more 'racy' biographers suggest that Olivier's bisexuality drove them apart or that Leigh herself was promiscuous (see Porter and Moseley, 2011). Their film partnership ended early in the 1940s: she was under contract to Selznick but wanted to be near Olivier – now conscripted – in Europe, and Korda, to whom Leigh was 'lent' by Selznick's studio, didn't cast them together after *That Hamilton Woman* (1941). Somehow they had less marketability as a film partnership than Leigh would have liked. It is clear that as the 'golden couple' of theatre their personal relationship was fading at the point at which their professional drawing power was at its height in theatre. Olivier claims Leigh told him she no longer loved him as early as 1948 (Olivier, 1982: 131), but they did not divorce until 1960: he had numerous affairs, and opinion is varied as to how much Leigh indulged in extra marital activity. Either way, their professional cachet as a couple far outlived, it would seem, a consistently intimate marital connection.

Extant biographies: re-inscribing Vivien Leigh

> So much has been written about Vivien already and so much of it dwells on the so-called 'dark' side of her life that I felt it was time there was some light. I never experienced the 'dark' side of her – except for a glimpse on one or two occasions – and I see no reason why we should continue to concentrate on what, in her case, was a condition caused by actual physical illness. (McBean, 1989: 10)

Leigh's friend and collaborator Angus McBean's response to accounts of the 'dark' side of Leigh was to produce *Vivien Leigh: A Love Affair in Camera*, a fond account of one of his favourite subjects beautifully illustrated by his own photographs. The book was not his first foray into defending Leigh's reputation. A decade earlier he wrote to the *Observer* to express his shock at an article in their magazine publicising Anne Edwards 'unnecessary, unpleasant and, except at the most superficial level, deeply untruthful book'.[9] He was responding to the magazine's feature on Edward's 1977 biography described as revealing

> quite another Vivien Leigh: a wild screaming vixen who suddenly lashed out at people with obscenities, kicks and punches: even at Larry, the man she loved most in the world. The ultra-fastidious convent-trained paragon

of deportment turned into a promiscuous slut, hungry for one-night stands with working class pick-ups. The masterful controlled beauty – rebuked by critics for her 'artshop daintiness' – would suddenly begin to strip off in public, or try to throw herself out of trains and aircrafts. The Gainsborough Lady was afraid of going mad.[10]

As this offensively sensationalist summary suggests, the book was very different to the respectful volumes that had preceded it and marked the beginning of establishing a new narrative of Leigh. Gwen Robyns's *Light of a Star* (Robyns, 1968) and Alan Dent's *Vivien Leigh: A Bouquet* (Dent, 1969) had painted a picture of an ethereal beauty who worked too hard and consequently suffered from nerves, but was also an intelligent woman with a lightning sense of humour. Dent – journalist, scriptwriter and old friend – drew on answers to a 'set of six questions to a hundred or so of the actress' best friends and colleagues' to outline her public and private faces and then used his experience as a theatre and film critic to consider her as a stage and screen actress. The book is the source of many anecdotes about Leigh that appear in subsequent accounts, notably the contributions from Oswald Frewen, a close friend of Leigh and her first husband. Dent's biography is, as its title suggests, a mixed affair combining unpublished testimony with fillers from critics. He readily admits in the introduction that although he loved her as a friend he was less enthusiastic about her professional accomplishments, and his questions reflect this ambivalence:

1. When did you first see or meet Vivien, and what was your immediate first impression?
2. What were the qualities you most admired in her personality?
3. Did you have any serious quarrels or misunderstandings?
4. How highly did you rate her as an actress (a) for the stage and (b) for the screen?
5. Where would you place her among the most beautiful women of her time?
6. Have you any anecdote or story about her? Or anything else to say of her?

(Dent, 1969: 12)

There are positive responses from Alfred Lunt (who with his wife Lynn Fontanne were the American equivalent of the Oliviers), Michael Redgrave and Rachel Kempson, Athene Seyler, Terence Rattigan, Nöel Coward, Isabel Jeans and George Cukor among others. All comment on her star quality and continual efforts to improve her acting. Dent, a journalist like Robyns, also included much cooler accounts from Anthony Quayle and Kenneth More who disapproved of her ambition and self-assurance.

Edwards's book is the start of a series in which each biographer devotes as much space to Olivier as they do to Leigh. The *Observer Magazine* notes that,

> to write this workmanlike, sympathetic but superficial biography she has listened to many people very close to Vivien Leigh. Ms Edwards did not get to see Sir Laurence; and she never met Vivien. It shows. Still, her book is indispensable to an understanding of the Olivier myth.[11]

Ten years after her death, Leigh was already subsumed into the Olivier myth. This was compounded by Garry O'Connor's *Darling of the Gods: One Year in the Lives of Laurence and Olivier* (1984), in which Leigh and Olivier assumed their now familiar and un-nuanced roles. In 1987, to coincide with the twentieth anniversary of Leigh's death, *Evening Standard* film critic Alexander Walker released *Vivien: A Life of Vivien Leigh*. His book paints a picture of a couple for whom the strain of juggling joint and separate careers is added to by the need to make money and maintain a golden image. What emerges is a suggestion that Leigh was a liability after her public breakdown in 1953, that she had to be 'carried' by Olivier, and this becomes embedded in the myth of their imbalanced relationship.

Cecil Beaton's biographer Hugo Vickers had full access to family papers and, as reviewers noted, more sympathy for Leigh. Rachel Billington reviewing his book in 1988 suggests he,

> makes less of a tragedy of Vivien Leigh's life – the drinking, the hopeless lack of discipline – than other biographers. He is at pains to establish her education and culture and her practical kindness. He builds up this image through concentrating on her background and her long-lasting friendships. However, he does seem to have achieved this at the expense of a true understanding of her manic urge towards self-destruction [...] Vickers is not keen to show his beautiful and brilliant heroine as a neurotic victim. Yet, finally that is exactly how she appears: victim to a beauty that was always just a bit more evident than her talent.[12]

It is difficult to ignore the underlying agenda that Billington brings to her assessment of this work. Obviously, for her, Vickers's biography is not enough to undo the popular myth – Vivien Leigh as a tragic but beautiful victim – in which she, it would appear, is a strong believer. Kendra Bean's celebration of Leigh marking the centenary of her birth is the first to make use of the Laurence Olivier archive at the British Library, noting:

> This previously untapped treasure trove of archival material, which includes everything from personal correspondence between Vivien and Olivier to film contracts, director's notes, interview transcripts, and legal and medical records, sheds new light on these two topics [her mental illness and personal and professional relationship with Olivier]. (Bean, 2013: 14)

Written by a devoted fan without an agenda of negativity, Bean uses the Olivier archive with the express purpose of accruing more evidence of Leigh's professional practice: to open out more dimensions for our readings of her life and work.

Perspectives on Leigh

There are a number of books on Vivien Leigh which collate anecdotes and recollections of her as a colleague and friend or trace her career as a film star and her working and domestic relationship with Laurence Olivier; but there are none which assess the different aspects of Leigh's life and career from a critical perspective. While many biographers approach Leigh with the clear intention of talking about her career, they inevitably end up focusing on her work and personal life as if the two are inevitably the same thing rather than two co-dependent 'lives' entwined. Thus John Russell Taylor, for whom there 'never was, and never has been since, anyone remotely like her on the British stage or the English speaking screen', suggests that the revelations about her mental health should make 'little or no difference to our evaluation of her professional career' (Russell Taylor, 1984: 10). He then, however, moves on to describe her illness as 'disruptive forces in her psyche', which presented some 'cost to her abilities as an actress' (ibid: 81). To some extent he too is caught up in the predicament shared by other critics of Leigh's career: they have to find a balance between being drawn to anecdotes about her ascribed, or predetermined, celebrity, as compared with analysing the evidence of her achieved celebrity. Leigh had a great deal of ascribed celebrity: a form of celebrity status which is less to do with achievement and more to do with existing assets or assigned roles. So her ascribed celebrity was constructed around her dazzling beauty, the publicity generated from her being cast in high-profile screen roles – just being *cast* as Scarlett O'Hara ascribes one celebrity status – and, of course, by her marriage to Olivier. Her *achieved* celebrity is never as clear cut. She can't just be a fabulous stage and screen actress, a box-office draw and have an extraordinary ability to play a range of challenging roles over a career spanning more than thirty years. Instead she has to be 'mad' in performance because she is 'mad' in life, a tragic beauty plagued by a fatal flaw – either ambition or her illness. Thus her achieved celebrity is not just shaped by her professional accomplishments, but also by her social notoriety. McBean and Russell Taylor avoid this trope as far as possible, but it is often lurking in the background (see McBean, 1989). In part this is a problem with historiographical approaches to the analysis of performing women's professional lives more generally: the domestic often ends up being foregrounded over the professional and questions of the nuanced quality of labour. With Leigh this foregrounding has hardened into an established narrative of her life and one can sense that the few who have written about her work in an evaluative or critical mode – Vickers and Bean might be counted among these – have had to persistently attempt to escape this narrative, structured like a three-act play: Act I: early life and rise to fame; Act II: being famous and married to Olivier – one half of the golden couple of theatre; Act III: tragic decline and early death. This constant over-privileging of life over art is a typical part of what Michael Quinn identifies as the quality of 'celebrity':

> Celebrity in its usual variety [...] is not composed of acting technique but of personal information. The first requisite for celebrity is public notoriety, which is only sometimes achieved through acting. In the context of this public identity there then comes to exist a link between performer and audience, quite apart from the dramatic character (or in only an oblique relation to stage figure and character). (Quinn, 1990: 156)

As the archives show, Leigh's connection to her audience was strengthened by their identification with the roles she played and, later, with the struggles she appeared to be having with her health and her marriage. Among the many touching letters written to Leigh and Olivier after news of her breakdown during the filming of *Elephant Walk* in 1953, Sara Dallwin, a 'young drama student' from Rotherham, writes to offer her comfort:

> Oh Miss Leigh, if you knew how much you are loved – not merely admired or envied, but loved. Here, in this industrial Northern town, where the words 'theatre' and 'drama' mean nothing to most people, during your illness your name was on almost every tongue, the tongues of men and women who have seen you only on celluloid.
> This makes everything 'the weariness, the fever and the fret' all worthwhile. For to be loved by thousands, millions of people, not only as an actress, but as a woman, is a blessed thing.[13]

As Kendra Bean's chapter in this volume investigates, Leigh knew what it was to be a fan and responded generously to her own. But the blurring of actress and woman voiced in Dallwin's letter was achieved at some cost. Access to Leigh's veridical or 'true' self, her 'I' as Chris Rojek, following George Herbert Mead, names it, was either limited or carefully stage managed in terms of press coverage during her lifetime (Rojek, 2001: 10). Her 'public' often assumed or treated her 'me' – the constructed self presented to the world – and her 'I' – her 'veridical', true or private self – to be one and the same. Leigh, like many celebrities, is someone for whom both her constructed self and her veridical self have been 'the site of perpetual public excavation' (ibid: 19).

Unlike many actresses and performers whose careers began in the late nineteenth or early twentieth centuries, Leigh left no autobiography and never engaged a biographer. It is ironic that while she may not have had any interest in writing such a volume, her letters, speeches and notes indicate that she would have had a commanding, intelligent and acerbically witty authorial voice as the writer of an autobiography. The construction of her auto/biographic narrative thus far has been created without interventions from Leigh herself: although of course one might argue that in keeping so many of her private and professional papers she was effectively 'self-archiving'. Even though we cannot be certain of her role and intention in the gathering and keeping of such materials, the breadth and depth of extant materials, beyond the usual scrapbooks of reviews and interviews, is extraordinary. Her business-like attitude to life is evidenced through her orderly approach to maintaining correspondence and household administration: letters from and to fans, to her employees, friends and professional acquaintances, lists of the contents of luggage, invitations to exhibitions, lists of instructions for household items to be repaired while she is on tour, of clothes and shoes to be sold and so on.

Her life story has also been heavily framed by the auto/biographies of Olivier, and others who worked with her, or encountered her professionally (see Maggie B. Gale's Chapter 4). Auto/biographical reference to iconic professional collaborations often legitimate the career of the writer or the subject of the biography; while they might provide useful insights they are not 'truths'. Outside of her own archive, and apart from numerous and often unsubstantiated screen and theatre anecdotes, Leigh's own voice is largely absent. In Chapter 2 in this volume, Kate Dorney provides an analysis of Leigh's voice as expressed in letters and interviews and the strategies she employed to stage manage her encounters with the press and, through them, the public. She often charmed interviewers, going out of her way to put them at ease because she had a clear understanding of the importance and the nature of the professional exchange that such encounters signify. While at pains to create a pleasant atmosphere in interviews, there is sometimes a quality of defensiveness in her voice caused, in part, by her sense of needing to steer the questioning or defend herself as an artist. Not dissimilar to other actresses of her era – and some would argue that this approach persists even today – interviews are often framed by questions about how she manages motherhood and work, or about how she manages the pace of her work while maintaining her social life, about how she manages the balance between her beauty and the requirements of a part, and whether she 'is' in fact the parts she plays.

Leigh sought out many of the roles she played, not just Scarlett O'Hara or Blanche DuBois in *A Streetcar Named Desire*. Not only did she design and define her career as much as was possible for a woman of her generation, but she was also meticulous in the method and level of preparation she undertook for both stage and film roles. This narrative does not sit comfortably with the popular image of Leigh as an unstable and fragile beauty, the jilted wife of one of the most renowned actors of the twentieth century. A voracious reader, Leigh had her own views of the construction and function of biography expressed here in her review of a biography of Emma Hamilton whom she played on screen:

> It is no pleasure to me to add that – but I do feel it strongly [...] the scope of this book seems to me to be out of all proportion to Emma's importance. She lived for another 15 years after this book had done with her [...] this biography, you see, tells only the first half of Emma's story, and my chief contention here is that the book should have told the whole story in *half* the number of words. (Dent, 1969: 124–5)

We might make a similar observation here and suggest that in focusing chiefly on Leigh's personal life, we have only half the story. Or, that half the number of words might be devoted to her life and half to her work. The acquisition of Leigh's archive by the V&A in 2013 was the subject of great press and public interest. Purchased from her daughter, Suzanne Farrington, it includes more than 7,000 letters,

Figure 1.1   Vivien Leigh on tour during the Second World War.

postcards and telegrams, over 2,000 photographs and a number of scrapbooks, annotated scripts, appointment diaries and awards. The collection reveals an astonishing range of correspondents and projects with whom, and with which, Leigh was engaged and offers remarkable insights into the film and theatre worlds in which she moved. Equally, the materials offer a very differently nuanced version of the intersections between Leigh's domestic and professional environments during a career that spanned the early 1930s to the late 1960s. Leigh ran her household with military precision instructing secretaries, housekeepers and maids in the management of her homes, clothes, jewellery and artworks as well as keeping up correspondence with friends and hundreds of fans. The authors who had access to this material, or parts of it (Edwards and Vickers), make little use of this information. Instead they have used the correspondence and interviews with friends and colleagues to add weight to the established narrative of Leigh as a determined and ambitious beauty who was professionally opportunistic, chased after a married man from whose professional shadow she could not extract herself, and suffered from an unmanageable illness. In other words she was a tragic beauty and a ruthless operator.

The press release issued by the V&A announcing the acquisition of the archive stressed the variety of Leigh's correspondents – from T.S. Eliot and Winston Churchill through to schoolgirl fans – and the insights the archive offered on productions like *A Streetcar Named Desire*, but very few of the journalists eagerly awaiting the opening of the archive to the public were interested in this.[14] What they wanted to know was what further light the archive might shed the established narrative; on her frequently documented relationship with actor-director Laurence Olivier and on her mental health. Over the next year or so, it became clear that the media were happy with the version of Vivien Leigh that they knew: beautiful and mad, the woman who had risked everything to pursue her career and the man of her dreams. In short, a version of Scarlett O'Hara.

While waiting for the archive to be catalogued and made available, *Mail on Sunday* journalist Chris Hastings marked the centenary of Leigh's birth by publishing an article headlined 'Frankly my dear, you won't be a dame! How Vivien Leigh was snubbed for the ultimate honour ... and why cuckolded husband Laurence Olivier might be to blame'.[15] The article was based around Hastings' discovery in Cabinet Office papers that Leigh had twice been considered for a DBE but deemed only to be worthy of a CBE by the two anonymous reviewers. One suggests: 'Personally I think she is underrated, and see no reason why she should not have a CBE, but certainly not a DBE.': the other declared that although a 'great admirer of her work and acknowledging that, 'she has won great public admiration for the courage with which she has in recent years faced illness [...] I doubt whether she is at present quite what may be called "The Dame Class", e.g. Edith Evans, Sybil Thorndike. I, therefore, venture to express the view that CBE appears to be more appropriate than DBE.'[16] Hastings goes on to suggest that it was her adultery, and, working on a suggestion from Vickers, Olivier's professional jealousy, that were behind the decision. It is depressing, but not entirely surprising that Leigh was not considered to be in the 'Dame Class' in either 1952 or 1954. The actresses she is compared to, Evans and Thorndike, were more than twenty years her senior and had impeccable stage pedigrees untainted by the suspect touch of Hollywood.[17] Of Leigh's close contemporaries, Peggy Ashcroft, Wendy Hiller and Celia Johnson, only Ashcroft received the honour under the age of 40, and she too was very much a classical stage rather than screen actor at the time.[18] Whatever the reasons for the Cabinet Office's decision, it is clear that from the point of view of selling papers, the story is 'Leigh in relation to Olivier'. Once the Vivien Leigh Archive was catalogued and opened to researchers, Hastings was first in the queue to access it and first into press with: 'From Larry with lust ... Olivier's X-rated letters to Vivien Leigh seen for the first time'.[19] Billed as 'a revealing selection of Olivier's correspondence', the focus is once again on Olivier and also on re-inscribing the same narrative of grand passion that ends in Leigh's undignified scramble to keep her prize. The contents of the article were then repeated in articles in the *Guardian* and the *Express* – the old stories, it seems, are still the best.

The archive

Some of the material in the archive clearly forms part of the Suzanne Farrington Papers referred to by Hugo Vickers in his biography, which he described as including the following:

> all the letters that Vivien wrote Leigh Holman between 1932 and 1967, the diaries of Vivien's mother, Gertrude Hartley, from 1920–1972, the letters from friends which Mrs Hartley kept, and the albums of press cuttings and photographs compiled (and frequently annotated) by Mrs Hartley. Amongst these papers were a number of letters written by Vivien to her parents and to her daughter, and similar letters from Laurence Olivier, Leigh Holman, and John Merivale. There were theatre programmes and all the letters of sympathy received by Mrs Hartley at the time of Vivien's death. (Vickers, 1989: xiii–iv)

The V&A collection does not contain Gertrude Hartley's diaries nor letters from Leigh to Holman, her parents – although there are some notes and cards from each of them to Leigh – or her daughter. It is assumed that these, if they still exist, are in private hands. But the letters from Leigh's friends and family are now in the V&A along with letters from Jill Esmond to Olivier and condolence letters to Olivier on Leigh's death, suggesting that when Leigh and Olivier divorced, their papers were never fully separated. This is borne out by the contents of the Olivier archive purchased by the British Library in 2000, which contains letters written by fans to Leigh after her nervous breakdown, and indeed letters from various doctors to Olivier about Leigh's health.[20] His archive has been a valuable source of information on Leigh's relationship with fans, the business details of LOP Productions, of which Leigh was an employee, and in evaluating their collaborative endeavours. The vast majority of the letters relating to her health in the Olivier collection appear to be from fans and medical practitioners who have written directly to Olivier about his wife. There is a sense in which the dutiful curatorship of this correspondence was underpinned by whoever kept them originally needing to display Olivier's role as gatekeeper or carer. Some of the correspondence from medical practitioners is very personal with an odd sense of Leigh's behaviour being meticulously dissected in her, especially now, ghostly absence.

Often actors' archives contain a small proportion of correspondence compared to photographs, press cuttings and annotated scripts. Leigh's archive is light on annotated scripts but rich in letters to and from colleagues and friends discussing every aspect of her life. As the chapters in this volume explore, Leigh was an active collaborator in her public presentation whether it be through costume and clothing, domestic decoration, roles, interviews or interaction with fans, and the letters in the archive demonstrate her wit, intelligence and commitment to her work. The archive also stands as testament to qualities often pointed out by her close friends, qualities that Leigh's sister-in-law Dorothy Holman (sister of her first husband Leigh Holman) noted when commenting on the booklet produced after the memorial event at the University of Southern California:[21]

> The book is very well done [...] what is missing is how clever she was in ordinary life, lovely little meals, just the present you like, the way she paid attention to people she was with, drew them out. No wonder she had hundreds of friends. (Quoted in Vickers, 1988: 360)

Since that book was produced, the clever, funny, considerate woman has receded to be replaced by the accounts we are familiar with today. Our aim with this volume is to try and restore some of the 'ordinary life' qualities that Dorothy Holman identifies. As Holman notes, Leigh was known to be lively, witty and charming – a prolific giver of thoughtful gifts to her friends and those she loved: her archive is full of letters of instruction to buy opulent gifts and letters of thanks from those who received them. She took great care to make sure those around her knew she appreciated them, that they were loved. She was intelligent and sociable: she invested in productions of plays, spoke a number of European languages, was musically trained and could dance well. She read voraciously, and had done so since childhood.[22] Leigh was a knowledgeable art collector and an accomplished interior decorator (see Hollie Price's Chapter 10).[23]

Actresses of an age

One of the pressing realities to which we have returned as editors of this collection, both in the commissioning and editing stages, is that there is very little written about actresses from the mid-twentieth century that attempts to contextualise and critique their professional practices. While there are studies of actresses from the nineteenth century that address technique, development of professional profile, self-fashioning, celebrity, artistic partnerships and so on, this historiographic process has not as yet mapped so well onto academic treatments of actresses and performers working in the twentieth century. Some comprehensive studies of individual actresses have emerged in recent years, such as Margaret Leask's on Lena Ashwell (Leask, 2013) or Helen Grime's work on Gwen Ffrangcon-Davies (Grime, 2013), but these have often struggled with the relationship between individual careers and the critical integration of assessments of historical and contextual materials about women's working lives and the development of professional practice in theatre more generally. There are more studies of popular screen actresses, but these often neglect crossovers with stage work or indeed necessarily focus on actresses whose work happens almost exclusively in film. Some useful recent approaches to reading screen women's' lives offer 'new' readings of the ways in which actresses 'self-fashion' beyond the textually autobiographic: for example Amalie Hastie's work on Colleen Moore and Louise Brookes in *Cupboards of Curiosity* (Hastie, 2007). Biographies tend to focus more on lives – tragic or otherwise – friendship, professional networks and sequences of acting achievements more than they do on questions of labour or ideas of professional practice and, as we suggest here, this is certainly the case with Vivien Leigh's numerous biographies.

Studies of actresses in the twentieth century would be well served, therefore, by a second volume of Tracy C. Davis's *Actresses as Working Women* (Davis, 1991), because of its critical emphasis on the sociohistoric and the economic contexts of actresses' labour and working lives. Similarly, the paucity of contemporary academic analyses of the theatre industry in the first half of the twentieth century more generally has created a vacuum in terms of readings of the commercial sector, and its cross-overs with the more experimental or independent aspects of the industry which have historically received more attention. It should be noted here that both actresses and women playwrights predominantly made a living in the commercial sectors of the theatre industry of the time. In terms of the discipline of theatre and performance studies as a whole, the *works* often receive more attention than the *worker*, the director and the writer more than the performer.

When it comes to different perspectives on actresses working lives in the twentieth century, we have numerous autobiographies which, while some focus on networks, partnership, friendships and domestic life, also offer extraordinary considerations of the working practice of many female performers. The list of these is endless but many offer detailed insights into rehearsal, touring and performance booking, marketing, dealing with the press, with fans, with managements, production as well as offering anecdotes of encounters with professional colleagues and the management of family life (see Gale in Gale and Dorney, 2018). These autobiographic 'histories' provide useful ways into understanding the shifts in practice and labour for working actresses. Many were written at turning points in the professional lives of their authors – Gladys Cooper's *Gladys Cooper* (1931), for example, was written in her early 40s; having reached the end of her management of the Playhouse Theatre in the West End, she was moving towards Broadway and Hollywood.[24] Constance Collier, who became a friend of Vivien Leigh's, wrote *Harlequinade* (1929), in her early 50s, having recovered from a life threatening illness and in the wake of her hit collaborations with Ivor Novello, which began with the stage and screen version of their play *The Rat* (1924 and 1925). It was published just prior to her moving to the US to begin a new career in the film industry. These actresses, however, were from the generation before Leigh. Born in 1913, Leigh's career moved far more swiftly into film – still in its silent era when Cooper and Collier were predominantly working on stage. Her formal training took place primarily at RADA, although it was not extensive, and her other training took place outside of the framework of a stock company or any extended period working with a particular group of actors, with individuals from whom she sought advice. She moved into film within the first ten years of sound and, in a way, developed her stage work in reverse – after having etched a place for herself in the film industry.

While later in her career Leigh took on the more traditional role of theatrical wife and company manager, or investor in productions,[25] her early career maps more onto the fault lines of the historical shifts in practice and employment for actresses in the mid decades of the twentieth century; this slippage impacts on our understanding of her career. Taking Cooper and Collier as oppositional examples, they etched out later careers in film as 'older' women, having both had their early careers equally bound by their market value as stage or 'postcard' beauties. Less known to American audiences from their early work, both had successful careers from middle age onwards in Hollywood – Collier's was as a mixture of sought-after voice-coach and playing niche roles as the older woman. Cooper also returned to stage work in the UK in her 60s and 70s. Others of their generation, such as Irene Vanbrugh and Sybil Thorndike, for example, did not make such an easy or successful relocation into film.

Leigh's high-profile screen career from the late 1930s was originally composed around two key film producers – Selznick and Alexander Korda – and unusually for an actress in this position, she was to some extent able to use the currency created by her playing of Scarlett O'Hara. Despite the critical hounding from Tynan (see Maggie B. Gale's Chapter 3 and John Stokes' Chapter 4 in this volume), stage productions in which Leigh starred usually did extremely good box office both in the UK and the US: she chose her parts with care, often taking roles she found technically challenging. Her illnesses created a hiatus in her career, as motherhood might have done for other actresses, and the momentum created by her success as Scarlett was punctuated by the Second World War, as were the careers of other actresses of her generation who stayed in the UK. However, Leigh tried to negotiate the type-casting of which she might have become a victim in her 40s, overly conscious of her ageing perhaps because so much had been made of the outshining of her talent by her beauty. When we see photographs of her from the 1950s, after her breakdown and her further bouts of tuberculosis, it is clear that her health conditions and the ensuing medical treatments have aged her prematurely, even taking into account the fact that the appearance of youthfulness was often undermined by the ways in which women beyond 40 were fashioned and photographed compared to today. There were not distinctive fashions for women in mid life: the same clothes might be worn by women from the upper-middle classes in their 40s through to old age. Generally speaking, it was less easy for women in their 40s who had made their names in film rather than on stage, to find 'new' careers beyond being ingénue or lead romantic heroine once they hit middle-age: a frequent complaint of our own contemporary actresses, older women in the mid-twentieth century were not as easily marketable on screen and age was more discernible on screen than on stage.

Some of the actresses of the era in which Leigh was working have left, often in autobiographic form, frequently anecdotally, the kinds of articulations of professional experience and even theoretical and practical advice on their art and forms of labour as actors. Leigh's ideas on acting, however, are woven throughout her interviews and correspondence as opposed to being written down in one place, as Kate Dorney (Chapter 2) and John Stokes (Chapter 4) explore in this volume. The Leigh archive at the V&A testifies to the manner in which her questions and ideas – about performing, about the many scripts she read and rejected, about her assessments of audience responses – developed and deepened alongside her career. In her correspondence with directors – George Cukor, Glen Byam Shaw, Peter Brook, Elia Kazan – and with actors and writers – Nöel Coward, John Gielgud, Ralph and Meriel (Mu) Richardson – and with fans, she explores repeatedly over the years what works, what doesn't and why, on both stage and screen.

Conclusion: 'Riding the crests of waves with grace and skill'

In Dent's *Vivien Leigh: A Bouquet,* actor Brian Aherne gives a wonderful summary of the way in which many of her friends and colleagues viewed Leigh:

> we should not grieve for Vivien. As I came into the University this evening, I saw a young man taking a surfboard from a car, and the thought came to me that Vivien had ridden all through life like a brilliant surfrider. All of us who knew her had watched, spellbound, while she rode the crests of the greatest waves with grace and skill, and then, when often happened, she fell off and then disappeared from sight we shook our heads sorrowfully. 'Poor Viv' we said 'She's gone this time!' but no – even as we turned to look, there she was, up again in the sunshine, riding another great comber, as we gasped with astonishment, admiration and relief. (Dent, 1969: 52)

Without wishing to over-extend the metaphor, our intention as commissioning editors has been to try and bring Vivien Leigh 'up again in the sunshine': questioning and challenging the established narrative and inscribing her in a feminist theatre history. Our goal is not to rewrite history and to canonise Leigh in the process, but to look again at the woman in relation to her professional world. To analyse her work on stage and screen, her collaborations with designers and photographers, her fans and her own artistic work with the interiors she created, within which to live and to accommodate and nurture her many and long-lived friendships with her professional colleagues.

The chapters in this volume have been divided into three sections. The first, Re-reading Vivien Leigh, includes two chapters which unpack the complex relationships between our understandings of Leigh's private and public persona, the construction of her mediated self and her issues with two health conditions which impacted on her work, or at least became part of the rhythm and practice of her working life. In Part II, 'The actress at work', John Stokes (Chapter 4), Lucy Bolton (Chapter 5) and Arnaud Duprat De Montero (Chapter 6), consider Leigh in performance, not just in terms of the reception of her work, but also in terms of her collaborative qualities as a performer. She had continuous working relationships with directors on stage and screen, as well as an impressive range of roles, especially in Shakespeare and in comedy, in addition to her iconic playing of Scarlett O'Hara and Blanche DuBois. Bolton suggests the roles played by Leigh on screen as epitomising a chronology of age and maturity. Stokes and Duprat de Montero assess her work from the perspective of reception: the latter focuses on her, as yet unconsidered, work with French directors, and on her particular reception as an actress and artist with French audiences. In Part III: Constructed identities, Susanna Brown (Chapter 9) and Keith Lodwick (Chapter 8), both curators based at the V&A, navigate us through and around Leigh's relationships with portrait photographers and costume designers in terms of collaboration and self-fashioning. Film scholar Hollie Price theorises the ways in which Vivien Leigh's feel for interior design, her collecting of paintings and antiques, afforded the creation of, sometimes, lavish interiors which were almost theatrical in their composition (Chapter 10). While film scholar and seasoned Vivien Leigh fan Kendra Bean's Chapter 7 takes us on a personal journey into the particular world of fandom that surrounds Leigh's work and life. Her approach operates as a dismissive to the fact that, as her *Guardian* obituary suggests:

> There was division among critics about whether or not Vivien Leigh could be called a 'great' actress. She often chose to play in an emotional undertone where others had preferred something more electric. In doing so, however, she impressed herself and her 'star quality' on playgoers who never shared the critics doubts, and at any time after 1945 her name alone could fill a theatre.[26]

Our hope here is that this volume goes some way towards re-viewing and re-appraising Vivien Leigh as the quote above demands, and that in doing so it opens out her work and, by implication, possible approaches to the work of other actresses from the twentieth century to a new generation of scholars, critics and enthusiasts.

Notes

1 This book is not the only outcome of the acquisition. The V&A mounted a number of events shortly after acquiring the archive and launched a touring

exhibition, *Vivien Leigh: Public Faces; Private Lives*, curated by Keith Lodwick in November 2015.

2 In the Vivien Leigh Archive, there are very few letters to or from her father Ernest Hartley, who when the family returned to England lived separately from Gertrude Hartley, Vivien's mother.

3 The film's global release was later – (see Arnaud De Montero's Chapter 6 in this volume).

4 There are numerous letters from fans expressing their opinions about the parts she has chosen, and indeed assessments of her performances: Leigh often answered this with barbed tact. One Mrs Watts, who had written to complain of her dislike, on moral grounds, of *A Streetcar Named Desire* on its pre-London tour in Manchester in 1949, received a polite but firm reply from Leigh suggesting that because of the size of the theatre 'crudities are always more apt to survive than subtleties ...'. Vivien Leigh Archive THM 433/3 'Other Correspondence'.

5 Letters from Joynson-Hicks and Co. to Olivier's lawyers between 21 September 1945 and 9 October 1945 – at the end of the Second World War – suggest Selznick wanted to end one such legal dispute in case of poor publicity while Leigh was suffering with TB. Vivien Leigh Archive, THM/433/3.

6 Correspondence in the Laurence Olivier Archive suggests that Leigh spent a great deal of time researching possible projects and roles, especially through Vivien Leigh Productions, a subsidiary of Laurence Olivier Productions (LOP) in the 1950s.

7 Jill Esmond (1908–1990) was the daughter of actor manager and playwright H.V. Esmond and actress and activist Eva Moore: Olivier had become part of an emerging theatrical dynasty through marriage. Her son, Olivier's first child Tarquin (b. 1936), suggests that Jill Esmond was 'ruined [...] for serious relationships with men', and that certainly by the 1950s she 'had become bisexual: anything for company' (Tarquin Olivier, 2012: 24).

8 Telegrams sent to Vivien Leigh as Mary Holman during the filming of *Gone With The Wind* opened variously with phrases such as 'Dear Little grey Squirrel'; 'Dear Little Herring'; 'Wee Spider' with comments such as 'Naughty, Keep your tail brushed' or 'A stout of heart little pussling, keep ears up and whiskers bristling my love washing your face'. In the early war years Olivier signed himself her 'most loving ... hysterical boy', Vivien Leigh Archive, Correspondence from Laurence Olivier to Vivien Leigh, THM/433/1.

9 'The Legend of Leigh', *Observer*, 14 August 1977, Vivien Leigh Biographical File, V&A.

10 'The Private Hell of a Golden Couple', *Observer Magazine*, 31 July 1977, 26, Vivien Leigh Biographical File, V&A.

11 Ibid, p. 27.

12 Rachel Billington, 'Beauty and the Manic Beast', *Financial Times*, 29 October 1988, Vivien Leigh Biographical File, V&A.

13 Sara Dallwin, to Vivien Leigh, 22 March 1953, Laurence Olivier Archive, Add MS 80634.

14 http://www.vam.ac.uk/__data/assets/pdf_file/0003/236217/Vivien_Leigh_acquisition_press_release.pdf, accessed 23 August 2016.

15 Chris Hastings, 'Frankly My Dear, You Won't be a Dame!', *Mail on Sunday*, 22 March 2013.

16 Ibid.

17 Edith Evans (1888–1976) was awarded a DBE in 1946 at the age of 58. Sybil Thorndike (1882–1976) was awarded a DBE in 1931 at the age of 49.

18 Peggy Ashcroft (1907–1991) was awarded a DBE in 1956 aged 49; Wendy Hiller (1912–2003) in 1975 aged 63 and Celia Johnson (1908–1982) in 1981 aged 73.

19 Chris Hastings, 'From Larry with Lust', *Mail on Sunday*, 1 February 2015.

20 Olivier Archive, British Library Add MS 79766-80750.

21 Alan Dent explains that the event, at the University of California in the summer of 1968, was set up as a 'Symposium' in celebration of Leigh's life and work (Dent, 1969: 12). His biography is in large part built on his correspondence with her colleagues and friends who attended the event, as well as his own reminiscences of working with Leigh.

22 During her first diagnosed bout of tuberculosis, she managed the total refurbishment of Notley Abbey, an estate bought at Olivier's insistence, and read through the works of Charles Dickens during the year she was supposed to be recuperating (see Vickers, 1990 [1988] and Walker 1994 [1987]).

23 Leigh left a number paintings to the state in her will, including a Renoir and a Degas – reportedly worth some £100,000 at the time (roughly over £1.5 million in today's money) see *Sunday Express* 'Vivien Leigh's Secret – She Left Art Treasures to the Nation', 25 August 1968; she also left paintings to friends: for example, she left Godfrey Winn a painting by Sickert (see Winn, 1970: 396).

24 Leigh worked with Cooper on the film *That Hamilton Woman* (1941). Leigh also had an affair with Cooper's son, John Buckmaster, and her last partner, Jack Merivale, was Cooper's stepson.

25 Vivien Leigh provided financial backing for a number of productions of note, including Shelagh Delaney's *A Taste of Honey* and Brendan Behan's *The Quare Fellow*. Laurence Olivier Archive, Add MS 80096, Correspondence on Laurence Olivier Productions and Vivien Leigh Productions.

26 'Vivien Leigh – Actress with an Intelligent Approach', *Guardian*, 10 July 1967, Vivien Leigh Biographical File, V&A.

References and bibliography

Bean, Kendra (2013) *Vivien Leigh: An Intimate Portrait*, London: Running Press.

Collier, Constance (1929) *Harlequinade*, London: John Lane and The Bodley Head.

Cooper, Gladys (1931) *Gladys Cooper*, London: Hutchinson and Co. Ltd.

Davis, Tracy C. (1989) 'Questions for a Feminist Methodology in Theatre History', in *Interpreting the Theatrical Past*, Thomas Postlewait and Bruce McConachie, eds, 59–81, Iowa City: University of Iowa Press.

———— (1991) *Actresses as Working Women*, London: Routledge.

Dent, Alan (1969) *Vivien Leigh: A Bouquet*, London: Hamish Hamilton.

Drazin, Charles (2011 [2002]) *Korda: Britain's Movie Mogul*, London: I.B. Taurus.

Edwards, Anne (1977) *Vivien Leigh: A Biography*, New York: Simon and Schuster.

Gale, Maggie B. and Kate Dorney eds (2018) *Stage Women: Female Theatre Workers, Professional Practice and Agency in the Twentieth Century, 1900–1950s*, Manchester: Manchester University Press.

Grime, Helen (2013) *Gwen Ffrangcon-Davies: Twentieth-Century Actress*, London: Pickering and Chatto Publishing Ltd.

Hastie, Amalie (2007) *Cupboards of Curiosity: Women, Recollection and Film History*, Durham and London: Duke University Press.

Lasky Jr, Jesse and Pat Silver (1978) *Love Scene: The Story of Laurence Olivier and Vivien Leigh*, Brighton: Angus & Robertson.

Leask, Margaret (2013) *Lena Ashwell: Actress, Patriot, Pioneer*, Herefordshire: Hertfordshire University Press/The Society for Theatre Research.

McBean, Angus (1989) *Vivien: A Love Affair in Camera*, Oxford: Phaidon.

O'Connor, Garry (1984) *Darlings of the Gods: One Year in the Lives of Laurence Olivier and Vivien Leigh*, London: Hodder and Stoughton.

Olivier, Laurence (1982) *Confessions of an Actor*, London: Weidenfeld and Nicolson.

Olivier, Tarquin (2012) *So Who's Your Mother?* London: Michael Russell Publishing Ltd.

Porter, Darwin and Roy Moseley (2011) *Damn You Scarlett O'Hara: The Private Lives of Vivien Leigh and Laurence Olivier*, US: Bloom Moon Productions Ltd

Quinn, Michael (1990) 'Celebrity and the semiotics of acting', *New Theatre Quarterly*, 6 (22): 154–161, Cambridge University Press.

Robyns, Gwen (1968) *Light of a Star: The Sensitive and Intimate Story of the Bewitching Vivien Leigh*, London: Leslie Frewen Publishers.

Rojek, Chris (2001) *Celebrity*, London: Reaktion Books.

Russell Taylor, John (1984) *Vivien Leigh*, London: Elm Tree Books.

Vickers, Hugo (1990 [1988]) *Vivien Leigh*, London: Pan Books Ltd.

Walker, Alexander (1994 [1987]) *Vivien Leigh*, London: Weidenfeld and Nicholson.

Winn, Godfrey (1970) *The Positive Hour*, London: Michael Joseph.

2

Public faces/private lives: performing Vivien Leigh

Kate Dorney

Reports of Vivien Leigh's untimely death in the British press reflected an uneasy attitude to a global superstar celebrated chiefly for her beauty rather than her acting abilities. Leigh occupied a unique position in Britain, partly because of her embodiment of roles on stage and screen and partly because of her offstage role as 'Lady Olivier', the professional and private consort of actor and director Sir Laurence Olivier until their divorce in 1960. The Oliviers were a celebrity phenomenon and global export dubbed 'theatre royalty' by the press, and received with similar levels of adulation and pomp as British royalty on their tours.[1] He was generally acknowledged as Britain's leading theatre actor – dynamic, daring and instinctively brilliant – she was usually cast as his dutiful pupil, at best always overshadowed by his genius and, at worst, holding him back.[2] Her well-publicised bouts of mental illness and later grief at their divorce saw obituaries present her as a tragic, unstable, but much-loved figure. Her unexpected death from tuberculosis at the age of 53 presented editors and journalists with a quandary about how to represent her: as a 'lass unparalleled' in beauty, certainly, but as an actress? The *Illustrated London News* opted for 'Vivien Leigh: An Unforgettable Beauty' surrounded by pictures of her in role and the sober reflection that, as an actress 'she seldom received the fullest honour'.[3] Elsewhere, J.C. Trewin reported that:

> Vivien Leigh's death has taken from the English stage not only the most physically beautiful of its actresses but also an artist with a mind. A thwarted intellectual, she had through her life been undervalued because people said, in the oldest of clichés, that her face was her fortune.[4]

Leigh repeatedly told interviewers that she considered her looks a hindrance. As other contributors to this volume explore, they occupied her fans and critics and were, and are, inextricably bound to assessments of her performance and personality. But they also worked to her advantage: getting her work as a model, bit parts in early films and clinching her the breakthrough role of Henriette in *The Mask of Virtue* which called for a very beautiful young woman. Described as 'the most exquisite person I have ever seen' by the equally exquisite Ivor Novello, she was then cast as the beautiful and virtuous Jenny Mere opposite him in *The Happy Hypocrite* (Robyns, 1968: 32). Looks were not integral to her abilities, but they gave her the chance to demonstrate them. What frustrated her, and has frustrated many generations of actress on either side of her, is the extent to which her looks, and her private life, dominated assessments of her professional achievements. As Kenneth Clark, represented anonymously in Alan Dent's posthumous appreciation of Leigh, remarked: 'It must have been discouraging to read always the same notices, praising her beauty and dismissing her acting with a pitying headshake' (Dent, 1969: 38). Despite the two Oscars awarded her for her most famous roles – *Gone With The Wind's* Scarlett O'Hara and Blanche DuBois in *A Streetcar Named Desire* – in press reports, interviews, books and articles she remains chiefly characterised in relation to her beauty and to Olivier, who, by the time of her death was director of the newly formed National Theatre, a post that confirmed him as the *de facto* head of British Theatre. A 1951 article in *The Sunday Times* is a rare example of a piece which suggests they are equally matched:

> Like her husband Sir Laurence Olivier, Vivien Leigh is at home in both worlds, amidst the majestic artifice which is the theatre and before the cinema camera's inquisitive stare [...] In private life the Oliviers wear the easy manners of people with distinguished aesthetic tastes and the ability to gratify them. Their professional partnership is a matter of constant and exacting effort; and of the two, Lady Olivier with her elegance, her irony and her drive is not the less formidable force.[5]

The oddly emphatic final note is eloquent testimony to the unusual sentiment being expressed and also hints at another constantly repeated trope about Leigh: her ambition.

Biographies, interviews and features focus on her personal life, appearance, ambition and skills as a hostess. Her charm made her attractive to interviewers but few seem to have been inclined to ask her to analyse how she worked unless it is to suggest that she was coached by Olivier or Elia Kazan, George Cukor or Alexander Korda.[6] Yet Leigh herself was careful to note her appreciation of advice from other women, telling one reporter

> it has always been a deep pleasure – and a considerable profit – to me to talk to mature and older actresses. I have derived profound benefit from long conversations with the late Lady Tree and with actresses like Ethel Barrymore and Constance Collier. I have, in short, a great reverence for experience – whether in players or in critics (and I suppose a corresponding disregard for inexperience).[7]

Notions of experience and inexperience are crucial to considerations of Leigh's critical reception. When she became an overnight sensation, critics, even the hypercritical James Agate, fell over themselves to hail her as a great actress despite her lack of experience. As she gained experience their criticism of her craft increased and her beauty assumed ever greater importance in their assessments of her work. The *Guardian* obituary is a good example of this, headlined 'Vivien Leigh – Actress with an Intelligent Approach', and illustrated with a picture of her taken recently, unlike many other obits which showed her at 20 years old, it notes:

> In the early stages of her career, critics had to fall back on simile in describing Vivien Leigh's prettiness and vivacity. She was 'like a flower' or 'like a kitten'. What was sometimes overlooked was she was like a woman and remarkably like an actress even in the days when she had to rely on looks rather than technique to advance from part to part.
> The technique came later, but was never as highly developed as her undoubted talent for exploiting a stage presence and doggedly studying lines until she mastered the meaning of the subtlest ones. In the end she was able to combine her pretty face with a sharply intelligent approach which fortified her in difficult roles.[8]

As John Stokes explores in Chapter 4, stage presence is usually considered a highly desirable quality in an actor, and part of their repertoire of techniques. In Leigh's case, however, if we believe the press, it is simply a device contrived to disguise a lack of 'technique'. 'Lack' is another recurring construct in accounts of Leigh's life and work: she is a woman constantly found wanting, whether the lack is of technique, the right partner, maternal feeling, more children, or the right part.

Central to this chapter, then, is an exploration of the way in which Vivien Leigh has been constructed in the public eye and, indeed, her participation in this construction and mediation. Beginning with a consideration of the context in which she first came to public attention and relating it to the experiences of other actresses of the period as a means for comparison, the chapter goes on to examine how she played her public role throughout her life. The contention is that although Leigh is often characterised in terms of her most famous roles: the ruthlessly ambitious Scarlett O'Hara, conniving and controlling Cleopatra and, finally, the mad and desperate Blanche DuBois, she is at the same time denied the agency these women had in determining their life courses. Alongside these characterisations, the chapter explores the strategies Leigh employed to create her own public image and, finally, the legacy created by authors, journalists and scholars.

The actress in the mid century

Leigh's adulthood coincided with an extraordinary period of change in social mores and professional practice. Her life is one example of the way in which

> social change between 1918 and 1962 affected women's own expectations, the social expectations which others had of them and, at times, even the defining of the sign *woman* itself [...] Two world wars, legislation and ideological change had gradually produced an altered role for women. (Gale, 1996: 21)

Born in India in 1913; educated at a convent school in Roehampton; sent to finishing school in France and Germany; trained at the Royal Academy of Dramatic Art (RADA); an international star from the age of 26 until her death less than thirty years later; married and divorced twice – Leigh was a witness to these changes.[9] The ease with which she was able to resume work after her first marriage, aged 18, to barrister Leigh Holman, is just one example of legislation which directly benefited her. The fact that she was able to keep working after her first divorce following a long and reasonably public adulterous affair with Olivier is evidence of a transition in social mores. Leigh's experience is not, of course, by any means typical of the average 'woman in the street' but it is not wholly untypical of the way in which actresses were trained, groomed for stardom and traded and marketed by film studios in the early 1930s. When she graduated in 1933 it was becoming more common for actresses to work in theatre and film, although film was treated with some suspicion by many classically trained performers, including Olivier, and generally seen as a way of making money, rather than advancing craft. Some actresses, like Sybil Thorndike (1882–1976), had appeared in silent films in the 1920s having first established their credentials on stage, others like Peggy Ashcroft (1907–1991) didn't engage with the medium until decades later. Leigh's closest contemporaries, Celia Johnson (1908–1992) and Wendy Hiller (1912–2003), combined stage and film stardom as Leigh did, but produced a greater body of work (Leigh was frequently denied permission to work because of studio contracts). Appearing in a huge number and range of plays, Hiller was the first British woman nominated for the Best Supporting

Actress Oscar in a British film for her role as Eliza Doolittle in *Pygmalion* (1938) and won the award in 1959 for her portrayal of Pat Cooper in Terence Rattigan's *Separate Tables* (1958). Celia Johnson began her career on the stage, turned to film and radio work during the Second World War, and is now best known for her portrayal of Laura in *Brief Encounter* (1945). Significantly, both women maintained low-profile private lives which protected them from the scrutiny brought to bear on Leigh.

Many actresses, Leigh, Johnson and Ashcroft among them, received training in the relatively new drama school system: RADA for Leigh and Johnson, Central School of Speech and Drama for Ashcroft. Others, like Hiller, trained with repertory companies and actor-managers, learning on the job as the majority of actresses had done in the nineteenth century. In both cases, it was recognised that actors honed their technique during their employment. Throughout her career, Leigh sought advice and formal training, from those she worked with, from theatrical biographies and histories and from voice and singing teachers.[10] Her approach to the craft is analogous to that of musicians and dancers for whom training and practice are lifelong preoccupations: she noted

> I go into a sort of little training before every big role. I find it essential because I'm, I guess, out of practice – like you do anything else. I mean, athletes go into training, and actors should go into training. (Funke and Booth, 1961: 214)

Her close contemporaries seem not to have had this approach, or at least not to have discussed it in public. In fact, continuous practice seems to have been regarded on some level as evidence of ambition (suspect in a woman) and an admission of lacking natural talent. Hiller and Johnson are presented as being unconcerned about their careers, while Ashcroft and Edith Evans are seen as naturally talented and rightly devoted to their work, like theatre nuns fulfilling a vocation (Figure 2.1).

Physical appearance, then as now, could have a decisive effect on an actress's career – determining the kind of parts they were offered and therefore their ability to develop a range of professional experience. Hiller and Johnson's less remarkable looks, in comparison to Leigh, and independence from leading actors of the day, meant that they attracted less press coverage in general, but more considered critiques of their work. Hiller got her break in *Love on the Dole* (1935), produced by the Manchester Repertory Company. Shaw then invited her to Malvern to play in *Arms and the Man*, *Pygmalion* and *Saint Joan*. Gielgud later described her as 'modest to a fault, punctual, reliable,

Figure 2.1 Vivien Leigh studying her script for *Caesar and Cleopatra*.

deeply professional [and] loyal'.[11] 'Professional'– a term frequently applied to Leigh – seems always to be a term of faint praise in the description of actresses. It smacks of competence rather than brilliance, and solidity rather than spirit. According to her *Oxford Dictionary of National Biography* (ODNB) entry, Hiller was: 'the least self- or career-obsessed of great actresses' (Jennings, 2007),[12] 'preferring to spend time with her family, gardening, or playing golf to enjoying the trappings of stardom'.[13] It may be that Hiller was the least career obsessed of actresses, but her career spanned five decades which suggests her success wasn't entirely a matter of chance. Similarly, Celia Johnson worked consistently and to critical acclaim over a long career and is also described in her ODNB entry as able to detach from work:

> Although Celia Johnson's dedication to her calling was immediately apparent to her public in the theatre, it rested on her shoulders lightly in her private life, which was devoted to her family, who lived at Merrimoles House, Nettlebed, Oxfordshire. She would often come out of a play before the end of its run in order to be with them. She seldom talked about the theatre and, when she did, approached the subject with a gay irreverence. (Douglas-Home, 2004)

Gay irreverence, it seems, is a more suitable approach for these actresses to take towards their work, or appear to take, than seriousness and dedication. Classical actresses like Ashcroft and Thorndike are permitted to be serious, but the kind of broad coverage that Leigh achieved is seldom recognised as an admirable, or professional, approach

'As a schoolgirl it was my permanent daydream to become an actress, and I never at any time had any shadow of doubt that would be the destiny I should work out.'[14] Every biography of Leigh notes her determination to become an actress from an early age, usually quoting school-friend and fellow actress Maureen O'Sullivan: 'Vivien always wanted to be an actress. She was single-minded. She was the only girl in the school to take ballet, for instance. She took it alone, the only one. I thought that was rather brave of her' (Bean, 2013: 20). Her first step on the path beyond school productions was the decision to enrol in RADA. At Holman's request she initially left the course after her marriage but soon re-enrolled – ostensibly to keep up her French – and did so again after the birth of her daughter Suzanne in 1933. She studied Shakespeare with Ethel Carrington and French with Alice Gachet – the only teacher at RADA for whom Joan Littlewood had any time (Walker, 1994: 64, 66). In interviews, Leigh claimed to have been a poor student dogged by accidents and bad luck, but we ought not to read too much into this as it's a common trope of actor's accounts of their training.[15] After graduation, she had her photos taken by Lenare (renowned photographer of theatre and society figures), looked for work and acquired an ambitious agent, John Gliddon. Gliddon and Holman negotiated Leigh's contract and agreed on her stage name 'Vivien Leigh'. She got her first part in the film *Things Are Looking Up* (1935) playing 'girl who puts her tongue out' (see Lucy Bolton's Chapter 5 in this volume).

She made her breakthrough playing Henriette in *The Mask of Virtue* (1935), in which her appearance was rapturously reviewed by the critics, with few comments on the performance. She became 'the fame in a night girl', lauded for the talent and beauty that secured her a £50,000 contract to make ten films in five years with Alexander Korda. Korda's biographer Charles Drazin suggests that the whole thing – the production and its reception – was contrived to get Leigh's career off on the right foot and ensure yet more publicity for his company, London Film Productions:

> According to Anthony Havelock-Allan, it was actually Alex who put on the production in the first place. He chose a director and a play which he knew could be easily and quickly staged, then gave Vivien Leigh the starring role. 'He wanted to see if she could carry it through, and she did. She looked very good. But nobody said what a wonderful actress, they said what a pretty little girl'. (Drazin, 2002: 161)

Havelock-Allan's memory was perhaps coloured by his estimation of Leigh's talents which he'd formed while producing her in the quota quickies *The Village Squire* (1935) and *Gentleman's Agreement* (1935). Drazin reports that, 'Leigh, he felt, was not a natural actress, but on film an acting experience could be manufactured' (ibid). Leigh never claimed to be a natural actress, not even at the height of her fame, and always reiterated in interviews that she was keen to gain experience. She also took the development of her offstage persona as seriously as that of her screen and stage roles and learned, no doubt with the help of Korda, Gliddon and *Mask of Virtue* producer and journalist Sydney Carroll, to work with the press. Even while trumpeting the 'fame in a night girl' the newspapers were simultaneously acknowledging it as a cliché and insisting that in Leigh's case it was different. Everyone spoke of her beauty, poise and ambition and how she was keen to reassure them that it was possible to have a husband, baby and a career – provided you had the staff to support you: 'You can be happily married and work terribly hard too'.[16] In the 1950s, she was more candid about the demands of juggling motherhood and ambition:

> I loved my baby as every mother does, but with the clear-cut sincerity of youth I realised I could not abandon all thought of a career on the stage. Some force within myself would not be denied expression. I took the problem to my husband and asked his advice. He was many years older than I was, a deeply kind and wise man, with that rare quality of imagination that implies tolerance and unselfishness. We decided that I should continue my studies at the Royal Academy of Dramatic Art. We took a tiny house in Little Stanhope Street and got a good nannie for the baby.[17]

As her career progressed, mentions of motherhood receded, the glamorous image that Leigh was cultivating was not consonant with maternity. When she became a grandmother, commentary centred again on her glamour.[18]

As mentioned above, Leigh's mental and physical application to the process of acting was, and is, frequently presented as an indication of her lack of talent. In his posthumous tribute to Leigh, critic J.C. Trewin raises the intriguing prospect that a possible explanation for the mixed reaction to Leigh's merits as an actor lie in the hype surrounding the *Mask of Virtue*:

> Vivien Leigh, even in immaturity was thinking her way through the theatre; she never ceased to do it. Seven years later she triumphed as the Cornish-born Jennifer in *The Doctor's Dilemma*. We must not suppose that on the stage she had done nothing else worthwhile; I imagine that some critics, recalling guiltily the dazzling 'slip of a girl' at the Ambassadors, were not going to get caught again. (Trewin, 1967: 38)

Leigh knew that and reflected on it in a number of interviews and it goes someway to explaining a curious gap in her public profile after her debut. For the next few years it is not so much that she got mixed reviews from the critics, more that they rarely mentioned her performances at all and, when they did, their comments were perfunctory.[19] She re-emerged in the public consciousness when she won the part of Scarlett O'Hara.

Merging the woman and the roles

Leigh's portrayal of *Gone With The Wind's* Scarlett O'Hara gave her an unprecedented public profile and abiding place in the public consciousness thanks to the film's phenomenal dissemination. As Helen Taylor notes the film,

> has been seen by more people than the entire population of the USA. It was given its first British screening on 18 April 1940, and has been an enormous favourite ever since. The film's gross earnings are estimated at approximately $300 million [...] 110 million people watched the first television showing. It had been subtitled in 24 languages, dubbed in six. (Taylor, 2014: 2)

It ran for four years at the Empire in London's Leicester Square offering a technicolour diversion from the bomb-damaged capital. Taylor describes the film as being, 'part of the regular war-pattern of London; something curiously secure and solid and blast-proof in the middle of the turmoil' (Taylor, 2015: 53–54). The ubiquity of the film, in which Leigh appeared in nine out of ten scenes, made her a star and guaranteed her recognition throughout the globe, but Leigh was not above poking fun at Scarlett. As well as performing the burlesque 'Scarlett O'Hara the Terror of Tara' as part of the Old Vic's 'Spring Party' troop entertainment in North Africa,[20] she told reporters

> Scarlett fascinated me but she needed a good healthy old fashioned spanking on a number of occasions and I should have been delighted to give it to her. But she had courage and determination and that is why women must secretly admire her – even though we can't feel too happy about her too many shortcomings. (Robyns, 1968: 71)

Leigh's biographers nearly always equate the actress' determination to 'capture' Olivier and the role of Scarlett with the characteristics of the fictional character. Scarlett's pursuit of Ashley Wilkes is compared to Leigh's pursuit of Olivier, conveniently overlooking the key difference that Olivier was more than willing to begin an affair where Wilkes was not. The affair and subsequent marriage has received considerable critical attention in biographies of both actors and is not something I intend to revisit here, other than to note that Leigh is always cast as the pursuer, just as Scarlett was. Accounts of Leigh's interest in, and pursuit of, the role are equally well covered, but I want to offer a different reading of them here from the perspective of a mid-century actress rather than from the perspective of a 'Scarlett in waiting'. Accounts vary slightly in the details but all quote Leigh's retrospective account of her fascination with the book and the role in the interview 'What Success Has Taught Me' published in 1950.

> From the moment I read [it], I was fascinated by the lovely, wayward, tempestuous Scarlett. I felt that I loved and understood her, almost as though I had known her in the flesh. When I heard that that the book was to be filmed in Hollywood early in 1939 I longed to play the part. (Quoted in Vickers, 1988: 108)

We might well be justified in concluding that, by 1950, Leigh was adept at telling reporters compelling narratives that had the kind of aspirational arc beloved of fan and celebrity magazines and, indeed, *Gone With The Wind*. We should also ask ourselves why an ambitious actress with film experience being groomed for stardom wouldn't want to audition for what was already being talked up as the greatest role in the world? The 'facts', distinct from various anecdotes, are as follows. *Gone With The Wind* was published in Britain in October 1936. In February 1937, Leigh presented her fellow actors in *Because We Must* with a copy of the book as a first night present. The same month the film's producer David O. Selznick told his office manager that he 'had no enthusiasm for Vivien Leigh' but would watch *Fire over England* when it was released (quoted in Vickers, 1988: 110). In July 1937, Leigh told the film correspondent of the *Evening News*

> 'I'm reading *Gone With The Wind*', said Vivien, 'but if I brought it here I shouldn't be able to start working.'
>   Her voice grew ecstatic: 'I've never been so gripped by anything in my life. It's the finest book I've ever read, what a grand film it would make! I've cast myself for Scarlett O'Hara. What do you think? (*Evening News* quoted in Vickers, 1989: 92)

Sometime before April 1938, she approached photographer Angus McBean to capture her in a number of different poses so she could send the results to Hollywood as part of her campaign for the part. In December 1938, Leigh met Selznick during filming of the burning of Atlanta scene, was screen tested and finally won the role. Korda and Selznick negotiated a contract in which Leigh would make two films a year for Selznick and one for Korda.[21] An increasingly familiar contradiction appears again in the narrative. As well as endorsing Leigh's vaulting ambition, the anecdotes surrounding the facts attribute agency to John Gliddon, her agent – who stood to benefit financially – and to Korda whose company would profit from her enhanced profile. Drazin suggests that the producer went to considerable lengths to help her gain the role, quoting Eve Phillips, an actress and model who had worked as Leigh's stand-in:

> Her entire characterization in *A Yank at Oxford* was worked out as a kind of screen test for Scarlett O'Hara [...] Larry helped her some, but it was Korda who really coached her. Her part was that of an English-woman, yes, but really an atypical Englishwoman ... she had this vision that she had to do an English version of Scarlett O'Hara. (Drazin, 2002: 164–165)

Again, why wouldn't an ambitious film producer and acting agent want their talent to get the leading role in the world's biggest movie? Leigh has been justly criticised for the unscrupulous way she dumped Gliddon as her agent once in the US – echoes of Scarlett. Like other Hollywood actresses, she also engaged in a long struggle with both Korda and Selznick over creative control of her career. We might regard the outcome of this struggle as a draw. She didn't get to make the films she wanted to with Olivier, apart from *Lady Hamilton*, but she didn't make the films she didn't want to either.[22] She played brave but pathetic women who came to a bad end: Myra in *Waterloo Bridge* (1940) and Emma Hamilton in *Lady Hamilton* (1941). Her casting as Cleopatra in Gabriel Pascal's version of George Bernard Shaw's *Caesar and Cleopatra* (1945) cemented her reputation as part kitten, part viper. Playful and endearing with Claude Rains' Caesar, she is imperious and ruthless with everyone else. Her next film role, as Anna Karenina, marks the shift from strong-willed beauty to a mentally unstable and sexually incontinent woman that encompasses *Anna Karenina* (1948), *A Streetcar Named Desire* (1951), *The Deep Blue Sea* (1955) and *The Roman Spring of Mrs Stone* (1961). It was only on stage that Leigh was able to pursue a greater variety of roles. Small wonder then that she could often be found declaring her preference for theatre over film.

Managing the brand

From her earliest 'fame in a night' interviews until the end of her career Leigh seems to have made a concerted effort to charm interviewers and to stage manage the occasions to the best of her abilities. This was unusual among stage actors – Olivier was famously taciturn, Ralph Richardson went out of his way to appear gnomic and, as noted above, her female contemporaries appear not to have attracted the same attention – but then Leigh was not usual among stage actors. It was unusual in any case for a film star to devote so much time to stage work, and the potent combination of Leigh and Olivier's marriage, fame and box office power made them especially fascinating to the press. Ever the professional, and increasingly conscious of the responsibility of 'brand' Olivier, Leigh attempted to simultaneously emanate grace, grit and intellect in her dealings with the press. The archive at the V&A attests to the care and effort that went into managing interview requests and approving copy, revealing correspondence between Leigh, Olivier and various journalists and amended drafts of articles about them.

A draft for an article entitled 'An Actress's Dilemma' reveals Leigh's nuanced understanding of the demands of critics and the public and the difficulty of finding roles that please them all:

> When an actor or actress has a certain amount of experience on the stage, and, perhaps, a little success, it becomes increasingly important and difficult to choose the right part and the right play. The audiences expect more and they want to see new facets of an actors [sic] art, new sides to his or her personality and, quite rightly, they become more critical and on their guard against unceasing praise.
>
> At the beginning of an actress's career, provided she is given a fair chance to show her mettle, it is all much easier. She has little to lose in the way of reputation and everything to gain. The critics and the public are eager for new personalities, and what accomplishments the beginner may show are liberally praised in the light of the promise they suggest rather than for the perfection of the immediate performance. In the early stages an actress can afford to experiment, mistakes are forgiven and there is still the novelty of a new personality to hold the interest of an audience.
>
> It naturally follows that after a time the selection of a play becomes more difficult.[23]

Leigh is referring here, as she did in several other interviews, to the difficulty of progressing as an actress in the face of extreme public adulation and the expectations of audiences and critics that each new role will affirm their enthusiasm without challenging their preconceptions about the actor. The article outlines her reasons for following the role of Scarlett O'Hara with Jennifer Dubedat and her own, not infrequently expressed, philosophy about the nature of drama and what audiences seek from the theatre. The tone is poised and measured, rather than apologetic or bombastic. As if it was a position she'd explained many times before, as indeed she had, and indeed, as she would do again and again throughout her career.

Ruth Fraser, who interviewed her in her dressing room during the filming of *Anna Karenina*, was invited to share Leigh's picnic lunch and treated to a surprise appearance from Alexander Korda, as well as being on the receiving end of Leigh's considered verdict on *Gone With The Wind*.

I adored the book ['the book' then crossed through in pencil], and of course it was tremendously exciting making the film, but I felt that I only achieved what I wanted in my performance in one or two parts of the film. But then [also crossed out] one is never satisfied with one's own performance, and enjoying playing in a film is no guarantee that one is going to enjoy watching it.[24]

This is characteristic of Leigh's frank assessment of the ups and downs of an actor's life and of her determination not to be typecast and to continue expanding her range.

In the late 1940s, Leigh's interviews and behaviour become increasingly stately as she and Olivier assume the role of theatre royalty, particularly during the 1948 British Council sponsored tour of Australia and New Zealand.[25] She, Olivier and the company played a range of parts, unusual now, but less so in an era still dominated by the repertory system. Leigh appeared as Sabina in *The Skin of Our Teeth*, Lady Teazle in *The School for Scandal* and Lady Anne in *Richard III*, but her greatest roles seem to have been as mother to the Old Vic company, arranging picnics, birthday celebrations and parties; and gracious representative of Britain attending receptions, recitations and banquets and giving speeches and press conferences. Privately she expressed fatigue at the constant round of social duties, telling Meriel (Mu) Richardson 'we are having a very strenuous time',[26] but publicly she held the company and Olivier's fraying patience together. Felix Barker quotes from Olivier's tour diary about a press conference organised for their arrival in Melbourne: 'Vivien carried the wretched thing off with superlative charm, starting by breaking up the formality of the arranged chairs and making us all mill around' (Barker, 1953: 276). As with the descriptions of the 'professionalism' with which she approached acting, these accounts, and those of her as a hostess, are always contrasted with the seriousness with which Olivier approached his work. There is still an unspoken assumption that nurturing guests, company members and friends is both trivial and more fitting for a woman.

Throughout the 1950s, Leigh's gracious exterior rarely cracked in public despite intense media scrutiny about her career and marriage. Her departure from the ideals of good behaviour to protest against the demolition of the St James's Theatre has since been variously reread as a symptom of her mental illness or menopause, but at the time the press merely reported it as they would later report other examples of celebrity activism. As well as orchestrating a public campaign against the demolition, including a march through London which she cheerfully admitted had attracted practically no publicity or interest from passers-by, Leigh also staged a much more newsworthy objection during a debate in the House of Lords about increasing arts subsidy. Violating the parliamentary rule by speaking despite not being a member of the House, she stood up and said: 'My Lords, I wish to protest against the St James's Theatre being demolished'. She was asked to leave and escorted from the chamber. As *The Times*' Parliamentary Correspondent reported:

> Within half an hour of speaking her one dramatic line in the House of Lords, Lady Olivier met reporters at the Stoll Theatre. Dressed in a long green and gold gown for her part as Lavinia in *Titus Andronicus* – in which she has her tongue cut out – she explained that her protest was made 'on the spur of the moment'.
>
> She said that she had had tea with Lord Bessborough and other peers and had then gone to listen to the debate. When she made her protest, she said Black Rod, sitting next to her, said 'Now you have to go'. She answered, 'Certainly, I have to get to the theatre'.
>
> Lady Olivier said: 'We have just come home from a tour of Europe where they are building theatres as hard as they can go. Yet here in London I saw British workmen pulling down the Gaiety on a Sunday'. She felt very passionately about the St James's Theatre [...] After last night's performance at the Stoll Theatre Lady Olivier, angered by a question about whether she would be apologising, repeated the word 'apologize' with eyebrows raised. 'I will tell you this,' she said. 'If the St James' Theatre is pulled down I will consider leaving the country. It may interest you to know that I can act in French, German and Italian, and even in Serbian.'[27]

Her courage in speaking out and her poise in receiving reporters do not suggest the ravings of a mad woman, but the calculated strategy of a star using her influence to stop one of London's few surviving Georgian theatres from being demolished. Not just by staging a public protest, but by reminding the public of her friends in high places and her star power which she threatens to take to another, more sympathetic, country. This might seem high-handed or arrogant but it's an entirely logical, and now commonplace, action to harness star power to a cause. Again, a comparison between Leigh and Ashcroft is instructive here. When Peggy Ashcroft lay in front of lorries to protest at an office block being built on the remains of the Rose Theatre in 1989, she was hailed as a brave and principled woman rather than an unhinged one. The St James's was pulled down in spite of Leigh's protests and lobbying and her anger at its destruction is palpable in her foreword to MacQueen-Pope's *St James's: Theatre of Distinction* (1958):

> It [the book] will surely fill readers of the future with nostalgia and astonishment. Nostalgia for the past, and astonishment at the apathy and levity with which our generation disposes of London's landmarks. For the death,

or more correctly, the murder of the St James's Theatre must be seen in the wider context of the ruin spread throughout the West End since the First World War.[28]

Leigh soon resumed the starry role expected of her in the press. 'Vivien Leigh's Recipe for Living' by Winefride Jackson, which appeared in the *Daily Telegraph* in 1958, begins as a frothy confection worthy of Barbara Cartland with a vivid account of being granted an audience with Leigh still in bed:

> [...] in a shell pink silk bed jacket, the speaker leaned across the rose pink and white draped bed, across the massed birthday cards, letters, writing cases, across the reclining Sabina (corgi) and Armando (Siamese cat) to shake hands.[29]

She goes on to describe her as 'one of the loveliest of young looking grandmothers-to-be' and discovers that Leigh's recipe for living is the occasional day in bed so you 'can get off all your correspondence'; keeping busy with lots of hobbies (gardening, painting, searching for antiques, racing) and having an hour's rest between 5 to 6 (ibid). The article ends with a telling phrase about Leigh's charm, potent while in its presence: 'Snowy River [the racing tip Leigh gave her] wasn't even placed. But I felt I had had a wonderful pep talk from an enthusiast in living, a leading lady in real life as she is on stage' (ibid). Perhaps Leigh was the victim of her own success in her relationship with the press and in her promotion of the Oliviers as an ideal couple. When the separation was formally announced, their attention was remorseless. Writing to Mu Richardson from the US in 1960 she pleads: 'Tell me all darling please – I am being pestered all the time by the press – English not American. Here they are much kinder and nicer and more tactful.'[30]

The tragic figure

> Olivier was about to embark on a new adventure of career, love and in due course of fatherhood. Vivien was already the victim of her illness. She was not at a good age or in a good condition for life to hold much hope of further happiness. Comfort, companionship she would find, but nothing could replace Olivier. (Vickers, 1988: 281)

From the moment the Olivier's marriage dissolved, the press cast Leigh as a tragic figure and successive biographies have continued this trend, however sympathetically, as the quote from Vickers above demonstrates. Physically and mentally frail, adrift personally and professionally – these were roles Leigh portrayed on stage and screen in *The Roman Spring of Mrs Stone*, *The Dame of the Camelias*, *Ship of Fools* and

La Contessa. As ever, there is an assumption of life following art or *vice versa*, with even her close friend Noël Coward apparently commenting at a preview of the latter: 'Why does Vivien keep choosing roles that cast her as a rejected fading beauty?' (Vickers, 1998: 343). One response to this might be to look at the range of roles open to a woman of 52 in the early 1960s, particularly a woman whose beauty is her most remarked upon characteristic. Leigh goes from playing the love interest in *Prince and the Showgirl* in 1953 to Hester 'a plain woman in her forties' in *The Deep Blue Sea* a year later. When Gladys Cooper, another noted beauty, played the gracious Countess of Marshwood in Coward's *Relative Values* in 1951 she was 63. It was the best role she'd had for ages and it was one of the only roles for a beautiful woman of her age. As debates in recent years have shown, more than sixty years on, the range of roles for older women has not progressed that significantly.

Posthumous accounts

The first biography of Leigh appeared a year after her death. *Light of a Star* (1968) was written by Gwen Robyns, a journalist who had pioneered 'human interest' stories about prominent figures.[31] She drew a sympathetic, if patronising, portrait of Leigh as a woman of unusual charisma, some talent and great beauty. Her suggestion that the Olivier's marriage might have endured is interesting, not only for the veiled way in which she references Leigh's mental health issues, but also because it once again demonstrates the entrenched attitude that men's careers and feelings came first.

> If Vivien had been prepared to slip into semi-retirement and only act occasionally, when a really irresistible part was available, there was a possibility that it could have worked out. But she had to work consistently and intensely to live, because work was her life. She became bored, depressed and difficult during the time she was not working. (Robyns, 1968: 188)

It's hard to imagine a biographer suggesting, even today, that the marriage could have been saved if Olivier went into semi-retirement and devoted himself to managing Notley Abbey and Vivien Leigh. Yet, unquestionably, the manifestations of Leigh's mental health issues stabilised during her relationship with Jack Merivale, an actor with a lower profile and fewer professional engagements than Olivier. Successive biographies and Olivier's autobiography revealed more details of Leigh's mental and physical health and sexual liaisons until her public image hardened as a beautiful, unstable nymphomaniac whose sexual appetite exhausted Olivier, creatively as well as physically – as Marilyn Monroe's was said to have worn out Arthur Miller – and whose affairs embarrassed him and all their friends. Unlike Monroe, however, Leigh has not been the subject of serious scholarship. Rather, she has been largely framed as an appendage or burden to Olivier, or stereotyped as a crazed chain-smoking nymphomaniac in accounts that are either sentimental, prurient or both. As noted in the introduction, the centenary of her birth in 2013 was marked in the media by the usual stories: a beautiful woman; a bad mother; always Scarlett O'Hara or Blanche DuBois, never an *artist* who rigorously honed her craft in order to portray these characters. Re-reading published sources and interrogating her archive show that Leigh was far more than the sum of her lovers and mental health issues; she was a consummate actress, off stage, as well as on, continually exploring ways of presenting herself to the world and to the writers, directors and producers she wanted to work with.

Notes

1 The Leigh and Olivier archives, as well as press cuttings held as part of the V&A's general collection, provide ample evidence of this, showing the couple with fixed grins at receptions across Europe (including with General Tito in Belgrade during the tour of *Titus Andronicus*), Australia and New Zealand (as part of a British Council tour).

2 This theory was first proposed by influential theatre critic Kenneth Tynan, who established his career with witty but cruel pen portraits of key figures in post-war British theatre, including Samuel Beckett and Leigh and Olivier's close friends and colleagues Terence Rattigan and Noël Coward. Tynan's accounts of Leigh's appearances as Titania, Lady Macbeth etc. have a memorable quality and still hold sway in public perception of the actress's work.

3 'Vivien Leigh: An Unforgettable Beauty', *Illustrated London News*, 15 July 1967, in Vivien Leigh Biographical File, V&A.

4 J.C. Trewin, untitled publication, Vivien Leigh Biographical file, V&A.

5 *Sunday Times,* 15 April 1951.

6 Leigh always gave credit to those who helped her, and they weren't always men. She praised her French teacher Mme Antoine for teaching her diction (Funke and Booth, 1961: 200), her *Mask of Virtue* co-stars Maud Tree, Jeanne de Casalis and Frank Cellier for helping her develop on stage (Bean, 2013: 27), and Lillian Braithwaite with whom she appeared in *Bats in the Belfry*.

7 Amended proofs for 'What Life Has Taught Me by Vivien Leigh' article for *Sunday Chronicle*, 28 July 1951, Vivien Leigh Archive, Personal Papers, Articles and Speeches. THM/433/9/1.

8 *Guardian*, 10 July 1967.

9 As was Peggy Ashcroft, who was first divorced in 1933 on the grounds of her adultery with Theodore Komisarjevsky ('Actress Divorced', *Daily Mail*, 11 May 1933); she later divorced Komisarjevsky on the grounds of 'misconduct' ('Actress Granted Decree Nisi', *Daily Mail*, 14 June 1937).

10 According to interviews and biographers, Leigh took elocution and voice lessons with Baraldi, Cunelli, Elsie Fogerty of the Central School of Speech

and Drama, 'a marvellous woman who Robert Helpmann told me about' (Funke and Booth, 1961: 214).

11 *The Independent*, 9 August 1992.

12 Jennings is quoting from Brian McFarlane's *An Autobiography of British Cinema* (1997).

13 Ibid.

14 Amended proofs for 'What Life Has Taught Me by Vivien Leigh' article for *Sunday Chronicle*, 28 July 1951, Vivien Leigh Archive, Personal Papers, Articles and Speeches. THM/433/9/1.

15 Leigh's friend and co-star Ralph Richardson gleefully recounted similar accounts of disaster, see Dorney (2008: 119) for details.

16 *Nottingham Journal*, 18 May 1935.

17 Vivien Leigh, 'What success has taught me'. In reading such interviews it is of course important to maintain awareness of their promotional purpose and constructed nature.

18 Vivien Leigh's Biographical File at the V&A contains a number of cuttings from 1959 and 1960 showing Leigh with Suzanne and her first grandson Neville.

19 Looking at the reviews, Leigh's beauty in *The Happy Hypocrite* seems to have been largely eclipsed by the sensation of that equally celebrated beauty, Ivor Novello, disguising his looks with make-up and masks to play the dissipated Lord George Hell. V&A Production file for *The Happy Hypocrite* (1936).

20 See Walker (1994: 227) and Bean (2013: 90) for more information.

21 The contract, the Second World War and Leigh's determination to continue her stage career and remain in proximity to Olivier resulted in her making only four films – *Waterloo Bridge* (1940), *Lady Hamilton* (1941), *Caesar and Cleopatra* (1945) and *Anna Karenina* (1948) – and appearing in six plays during a ten-year period: *The Doctor's Dilemma* (1942), *The Skin of Our Teeth* (1945), *Richard III* (1948), *The School for Scandal* (1948), *Antigone* (1949) and *A Streetcar Named Desire* (1949).

22 She hoped for the role of Cathy in *Wuthering Heights*, and refused Isabella, and also lobbied to be the second Mrs de Winter in *Rebecca*.

23 Typescript of 'An Actress's Dilemma', Vivien Leigh Archive. THM/433/9/1.

24 Typescript of an untitled interview with Ruth Fraser, Vivien Leigh Archive. THM/433/9/1.

25 The tour is the subject of both Felix Barker's *The Oliviers* (1953) and Garry O'Connor's *The Darlings of the Gods* (1984).

26 Vivien Leigh to Meriel Richardson, 15 May 1948, Ralph Richardson Archive. Add MS 82044.

27 'Lady Olivier's Cue in the Lords', *The Times*, 12 July 1957. Vivien Leigh Biographical File, V&A.

28 Proof page for the Foreword to *St James's: Theatre of Distinction*. Vivien Leigh Archive. THM/433/9/1.

29 Winefride Jackson, 'Vivien Leigh's Recipe for Living', *Daily Telegraph*, 1958. Vivien Leigh Biographical File, V&A.

30 Vivien Leigh to Meriel Richardson, undated, Ralph Richardson Archive. Add MS 82044.

31 'Gwen Robyns Obituary', *Daily Telegraph*, 6 November 2013.

References and bibliography

Barker, Felix (1953) *The Oliviers*, London: Hamish Hamilton.

Bean, Kendra (2013) *Vivien Leigh: An Intimate Portrait*, Philadelphia: Running Press.

Dent, Alan (1969) *Vivien Leigh: A Bouquet*, London: Hamish Hamilton.

Dorney, Kate (2008) 'Ralph Richardson', in *The Golden Generation: New Light on Post-war British Theatre*, edited by Dominic Shellard, London: British Library, pp. 117–151.

Douglas-Home, William (2004) 'Dame Celia Johnson', in *Oxford English Dictionary of National Biography*, Oxford University Press.

Drazin, Charles (2002) *Korda: The Definitive Biography*, London: Sidgwick and Jackson.

Funke, Lewis and John E. Booth (1961) 'Vivien Leigh', in *Actors Talk about Acting*, London: Thames & Hudson, pp. 194–224.

Gale, Maggie B. (1996) *West End Women: Women on the London Stage 1918–1962*, London: Routledge.

Jennings, Alex (2007) 'Dame Wendy Hiller', in *Oxford Dictionary of National Biography*, Oxford University Press.

O'Connor, Garry (1984) *Darlings of the Gods: One Year in the Lives of Laurence Olivier and Vivien Leigh*, London: Hodder and Stoughton.

Robyns, Gwen (1968) *Light of a Star, The Sensitive and Intimate Story of the Bewitching Vivien Leigh*, London: Leslie Frewin.

Taylor, Helen (2014) *Scarlett's Women*, London: Virago.

———— (2015) *Gone With the Wind*, London: BFI Publishing.

Trewin, J.C. (1967) Untitled publication, Vivien Leigh Biographical file, London: V&A.

Vickers, Hugo (1988) *Vivien Leigh: A Biography*, New York: Little Brown and Company.

Walker, Alexander (1994) *Vivien: The Life of Vivien Leigh*, London: Orion Books.

3

Making Vivien Leigh mad

Maggie B. Gale

... an artist with a mind. A thwarted intellectual, she had, through life, to be under-valued because people said, in the oldest of clichés, that her face was her fortune ... under-valued, under-rated: it was in the pattern of her life.[1]

Vivien seemed quite imperturbable, playing the innocent with her husband, the confident careerist with David Niven, the troubled idealist with Tyrone Guthrie ... and the single-minded lover with Olivier ... No one knew what she was really thinking and feeling, not even, probably, herself [...] Vivien was never, for a moment, a person whose reactions could be taken for granted. If she found it easy to behave like Scarlett on screen it was quite possibly because she found it easy to behave that way off [...] it was normal ... to regard all this as not only enchanting but necessarily feminine [...] there is no doubt that Vivien Leigh was the acme of femininity, delightful, maddening and of course by definition, incomprehensible to any mere man ...
(Taylor, 1984: 18)

During her lifetime, reports of Vivien Leigh's petulant or demanding behaviour rarely translated into actual insinuations of 'madness': her conduct might be euphemistically described as eccentric or caused by nervous exhaustion. The run of biographies published in the years immediately following her death (see Chapter 1 in this volume) often include anecdotes from friends and co-workers which allude to her behaviour as sometimes challenging or perplexing. It was, however, as Alexander Walker notes, largely after the publication of Laurence Olivier's *Confessions of an Actor* (Olivier, 1982) in which Olivier did not hold back in his portrayal of Leigh's instability and mental health issues, that her professional colleagues and friends talked much more freely and willingly about her behaviour on and off stage and screen. One might argue, then, that the process of 'making Vivien mad', gathered real momentum after Olivier opened the floodgates.

Since her early death in 1967, at the relatively young age of 53, from a recurrent and late-diagnosed episode of tuberculosis[2] (Walker, 1994 [1987]: 388), the proliferation of biographies of Leigh, or autobiographies of those who worked with her, often refer to her pattern of disturbed behaviour, which resembles what we might today see as a form of bipolarity exacerbated by extreme emotional or work-related exhaustion. She went through long periods touring abroad, had a fairly relentless schedule of performances and filming from the mid 1930s to her death, a discernible propensity for feverish socialising and refused to permanently stop drinking or smoking. She had two very public miscarriages in her 30s and 40s and a very public 'breakdown' in 1953, all of this in combination with, from the mid 1940s onwards, a definitive diagnosis of tuberculosis, from which she could only recover through treatment and rest. Despite her great beauty and her seemingly easy rise to fame, Leigh's was not an easy journey either personally or professionally.

Mentions of her depression begin with reports of stress and fatigue during the filming – over a period of a year – of *Gone With The Wind* in 1939; of odd behaviour during work on the film of *A Streetcar Named Desire* in 1951; the 'breakdown' during the filming of *Elephant Walk* in 1953; problems during the 1955 season at Stratford-upon-Avon with Olivier; manic episodes during the campaign to keep the St James' theatre in London's West End from being demolished in 1957; depressive periods during the years around her divorce in 1960 and during the run of *Tovarich* in 1963, the musical for which she won a Tony award. Jack Merivale, her last partner who also to some extent took on the role of 'carer', noted periods where Leigh swung between manic activity and low moods in the mid-to-late 1960s (see Walker, 1994 [1987] and Vickers, 1990 [1988]).

In terms of acknowledging or understanding her medical condition, her professional colleagues, such as Tennessee Williams, often depict her as a talented but tragic actress: she was 'dear to his heart' but 'having known madness she knew how it was to be drawing close to death' (Williams, 2007 [1972]: 226). Others, among them Stewart Granger, paint themselves as her intimates: 'real' and heroic companions in a time of need. The retelling of her breakdown in Hollywood, after returning from filming *Elephant Walk* in Ceylon, is at the centre of the mythologising about her mental illness. She was manic, out of control, hysterical and 'not herself', unwilling to accept help and in denial that there was anything amiss (Granger, 1981: 289–293). Peter Finch, the leading man with whom Leigh was having an affair during the filming of *Elephant Walk*, was, according to his biographer Trader Faulkner, mesmerised by the self same personality traits others related to Leigh's illness. He suggests she bewitched Finch, that theirs was both a manic and a passionate affair, and that he found it difficult to separate this from his understanding of what was clearly some form of manic depression: a 'flawed masterpiece' she had 'stretched him to the very limit and left him "confused": it took him "many years to re-adjust"'(Faulkner 1979: 156). Similarly, Elaine Dundy contextualises Finch's responses to Leigh's manic behaviour by suggesting he was both enchanted and attracted by her complex personality, but that when faced with her mental ill ease, he had no knowledge as to how he might help her (Dundy, 1980: 186).[3]

Others with whom Leigh had long-lived professional or personal relationships are more sympathetic to her condition. Thus, Noël Coward's editors have tended to shape his *Diaries* and collected journals, *Remembered Laughter*, to emphasise Coward's extreme irritation with Leigh at times, especially when she dropped out of a heavily booked production of his *South Sea Bubble* once it had opened, due to pregnancy in 1956 at the age 43 (see Coward 1982 and Lesley 1976). Yet the prolific correspondence between the two reveals an intimate friendship where Coward provided solace and encouraged Leigh to look after her health more conscientiously, as well as seeking her opinion in relation to work.[4] It was, in fact, Coward she turned to when she removed herself from the care of Dr Rudolph Freudenberg at Netherne Hospital in Surrey and checked into University College Hospital in London, after three weeks of induced coma and electric shock treatment on returning from the disastrous filming of *Elephant Walk* in 1953. Olivier had checked her in, handed her over to a doctor he had probably not met before, and returned to his holiday in Italy, supposedly to avoid the press. Her ever-absent father was in Ireland and her mother was holidaying in Paris with a friend. Leigh's biographer Anne Edwards, who had access to her mother Gertrude Hartley's diaries, suggests that Olivier removed himself because he was so traumatised by the whole event: he needed 'privacy to think things out' (Edwards, 1977: 198), but Oswald Frewen, an old family friend of Leigh and her first husband Leigh Holman, thought them all 'memory-losers and liars' for abandoning her, in the case of Olivier, 'address unknown' (Vickers, 1990 [1988]: 234). These narratives all contain elements of 'truth', but are flavoured by a misrepresentation of men in the role of carer, misunderstandings about both the nature of illness and treatment, and reveal a fear and ignorance around mental illness that often manifests as abandonment.

Leigh's struggles with the physiological disease of tuberculosis, from the mid 1940s, are less discussed than her mental health issues and the ways in which she and those around her coped with them, both professionally and privately. Leigh suffered from two forms of debilitating illness, both of which are better understood and better treated medically and socially today than they were in her own lifetime. Neither of these conditions, however, was conducive to the easy management of such a prolific and public facing career.

This chapter explores the many manifestations of Leigh's illnesses, how they were treated and how they have shaped our understandings of her work as an actress. The contexts of her medical conditions, in terms of the social and professional worlds in which she operated as well as in relation to the kinds of treatment she received from the medical profession, are in part responsible for 'making Vivien Leigh mad'. Here, the 'madness' of Vivien Leigh is mapped out in a gendered social and professional world far less tolerant, some would say, than our own. The focus on her 'specialness' as a victim often substitutes for the kind of analysis of her professional practice that might have been applied to an actor in the same position. She drank and smoked heavily and was known to love socialising well into the early hours on a regular basis, none of which are restorative for someone suffering from either tuberculosis or any form of depression, manic or otherwise. But they were very much accepted social behaviours in the high-profile stage and screen lives of successful performers of the day, especially those moving so frequently between screen and stage roles as Leigh did, and those whose lucrative studio contracts made them corporate and public property. While expensive and 'cutting edge' in their time, the treatments Leigh received did not provide her with a cognitively controlled journey to wellbeing. There was no investment in the kinds of 'talking cures' offered by the psychotherapeutic as opposed to the psychiatric in accounts of her failing health and its impact on her work – but evidence suggests this was in part a result of her own wishes to keep her condition out of the public eye.

Being Vivien Leigh: in retrospect

> Vivien Leigh's beauty was absolutely radiant, her elegance phenomenal. She was extremely cultivated, discriminating in her choice of paintings, furniture, beautiful objects; she was a highly gifted actress, a brilliant comedienne. She was also ... a terrified woman. (Bloom, 1996: 109–110)

As noted in Chapter 1, the personal and professional relationship between Leigh and Olivier forms a central focus of a number of biographical readings of Leigh and I have no wish to replicate this configuration here. However, her illnesses, both physiological and psychological, were largely tied in with the peaks and troughs of her associations with Olivier. The revelations of his *Confessions* imply a man incapable of dealing with the illness of loved ones, and even less capable of conceptualising the impact of the appalling terror of experiencing uncontrollable and debilitating forms of recurrent depression. After her first series of electro-convulsive therapy (ECT) treatments in the early 1950s, Olivier claims that Leigh 'was not, now that she had been given the treatment, the same girl that I had fallen in love with ... something had happened to her, very hard to describe, but unquestionably evident' (ibid: 160). Indeed, as explored in the following pages, something had happened to Leigh: Olivier had sanctioned, without her informed permission, the first of many ECT interventions.

Two forms of illness

Accounts of Leigh after her death – without exception – refer more often to her mental rather than physical health issues. While praising her talent as one of a handful of English actresses whose talent she admired, for example (Bacall, 2005: 436), Lauren Bacall also hints at the background presence of Leigh's depressive condition and its central role in the ending of Leigh's marriage to Olivier: '... he knew he would not survive if he did not get away' (ibid: 327). Actress Claire Bloom, born in the early 1930s and so of a different generation from both Leigh and Bacall, had an affair with Olivier of which Vivien Leigh was aware, but found him to be 'pedestrian and dull' with 'little interest in anything outside his own particular sphere of genius'. She talks of Leigh as Olivier's 'more brilliant wife' (Bloom, 1996: 94). In admiration of Leigh's management of her domestic and professional sphere, Bloom also felt that her *modus operandi* was built around the need to keep at 'bay and counter the torment of a mental illness that constantly threatened her fragile existence' (ibid: 109). In contrast, to some extent, Rachel Kempson, married to an equally iconic and troubled actor, Michael Redgrave, claimed that Leigh's illness 'had nothing to do with her work' – her performances could be magnificent – (Kempson, 1986: 227), but thought Leigh's 'fragile and sensitive nature' meant that she, a professional perfectionist, fell easily into depression when she believed her achievements to be less than they might be (ibid: 228).

Leigh spoke very little about her state of health in her lifetime: there are odd unattributed quotes such as, 'My birth sign is Scorpio and they eat themselves up and burn themselves out ... I swing between happiness and misery', but in general she did not view her state of health as a matter for public consumption.[5] She did, however, talk freely to intimate colleagues and there are odd mentions, sometimes throw-away comments, in her letters. For example, in 1953 while making *Elephant Walk* she wrote to Coward:

> I've had a cobra round my neck – sat on an elephant – swum in a pool on a hill 1600 feet high which I climbed before sunrise ... padded around temples – changed the script considerably and figure toi (sic) found a night club, called the 'Gilded Cage'. This is the most beautiful place I have ever been in my life. Shall I buy a house here? ... I think of <u>you</u> and Coley ... a very great deal – everyone is charming, except that they treat me as if I were a raving lunatic.[6]

And, in 1955 while rehearsing in Stratford upon Avon,

> ... My wretched chest has gone back on me again and I am not allowed to go to Barbados as planned but must stay in some boring mountains having nasty things injected, <u>but</u> it will only take a short while if I'm sensible and good – which I intend to be ready for the play.[7]

Her articulation of the impact of exhaustion and its contribution to her depression are more clearly and openly expressed in her sequence of letters to Merivale while she is working in *Tovavich* in the US in 1962 and 1963.

> I hope I did not depress you with my worries, but truthfully I do not know what to think. Perhaps it is only because I am so very miserable in myself that I am unduly depressed. You must not think that I am in despair all of the time. (New York, 28 December 1962)

> What an utterly wretched time this is ... I should never have taken on something so foreign. It is another world all together ... I am assailed by fears of what would happen if it should turn out to be a failure. (Philadelphia, 24 January to 6 February 1963)

> I have never felt so mortally ill & I wonder each performance how I shall manage ... I think the critics will be brutal (I shall agree with them) but the thing may run. They are doing very good business at the box office I understand. Oh dearest, I do absolutely hate doing something I despise & find distasteful. (Hotel Dorset, 11 March 1963, New York)[8]

These are the letters of someone worried about their ability to play a physically demanding role without the camaraderie of actors with whom they are familiar: anxious letters from an actress working in a role in a musical, the quality of which she is not convinced by. It is interesting that there are few extant letters to Olivier which express her desperation quite so frankly.

While very real both in terms of physiology and psychology, Leigh's fragility has been fastened onto by her critics and biographers. Phrases like 'her delicate constitution could not sustain a career single-handed ... her career had been interrupted from time to time from nervous collapse when she drove herself too hard ...' (Gaye, in Billington 2001: 201–204) do not do justice to her expansive career achievements. Equally, they erroneously suggest that her career was entirely tied up with Olivier's, and show no appreciation of the fact that illness was *part* of her career not separate from it. In Leigh's time, however, her illnesses were little understood and discussion of them socially taboo. However, even our contemporary press, as Kate Dorney suggests,[9] find ready-made headlines for articles on Leigh that equate her career with an irreconcilable conflict between beauty, talent and madness, as opposed to a critical appreciation or analysis of her artistic achievement. Thus we have titles such as 'Hollywood Hell'[10] or 'Frightened Butterfly ... the secret life of Scarlett O'Hara'; 'Struggles of the star who shone in the shadow of greatness';[11] 'The private hell of a golden couple'[12] and 'Beauty and the manic beast'.[13]

Leigh's physical health is framed by assertions of gendered fragility and her 'madness' is shaped in reference to her professional, personal and sexual aspirations: seen by some as shaping, in turn, her performances in films such as A *Street Car Named Desire* (1949) or *The Roman Spring of Mrs Stone* (1961) – she was a great Blanche DuBois because she was 'a bit mad' herself, who better to play a woman (Mrs Stone) with unfulfilled sexual longings than a once iconic beauty, now in her late 40s, looking aged and abandoned by her iconic husband, and so on. Of course Leigh was an actress, she was *acting* these roles because she practised a craft: playing 'mad' doesn't mean you are 'mad'. In her lifetime, fans and critics alike associated her with her roles, but they also connected with her as a person.[14] Her illnesses, however, created a professional landscape in which they were unspoken or unacknowledged by some – tuberculosis was the illness of the poor or the effete and depression something that was little understood and even less talked about. Depression was bad for studio press and investment. Both Leigh and Olivier's archives suggest, however, an overwhelming connection to, and empathy with, Leigh's condition from her fans – many of whom are reassuring that depression is more common than one assumes, and is a condition rather than death sentence.

In her biographies and the autobiographies of those who knew her, there is little attention to the ways in which her own mental illness may have been in part a reflection on the social and professional challenges of being a mid twentieth-century upper middle-class professional woman. After the release of *Gone With The Wind* in 1939, she swiftly became an actress with iconic status, unusually maintaining both a high-profile stage and screen career, awarded two Oscars, a Knight's Cross of the Légion d'Honneur in 1957 and a Tony for her role in a revival of *Tovarich* on Broadway in 1963. She lived almost entirely in the limelight but was also, like many other women in the mid century, tacitly expected to stay in the shadow of her husband Olivier: she was the more globally high-profile screen performer of the two but he was, for the theatre establishment, the leading actor-producer of the British theatre.

Without wishing to undermine the impact of what were clearly very real health issues, tuberculosis – or the 'white plague' – and a form of hyper-depression, the construction of Leigh as emotionally unstable, out of control or mentally ill relates directly to the generic context of professional, social and medical frameworks for the stigmatisation of women's professional conduct, social behaviour and mental health issues in the public realm of the day. A seminal early feminist work on women and psychiatry suggests that clinicians were 'likely to suggest that women differ from healthy men by being more submissive, less independent ... less aggressive ... more emotional ... less objective' (Chesler, 1972: 68). Chesler is writing of the same generation of clinicians as would have treated Leigh. She notes one contemporary study in which 'angry' women are often highly successful professionally, but considered 'neurotic' because they exhibit 'male' behaviours – 'bursts of uncontrollable temper ... use of foul language ... alcohol or drugs' (ibid: 70). Leigh, for all her hyper-feminine beauty and charm, did not always behave in what would have been considered a very 'ladylike' manner in the mid century: as well as having a number of long-lasting female friendships, she was also, I would suggest, 'one of the boys'. The photographic repertoire of Leigh's private and public life reflects this odd juxtaposition – posed in glamorous shots or production photos, close focus, still and timeless, looking into the distance or in pose for a publicity shot with or without her co-star; or laughing and joking with theatre friends, always a cigarette and drink at hand, looking joyful and sometimes a bit wild with Robert Helpmann, Coward or other professional colleagues (Plate 1). While recent studies of women's expectations of 'normative' life paths note that social 'changes in attitudes and behaviours have increased the diversity of life paths and have altered the meanings and implications of different life course experiences' (Koropeckyj-Cox et al., 2007: 325), Leigh was in the minority, a female artist among other artists, trying to design her career against a background of patriarchal establishment paternalism.

One might even suggest that if Leigh had been a man, her symptoms and their social and professional implications would have been diagnosed using different evaluative measures. Professional ambition, openly sexual sensation seeking and heavy drinking are more frequently, though not exclusively, associated with the male stars of the era. Leigh had genuine health issues, and unusually for a performer with such high-profile currency as a screen actress after *Gone With The Wind*, combined long periods touring theatre with working long and stressful hours on film sets: she was in fact rarely not working, or being a busy hostess and a prolific networker. None of this was conducive to a pensive or restful lifestyle, and it is the high-pressure, frenetic moments from which she appears to have descended into illness on a fairly regular basis from the mid 1940s onwards. Leigh was also, however, as the chapters in this collection testify, an award-winning, largely self-educated actress, whose career spanned more than thirty years across stage and film performances, and whose iconic status, and enormous fan base, was both a blessing and a curse. Equally, as her great friend Coward implied on more than one occasion, she was often her own worst enemy: he implored her to, 'cable me constantly and write to me constantly and above all take care of yourself, <u>really</u> take care of yourself'.[15]

Physical illness: tuberculosis

When her doctor finally diagnosed Leigh's returned tuberculosis (TB) in late May 1967, the X-rays showed 'there was a great black hole in her lung'. She had already been coughing up blood and refused treatment in a clinic, so was ordered bed rest. Jack Merivale suggested to Alexander Walker that there was a steady stream of visitors that sometimes built to the fevered pitch of a cocktail party: she was often found smoking. Nobody seemed to realise how serious her condition was. It appears odd to us now that Leigh, having suffered serious episodes of TB since the mid 1940s, was not taken in hand at the same pace – and with the same lack of personal agency being permitted – as she was when she had episodes of depression. One of her close friends, actor and playwright Emlyn Williams, told Walker that he was worried about her when he visited her after her final diagnosis and found her smoking, but that no one else appeared to be concerned (Walker, 1994 [1987]: 389). Coward also frequently suggested she should not smoke (Vickers, 1988: 353). Her early biographer Gwen Robyns proposed that no one realised how bad Leigh's prognosis was (Robyns, 1968: 240), whereas Anne Edwards claims that since at least 1965, her tuberculosis had been returning, 'but she refused to accept the seriousness of her condition' (Edwards, 1977: 278). Either way, this physiological illness was curable.

In tracing the history of Leigh's TB there appears to have been a fairly consistent lack of concern in terms of illuminating the means by which to outdo the disease. From the later nineteenth century onwards, TB was perceived as a disease of poverty, but was also conceptualised as having a 'redemptive-spiritual' nature, and almost fetishised as the disease of the bohemian artist, with its own kind of poetic beauty of the tragic (Barnes, 1995: 51). Treatments varied hugely, especially in relation to economics and social status. Those who could afford it might be diagnosed via X-ray, but state-run sanatoriums, where sufferers underwent strict regimes of bed rest, isolated the individual from their social milieu and had relatively poor survival rates (Sucre, n.d.). Other treatments by the late 1940s included chemotherapy and potent cocktails of antibiotics, as well as regimens of bed rest, careful diet and no alcohol or smoking. Tuberculosis was by this time more of a curable disease.

Leigh contracted TB in the closing years of the Second World War: Olivier makes scant mention of it in *Confessions*. He was unable to return to England for three weeks on hearing of her diagnosis, whereupon he took her to Scotland for a 'complete change of atmosphere' and was then concerned that while the 'holiday' was a good idea, he had missed valuable rehearsal time (Olivier, 1982: 115). Accounts vary, as Vickers claims that she was treated for six weeks at University College Hospital and that it was after this that Olivier arranged their sojourn. It is odd that a woman with money and access to expensive medical care should first contract the disease and second never fully recover from it. Perhaps TB was not so rare among her social circle: according to Vickers, Meriel (Mu) Richardson, wife of the actor Ralph Richardson, was also suffering from TB at this point and she and Leigh cemented their friendship further by doing *The Times* crossword over the telephone together with each other while convalescing (Vickers, 1990 [1988]: 176). Leigh periodically mentions the unpleasant medication she had to take, as in the letter above, and the fact that she resented the debilitating effects of the disease when she was forced to stop working and rest. In fact, her year recovering from her first infection was spent reading the works of various classical writers – Dickens, Montaigne – but also planning and overseeing the staggeringly complex overhaul and refurbishment of Notley Abbey, the decaying estate Olivier had insisted on purchasing at the close of war. When pushed by Stephen Watts of the *Sunday Express* for news of her health in early 1946, while one detects a sense of wanting to keep her condition private on Olivier's part, one also sees that he was perhaps simply completely ignorant of the potential impact of the illness on her future wellbeing. He reports:

> Her sort of trouble is veiled in mystery, and it is hard to get conclusive and satisfactory news ... I think that on the whole she is not doing badly, and is bearing up under her slow progress with her usual delightful good spirits ... it is all a bit worrying but it might be much worse.[16]

Perhaps the social stigma of TB prohibited discussion. Olivier is certainly at pains to detail Leigh's bouts of depression and her manic behaviour in great detail, but the physiological illness barely features in his, nostalgic but infrequently kind, autobiographic framing of Leigh. Biographers do not detail the chemical treatment she received or note that, by the late 1940s, these periodic treatments would have been combined with those administered for her depression. By the time she was in her 40s, Leigh was familiar with returning bouts of TB and the cocktail of drugs and ECT she was being given on, it would appear, a regular basis.

Mental illness: manic depression and medicalising Vivien Leigh

When she was good, she was very, very good, but when she was bad she was *awful*.

(Maxine Audley, quoted in Vickers, 1990 [1988]: 3)

... she suffered from recurrent bouts of insanity which turned her already wilful nature into something approaching that of a monster: cold, rude, spoiled and aggressive.[17]

Some who comment on Leigh's mental health lack any empathy or understanding: on a spectrum, Olivier's comments mostly come within this category. He certainly made little connection between his own behaviour, her environment and her mental illness, but rather distances himself, literally and mentally, on a regular basis. Others are more sympathetic, recognising the frightening and debilitating impact of her illness on her life and professional activity. Certainly the many letters from fans and colleagues sent during her first extended major breakdown in 1953 attest to both a professional network and fan base of those who had an empathic connection to her illness. Suggestions for remedies and offers of help and sympathy arrived on Olivier's desk from all quarters – from one Mr Magnée a 'specialist in massage of artistes, dancers and athletes' proposing the use of his services, to theatre director Theodore Komisarjevsky, writing to Olivier to say that Leigh needed 'centrying (sic), a very long rest and care. Theatre is a fearful business nowadays ...'.[18] Numerous fans offered advice and suggested the need for spiritual renewal. Friends and colleagues recommended intervention from outside of the Oliviers' circle. Thus, close friend and actress Constance Collier proposed that Vivien talk to someone, 'not a psychiatrist, but a spiritual man, that she could pour her thoughts out to without any self-consciousness'.[19] While friend and playwright Lesley Storm, who had been with Leigh in Ceylon, sympathised that the 'frustration of trying to make bricks without straw', on the production of *Elephant Walk*, had worn her out, and called the 'set-up' in Ceylon 'difficult and depressing'.[20]

This was not the first time Leigh had suffered with manic-depressive symptoms. Reports of exhaustion were not infrequent even as early on as on the set of *Gone With The Wind*, but we should take into account here that the work hours were phenomenally long with Selznick keeping up the pace, despite lack of sleep and through regular ingestions of Benzedrine.[21] The film was shot completely out of sequence, Leigh's original director George Cukor had been sacked in favour of one the male lead – Clark Gable – preferred, and Leigh was working with a team of people who were unfamiliar in a foreign country on her first large-scale film, on which numerous reputations were riding. Walker claims that Leigh was anxious about her bouts of 'alternating elation and depression' by the mid 1940s and that these could not be traced to 'any physical malfunction' (Walker 1994 [1987]: 244). She was acutely concerned by the stigma of mental illness, it would appear, and of course the kinds of support networks for, and understanding of, mental health that exist in the twenty-first century could not have been imagined in the mid twentieth. Robyns writes that Leigh reported feeling 'like an amoeba at the bottom of the sea', when in a depressive state: that she experienced a debilitating sense of disassociation (Robyns, 1968: 178). During her manic phases, it was noted that she drank and socialised more than normal and so became even more exhausted. Descriptions of Leigh in states of disarray vary in the depth of detail and intensity: David Niven described her most famous post-*Elephant Walk* breakdown in vivid terms in the first edition of his autobiography, *Bring on the Empty Horses*, only to remove it in subsequent editions.[22] Olivier, however, does not hold back in his *Confessions*, perhaps as a means of absolving himself from any real sense of responsibility for her care: he even appears to find it difficult to understand why her changed attitude to him was 'unquestioningly evident' her after he placed her in a clinic in 1953, with an unknown doctor who was permitted to administer insulin coma treatment and ECT (Olivier, 1982: 160).

Prior her incarceration in Netherne Hospital under the care of Freudenberg, Leigh had seen other doctors in the US, but had been unwilling to undergo psychiatric or psychoanalytic treatment. Doctors appear to have taken it upon themselves to offer their opinions, their diagnostic expertise and their propositions for treatment without recourse to consulting Leigh herself. Thus, Dr Kubie, a New York doctor they had previously consulted, commented that he had been thinking back to their failure during the previous year 'to persuade [Leigh] of the importance of accepting intensive treatment ...'. He notes that she was, 'desperately anxious and uneasy and fearful at the thought of my keeping records'. Claiming that he made 'informal' notes to pass on to another doctor anyway, should the need arise. Kubie goes on to note that he has already given these notes to a Dr Glover who he recommends fully, in the knowledge that there have been previous disagreements among her doctors in terms of diagnosis. He has discussed her case with a Dr Greenson, who they have also consulted, and suggests that Leigh does not necessarily need to know that any of this communication about her state of wellbeing has been happening behind her back.[23]

It is worth noting here that the extant correspondence about her mental health predominantly excludes Leigh and is written to her partners: first Olivier, and then, with far less ominous, careerist or arrogant intent, to Merivale – her partner from the early 1960s until her death. This would not have been unusual in that women were viewed as the 'property' of their husbands on whose care they should rely. Leigh appears not to have been given, nor to have taken, much agency in treatment. Similarly, Leigh has had little agency in the ways in which her mental health has been historicised. Biographers use the small number of extant available medical records but also rely on anecdotal evidence, such as that offered to Vickers, whereby

> Another [school] friend, who hid behind the veil of anonymity ... [said] ... Vivien would get along fine ... then, suddenly, a complete turnaround. Sometimes it would last only a few hours, other times a day or more ... a completely different girl – moody, silent, petulant, rude, often hysterical. None of us understood it ... she ... suffered from some mental peculiarity ... frightening, almost on the order of a dual personality. (Vickers, 1990 [1988]: 21)

The memories of a nameless school-friend, while half dismissed, are given enough page space to catch the eye and embed themselves into a narrative whereby Leigh was effectively always beautiful but 'mad'. It is difficult to extract Leigh from this narrative construction, but later diagnostic correspondence with Merivale is more persuasive in its assertion that Leigh had a condition that could be understood, controlled and treated. One can only assume that the correspondence excluded Leigh even though it discusses her medical condition. Dr Conachy is far more aware of environmental factors than her doctors in the 1940s and 1950s were, and is also more than willing to disassociate her illness from her 'personality', recognising also the pressures of her professional status. Thus he writes:

> This lady is normally a person of very high intelligence and education, nimble wit and extremely good reasoning power. She has a quality of

determination and ruthlessness which have helped her to reach and maintain eminence in her profession ... I do not think that psychoanalysis, special psychotherapeutic techniques, or anything more than supportive psychotherapy at the most is called for in this case.

The patient is suffering from a manic-depressive illness. This first manifested itself in 1949, when a sudden onset of elation caused confusion in her social, sexual, and professional life. Since then, up until 1960, she has had fairly regular cyclic periods of manic and depressive phases, which have been variously diagnosed in the United States, in the manic phase, as schizophrenia and hysteria ... I feel there can be no doubt that she has a cyclic manic-depressive psychosis.[24]

Thus, to suggest as did Evelyn Waugh (above) that Leigh suffered from 'recurrent bouts of insanity' or that she had, as her anonymous school-friend claimed, some sort of 'mental peculiarity', reveals more about social attitudes to mental illness at the time than it does about Leigh's actual condition. Such social attitudes, both to mental illness and to women in general, informed the treatments she was given from the early 1950s onwards.

The realities of illness for a working actress

When Olivier flew Leigh back for treatment in 1953, it was in part because the film studio would not foot the bill for her treatment in the US. Contracted performers were effectively regarded as economic collateral, and Leigh was not well enough to work. Her illness was bad for business, and the high-profile context of the 1953 breakdown may or may not have been Olivier's rationale for placing her under Freudenberg at Netherne. The hospital had pioneered psychosurgery in the 1940s – leucotomy and lobotomy operations – but also later became one of the first hospitals to use art therapy with inmates. It became part of the newly formed state-funded National Health System in 1948, and was in effect the county asylum. Freudenberg had only been at the hospital since the late 1940s and, although later known for his promotion of social-centred approaches, was a pioneer of a new treatment for mental illness which involved insulin-induced comas: on arrival under his care this treatment was administered to Leigh. She was also given ECT here for the first time (Vickers, 1988: 233). Freudenberg's treatment meant she could not have visitors and her ex-husband, Leigh Holman, was only called to see her so that he could persuade her to continue her treatment. Freudenberg was a 'truly artistic man' (Becker and Bennet, 2000: 196):[25] he was keen to connect with Olivier at the beginning of Leigh's treatment.

Thank you so much for your letter. I am very pleased to have your address ... Fortunately the treatment is progressing very satisfactorily and the prolonged sleep still continues ... It is still too early to say definitely how much time will be needed to get her well but I am very hopefully about the outcome. It will interest you that she has in the meantime agreed to stay on so that no extension of the order was necessary. I hope you are finding the rest you were longing for on Ischia which I used to know well.[26]

I do intend terminating the sleep treatment between about the 8th and 18th of April. Further psychological ... treatment will then be necessary. Preferably for a few more weeks here if she will agree to it.[27]

Leigh somehow managed to get herself released and transferred to a private room in University College, London, where it was Coward, not Olivier, who ministered to her needs. Freudenberg was still involved in her treatment, although by May 1953 he was unwilling to continue with home visits to his artistic but clearly 'difficult' patient, suggesting a number of alternative doctors for Leigh, one of whom, Dr Glover, had already been recommended by Dr Greenson from California:

the most practical thing would probably be if someone from Oxford could call perhaps once or twice a week. I ... wonder whether ... Dr. Tredgold or Dr. E. Glover could be approached ... Perhaps you could consider all the possibilities and maybe we could then make some final arrangements about future treatment on Thursday, 4th June.[28]

Thus the man who had made the most radical intervention in Leigh's medicalisation gave notice to wash his hands of the case, only a few months after taking it on.

It is easy in hindsight to see that Olivier's handling of the situation was driven by panic: many of Leigh's later biographers draw our attention to his admission that his 'duties' towards her care made him 'mortally sick' at the time (Vickers, 1988: 235). Freudenberg was a new voice in psychiatric care, but his methods appear brutal to us now: he only agreed to take Leigh on if she stayed in the clinic and underwent what was effectively a dehumanising treatment, discussion of which rarely mentions or considers the patient's experience. Freudenberg believed in the power of insulin and ECT in cases where there was an, 'admixture of depression, elation, apprehension and agitation', despite emerging medical research that evidenced negative results and side-effects for patients (Freudenberg, 1947: 12). Michel Foucault's general observation is useful here, that 'while the victim of mental illness is entirely alienated in the real person of his [sic] doctor, the doctor dissipates the reality of the mental illness in the critical concept of madness' (Foucault (1991 [1967]: 277). There was, as previously noted, a gender dynamic to the treatment of Leigh as with all other women in the psychiatric system.

While there had been, between the two world wars, recognition that the high number of women amongst depressive cases was in part due to their environmental circumstances, and more women had moved professionally into psychiatric practice, in reality little had changed. Elaine Showalter notes that diagnoses remained unreliable even toward the end of the twentieth century, 'to cover a vast assortment of odd behaviours, cultural maladjustments, and political deviations' (Showalter, 1987 [1985]: 204). Even kindly Dr Conachy later commented that what biographer Edwards called Leigh's 'terrible breach of protocol' (Edwards, 1977: 218) – her outburst in the House of Lords – in her campaign to save the St James' Theatre in London from demolition in 1957, was precipitated by a manic phase rather than being generated from a political position about the need for state support in the arts: 'She adopts lost causes, will parade in the streets in processions, invade the House of Lords, and talk freely with the press.'[29] Similarly, Leigh's much commented upon sexual drive was not perceived as 'normal' for a woman, while it was perfectly fine for men to seek partners outside of marriage. Social factors clearly melded with physiological factors in diagnosis, and Freudenberg, a research-based clinician rather than a Hollywood psychiatrist, is focused on here more because of the ways in which the treatment he carried out on Leigh set the pace for the treatment of her mental illness from this point on, rather than because he was somehow more patriarchal and ruthless than any other doctor. It was fortuitous, however, that the 'extension to the order' he refers to in his letter to Olivier was never made. The side-effects of ECT were notoriously problematic even in the 1950s: memory loss and seizures – destabilising for anyone, let alone an actress.

Vivien Leigh had bouts of depression well before the 1953 breakdown. A number of biographers talk of her unpredictable behaviour during her work on A Streetcar Named Desire, both on stage and while filming on set. While Selznick's biographer claims that Leigh was 'one of those actresses who, once into a role, were trapped by it' (Thompson, 1993: 313), Leigh was playing Blanche, written as a sexualised and deluded 'woman of a certain age' – on stage or on a film set – from mid 1949 through to late 1950.[30] The point here is that most actors, male or female, find it challenging to switch off from their 'role' when engaged in such long periods of work with it: Leigh would not have been unusual in this. But it is much simpler to reiterate the narrative option whereby Leigh 'played mad' so well because she was 'mad', and this made her even more mad: she was, supposedly, the parts she played. This is certainly what Marlon Brando added to the layered myth of Leigh: 'in many ways she *was* Blanche ... memorably beautiful ... vulnerable [a] wounded butterfly'. According to Brando, she also, in a rather unladylike manner, openly sought sexual partners during filming – although he claims he excluded himself as he did not want to cross Olivier, to 'invade his chicken coop' (quoted in Capua, 2003: 112). Underpinning such assessments is a clear assertion that Leigh was someone else's property – the studio, the director, the husband – and that displays of her own sexualised agency, whether such stories are true or not, were unacceptable in a woman. To some extent Leigh's beauty, her acknowledged talent and her outspokenness made her as much a victim of social and moral hypocrisy as did her mental illness. One can't help wondering if the various rumours and myths which grew up around her playing of Blanche would have been less colourful had she not won an Oscar for playing the role?

Reading illness, reading Leigh

> I have recently been in touch with both Dr. Childs and Dr. Shribman and I gather from them that there is little chance of broaching the subject of treatment with Lady Olivier. The most she seems to be able to tolerate as psychiatric help is an occasional semi-social contact with Dr. Shribman. She seems to be managing not too badly at the moment and will still hope that a major manic episode can be avoided.[31]

Leigh was unwilling to engage in any kind of long-term talking therapy. The combined drug therapies with which she was treated would be more cautiously advised today. Like many of her generation, she was a heavy drinker by today's measured standards, but the cocktail of chemicals she was given to maintain a state of equilibrium were dangerous. This was especially the case in the mid 1960s, when her doctor reportedly sent 'libraxin, seconal, seranace and marplan', *in case* she became ill (Vickers, 1990 [1988]: 344). While libraxin is intended to settle the stomach, seconal is now not recommended unless the dose is carefully calculated if you have suffered from depression or alcohol abuse, and useage of marplan is only advised under close medical supervision with risks for those already experiencing mood disorders. Each of these drugs has side-effects that would impact significantly on professional practice for a performer, including drowsiness, dizziness, fainting, fever, stomach pain, problems with memory and over-excitement. Along with the drug commonly administered for tuberculosis – streptomycin – and her regular ECT treatments, it is quite surprising that Leigh managed to maintain a career on stage or screen for as long as she did. Doubtless, we know more about the side-effects of these treatments now, but these would have been expensive drug treatments recommended by high-calibre medical practitioners in Leigh's day.

One cannot effectively 'read' the relationship between Leigh's mental health condition and her career without a sense of both her victimhood and her professional survival. She was still extremely good box office well into the 1960s and continued to choose her roles carefully, happily receiving scripts for potential productions and favouring parts which would challenge her. In some ways hers remained an unusual career trajectory for an actress of her generation, she continued to find and make work through her 40s and into her early 50s both on stage and screen. Depression was less well understood half a century ago, and women were much more likely to be diagnosed as schizophrenic or manic depressive if 'out of sorts': in many senses their lifestyles were more limited by gendered social expectations than many men's – women were really still required to be homemakers and mothers above all else. As the other chapters in this volume evidence: Leigh was an accomplished, business-like and artistic homemaker. While motherhood was not something at which she excelled in terms of her own daughter, we should note that Olivier's fathering of his first child, Tarquin, was almost entirely carried out at a great distance, but this was rarely mentioned in the press. Again, frequently referred to or implied by the press, Leigh's neglectful parenting here was no more extraordinary than most upper-middle class women whose children were looked after by paid help. Indeed her own experience of parenting involved being moved from one continent to another at the age of 7, to be visited by her mother and her mother's 'male friend' once a year until she was in her teens.

It is also impossible to read Leigh's condition without recourse to an analysis of her professional relationship with Olivier. Olivier was ambitious and driven, but he initially lacked the screen persona that made Leigh, with little training or experience, a box office dream early in her career. Irene Selznick who produced *Streetcar* found Olivier, as did many others, an inexperienced commercial director, unwilling to listen and unwilling to concede error (Selznick, 1983: 324–328). Many of Leigh's professional colleagues thought her work better by far than Olivier's – thus Godfrey Winn pointed out that while the critics thought her Lady Macbeth inferior to Olivier's Macbeth, many found her performance 'electrifying' and, despite the professional critics, the audience gave her a 'tumultuous reception' (Winn, 1970: 382). Olivier's domestic ambitions required a devoted and competent wife at home. He had originally married into a theatrical dynasty through his relationship with Jill Esmond, moved on to marry an emerging global film star and then retreated as her star began to overwhelmingly outshine his own. Determined to maintain and develop a simultaneous career in film and theatre, Leigh was a victim of the patriarchal ownership and middle-class snobbery which dominated both the British theatre industry and its critics during the mid century. As a screen actress with a massive fan base, she was theatre box office gold, an accomplished comedienne she was popular with audiences and producers alike. But the classical stage was traditionalist and maintained by those who looked down on film acting as less skilled, less intellectually viable and less artistic.

There are numerous reports of Leigh stressing that she is an *artist*, with the associative implications of this framed by hard work, intellectual vigour, research, practice and creativity, as opposed to a 'gifted beauty' who happens to work as an actress. This was quite an assertion for a woman of her generation, and for one who could have simply retreated to wealthy domesticity at any moment in her career. One of her old school-friends, Patsy Quinn, who married into the English aristocracy, bizarrely told Leigh's early biographer and friend Alan Dent that she thought Leigh would have even 'excelled and been very happy as a great hostess or wife of some famous person, and never yearned for the stage' (Dent, 1969: 47). On the other hand, Elaine Dundy claims that Leigh was 'religiously what might be called a "far seeker"', and that later in life 'she was to describe herself as a "Zen-Buddhist-Catholic"' (Dundy, 1980: 180). Indeed, archival holdings of letters, theatrical and domestic memorabilia attest to a woman interested in the spiritual – her use of Pelmanism for memory and concentration,[32] a thirteen-page astrological reading, a detailed palm reading completed in the late 1940s. She was close friends with many gay actors and writers, and was not 'typically feminine', other than in her much commented upon beauty and home-making: she was not passive, and carefully designed many aspects of her life, even though the treatment of her illness suggests she was 'managed' by others.

There is no doubt that Leigh suffered from manic depression – as did many other artists of her generation – Tennessee Williams, Sylvia Plath, Georgia O'Keefe. A number of recent studies emphasise the link between manic depression and creativity: while careful not to trivialise depressive disorders with a simple equation of 'madness and genius', Kay Redfield Jamison points to the unusually high percentage of established artists who meet the criteria for depressive illness (Jamison, 1997: 45), and to the fact that historically treatments 'dampen a person's general intellect and limit … her emotional and perceptual range'.

Even in the late twentieth century she notes the lack of 'meaningful choices patients are given in treatment' (Jamison, 1997: 45). For Jamison, 'Manic-depressive illness ... is a very strange disease – one that confers advantage but often kills and destroys as it does so' (Jamison, 1993: 240). Like other female artists on the 'depression continuum', such as Sylvia Plath, Leigh shared a history of distant parenting, overwhelming attention from male admirers, partners with artistic ambitions and a lack of commitment to sexual fidelity, as well as a need for prolific creativity, perfectionism and domestic security (see Cooper, 2003). For Irene Mayer Selznick, the 'gods had given Vivien every possible gift: at her best, there never was exquisite beauty and charm so combined. Then as if they had gone too far, they added a flaw, tiny but lethal – a recurrent emotional disturbance, which brought her tragic years' (Selznick, 1983: 328).

Perhaps, however, this 'flaw' underpinned Leigh's ability to play such a range of roles, roles in which she deliberately underplayed her 'beauty' and performed the 'flawed but unique' aspects of imagined lives (Bean, 2013: 245). While her affair and marriage to Olivier meant she was permanently in the public mind as one half of the 'golden couple' of British theatre, globally she was permanently in the public eye because of her film work – in which many felt she outshone Olivier. Photographer Angus McBean notes that she did not make another film with Olivier after 1941 (McBean, 1989: 36): he may well have been haunted by her overwhelming success as Scarlett O'Hara, just as she was haunted by her illness. As late as 1966, Olivier sought medical advice in terms of his relationship with Leigh, as if she was some kind of incontrollable monstrous presence.[33] While theatrical autobiographies rarely paint colleagues in a positive light and often delight in the failings of others, in retrospect one would hope, however, that Olivier's contribution to the many myths of Leigh's 'madness' were not ultimately fuelled by her rejection of his offerings as a husband or by the simple, professional jealousy of one actor for another. Any correctives to the various constructions and 'readings' of Leigh's illness do have to embrace the significance of the patriarchal and sexist context of her personal life and professional career: men and women were simply perceived and treated unequally. To be a beautiful actress was one thing, but to be intelligent, ambitious, witty, artistic and demanding as well, left actresses open to levels of critique that went beyond the journalistically snide or toxic commentaries that many actors expected. In re-positioning Leigh, her work and life – as chapters in this volume seek to address – speak for themselves: her medical conditions, both physiological and psychological, were part of her oeuvre, not separate from it.

Notes

1 J.C. Trewin 'Vivien Leigh', dated 1967. Vivien Leigh Biographical File, V&A.
2 Streptomycin was being trialled in the late 1940s as a chemical treatment for tuberculosis, and was in common use after the success of trials. Side-effects could include ataxia, vertigo and cranial nerve damage, tinnitus and involuntary movement.
3 Elaine Dundy, novelist, journalist and playwright, was the first wife of Kenneth Tynan, the critic who in the mid 1950s continually gave Leigh poor, even vitriolic, notices to the point of an almost obsessive quest to malign her work: even Olivier, who later employed him as Literary Manager at the National Theatre, thought him somewhat blinkered in his view of Leigh's work. By the end of the Stratford Season in 1955, Tynan had been 'won over' by Leigh according to Maxine Audley (quoted in Vickers, 1990 [1988]: 248).
4 Vivien Leigh Archive THM/433/2 Named Correspondence and also the letters between the two in the Laurence Olivier Archive at the British Library Add MS 80085.
5 Unattributed source, quoted in review of Alexander Walker's biography, see Vivien Leigh Archive THM/433/4 Material relating to Vivien Leigh's Career.
6 Vivien Leigh, to Nöel Coward, Vivien Leigh Archive, 8 February 1953, THM/433/2/3.
7 Vivien Leigh, to Nöel Coward, Vivien Leigh Archive, 12 October 1955, THM/433/2/3.
8 Jack Merivale, to Vivien Leigh, Jack Merivale Letters, BFI: Box 2.
9 See Kate Dorney's Chapter 2 in this volume.
10 *Daily Mail*, 2 March 1977, p. 16.
11 Laura Thomson, *The Daily Telegraph*, 18 November 2013.
12 *Observer Magazine*, 31 July 1977.
13 Rachel Billington, 'Beauty and the Manic Beast', *Financial Times*, 29 October 1988.
14 Numerous letters to Leigh suggest a deep sense of connection with her over her illness, see Vivien Leigh Archives, THM/433/2.
15 Nöel Coward, to Vivien Leigh, 30 September 1955, Laurence Olivier Archive, Add MS 80085. Concerned that Olivier would consider his play 'a fucker', Coward sought Leigh's honest assessment – he respected her professional thoughts as well as wanting to confirm their friendship.
16 Laurence Olivier, to Stephen Watts, 13 February 1946: Laurence Olivier Archive Add MS 80619. BL.
17 Evelyn Waugh on Alexander Walker's *Vivien Leigh*, *Independent*, 23 May 1987.
18 T. Komisarjevski, to Olivier, Vivien Leigh Archive, THM/433/1.
19 Constance Collier, to Laurence Olivier, Vivien Leigh Archive, THM/433/1.
20 Lesley Storm, to Laurence Olivier, Vivien Leigh Archive, THM/433/1.
21 See Selznick, 1983: 217.
22 See Vickers (1990 [1988]) who quotes Niven from *Bring on the Empty Horses* 1975, London: Hamish Hamilton, pp. 309–321. This section has been removed from subsequent editions of the book, such as the 1976, Book Club Edition and 2006, Hodder edition.
23 Letter from Lawrence Kubie MD (NY), to Laurence Olivier, 25 March 1953. Dr Greenson also strongly recommends that Olivier consults with Dr Glover in

England, see letter to Olivier from Ralph Greenson MD, Beverly Hills, California, 30 March 1953, Laurence Olivier Archive, Add MS 80619.

24 Dr Arthur Conachy, to Jack Merivale, 20 June, 1961, Jack Merivale Letters, BFI: Box 2. It is worth noting his diagnosis is not shaped by the kind of sycophantic, arrogant attitude previous doctors had towards Olivier. 'A most charming, able, intelligent woman inflicted by a manic depressive illness, who with courage and marked strength of character, has taken a heavy and continuous emotional strain in her stride during the past year. The one undesirable factor in this pattern is her tendency to take considerable and regular amounts of alcohol, particularly in moments of stress. She refuses to modify this, but is in no sense an alcoholic.'

25 The Wellcome Library in London has archive holdings of Freudenberg's working papers, but case notes from Netherne have been removed from these. See Wellcome Library Western Manuscripts PP/RKF Freudenberg, Rudolph Karl (1908–1993 [listed incorrectly as he died in 1983]) and Freudenberg, Gerda (née Vorster) (1906–1995).

26 Dr R.K. Freudenberg, Netherne Hospital, 29 March 1953, to Laurence Olivier, Laurence Olivier Archive, Add MS 80619.

27 Dr R.K. Freudenberg, Netherne Hospital, 5 April 1953, to Laurence Olivier, British Library, Laurence Olivier Archive, Add MS 80619.

28 Dr R.K. Freudenberg, 30 May 1953, to Laurence Olivier, British Library, Laurence Olivier papers, Add MSS 80619.

29 Dr Arthur Conachy, to Jack Merivale, 20 June 1961, Jack Merivale Letters, Box 2.

30 The film premiered in New York in September 1951. According to Capua, filming finished in August 1950. See Capua, 2003: 115.

31 H.M. Segal MD, to Laurence Olivier, 24 October 1958, Laurence Olivier Archive Add MS 80169.

32 Popular in the early part of the twentieth century, Pelmanism was a form of 'mind training', a sort of 'self-help' tool for enhancing memory and concentration and for controlling thinking – what we might now call 'mindfulness'. The 'system' was taught via correspondence and Vivien Leigh was trained in Pelmanism as a child (Robyns, 1968: 55). This memory system was developed by W.J. Ennever (1869–1947), and hugely popular among the artistic middle classes: a later popular memory card game was developed from its principles. See Senate House, University of London, Special Collections.

33 See Dr S.M. Whitteridge, to Laurence Olivier, 9 December 1966, where he advises that Olivier not allow Leigh access to his new children, Laurence Olivier Archive, Add MS 80169.

References and bibliography

Bacall, Lauren (2005) *By Myself and Then Some*, London: Headline Books.

Barnes, David S. (1995) *The Making of a Social Disease: Tuberculosis in 19th Century France*, California: University of California Press.

Bean, Kendra (2013) *Vivien Leigh: An Intimate Portrait*, London: Running Press.

Becker, Thomas and Douglas Bennett (2000) 'Rudolph Karl Freudenberg – from pioneer of insulin treatment to pioneering social psychiatrist', *History of Psychiatry*, xi: 189–211.

Billington, Michael (2001) ed., *Stage and Screen Lives*, Oxford: Oxford University Press.

Bloom, Claire (1996) *Leaving a Doll's House*, London: Virago.

Capua, Michelangelo (2003) *Vivien Leigh a Biography*, North Carolina: McFarland Publishers Inc.

Chesler, Phyllis (1972) *Women and Madness*, New York: Avon Books.

Cooper, Brian (2003) 'Sylvia Plath and the depression continuum', *Journal of the Royal Society of Medicine*, 96 (6): 296–301.

Coward, Nöel [Graham Payne and Sheridan Morley eds] (1982) *The Nöel Coward Diaries*, London: Macmillan.

Dent, Alan (1969) *Vivien Leigh: A Bouquet*, London: Hamish Hamilton.

Dundy, Elaine (1980) *Finch, Bloody Finch: A Biography of Peter Finch*, London: Michael Joseph.

Edwards, Anne (1977) *Vivien Leigh: A Biography*, New York: Simon and Schuster.

Faulkner, Trader (1979) *Peter Finch: A Biography*, London: Angus and Robertson Publishers.

Foucault, Michel (1991 [1967]) *Madness and Civilization: A History of Insanity in the Age of Reason*, London: Routledge.

Freudenberg, R.K. (1947) 'Ten year's experience of insulin therapy in schizophrenia', *British Journal of Psychiatry*, 93: 9–30.

Granger, Stewart (1981) *Sparks Fly Upward*, London: Granada Publishing.

Jamison, Kay Redfield (1993) *Touched with Fire: Manic Depressive Illness and the Artistic Temperament*, New York: Simon and Schuster.

——— (1997) 'Manic depressive illness and creativity', *Scientific American*, 7: 44–49.

Kempson, Rachel (1986) *A Family and Its Fortunes*, London: Duckworth.

Koropeckyj-Cox, Tanya, Amy Mehraban Peinta and Tyson H. Brown (2007) 'Women of the 1950s and the normative life course: the implications of childlessness, fertility timing, and marital status for psychological well-being in late midlife', *Aging and Human Development*, 64 (4): 299–330.

Lesley, Cole (1976) *Remembered Laughter: The Life of Nöel Coward*, New York: Alfred A. Knopf.

McBean, Angus (1989) *Vivien: A Love Affair in Camera*, Oxford: Phaidon Press.

Niven, David (1976) *Bring on the Empty Horses*, London: Book Club Edition and (2006) London: Hodder and Stoughton.

Olivier, Laurence (1982) *Confessions of an Actor*, London: Weidenfeld and Nicholson.

Olivier, Tarquin (2012) *So Who's Your Mother?* London: Michael Russell Publishing Ltd.

Robyns, Gwen (1968) *Light of a Star: The Sensitive and Intimate Story of the Bewitching Vivien Leigh*, London: Leslie Frewen Publishers.

Selznick, Irene Mayer 1983 *A Private View*. London: Weidenfeld & Nicholson.

Showalter, Elaine (1987 [1985]) *The Female Malady; Women, Madness and Culture, 1830–1980*, London: Virago.

Sucre, Richard (n.d.) 'The Great White Plague: The Culture of Death and the Tuberculosis Sanatorium', www.faculty.virginia.edu/blueridgesanatorium/death.htm accessed 12 June 2016.

Taylor, John Russell (1984) *Vivien Leigh*, London: Elm Tree Books.

Thompson, David (1993) *Showman: The Life of David O. Selznick*, London: André Deutsch.

Vickers, Hugo (1990 [1988]) *Vivien Leigh*, London: Pan Books Ltd.

Walker, Alexander (1994 [1987]) *Vivien Leigh*, London: Weidenfeld and Nicholson.

Williams, Tennessee (2007 [1972]) *Memoirs*, London: Penguin.

Winn, Godfrey (1970) *The Positive Hour*, London: Michael Joseph.

PART II

The actress at work

4

An actress prepares
John Stokes

'To be born woman is to know—
Although they do not talk of it at school—
That we must labour to be beautiful'

(W.B. Yeats, 'Adam's Curse')

'Il faut souffrir pour être belle'

(French proverb)

Inherited worries about Vivien Leigh's beauty continue to threaten our understanding of her achievements. Throughout her career, critics of her stage performances returned to the vexed question of her looks: were they more of a curse than a blessing? Was she, so the weary cliché would have it, 'fated to be beautiful'? As Laurence Olivier said long after her death: 'the critics have never been able to accept beauty and talent. You can have one or the other, not both. She had both' (Olivier, 1986: 100). In an especially cruel twist, her constant efforts to improve her technique, to undergo further training in middle age, to discover a perfect emphasis and stick with it, the seriousness with which she took personal criticism: all were used as evidence that she lacked any innate ability.

Her beauty was a matter of proportion and symmetry, perfect structure revealed in carefully maintained surface. But it was thanks to her talent that this beauty was able to cross gender (Viola in *Twelfth Night*) and to co-exist with dark motives (Lady Macbeth), could lend modernity to tragedy (*Antigone*) and energy to comedy (*The Skin of Our Teeth*). For one of her greatest performances, Blanche DuBois in *A Streetcar Named Desire*, she deliberately ravaged her face with make-up to suggest the endless effort that goes into looking good. Throughout her life she took steps to deepen her understanding of her art, to refine her skills and to explore different approaches. The overall process might be described, very broadly, as a shift from self-presentation, with its stress on 'personality' and on the priority of appearance, to a more psychological concern with the roots of characterisation that was at its most intense in the mid 1950s when Leigh took on a series of major roles, mainly Shakespearean.

That her loveliness could be exploited in new and highly theatrical ways was realised with a brilliant stroke of theatrical imagination by Peter Brook in 1955 when he directed *Titus Andronicus* with Leigh as Lavinia. Adopting a technique inspired by Kabuki – aestheticising the results of male brutality as if they were too horrible to show naturalistically – Brook turned her suffering into a terrifying and seemingly permanent admonition. Decades later, he recalled Leigh's ability to find 'a beauty and a poetry in her misfortune. So Lavinia, raped and with her hands cut off – which we suggested just with red ribbons falling from her fingers to the ground – turned this piece of Grand Guignol into a haunting moment of beauty' (Brook, 2013: 35). The production, which starred Olivier as Titus, began in Stratford-upon-Avon and later had a season in London as well as touring continental Europe. Everywhere it made an extraordinary impact. And, as always, whatever the play, Leigh received letters from members of her audience, many of them clearly overcome by what they had seen, even to the point of collapse:

'I can find no words in which to tell you how deeply you wrung my heart as Lavinia – I was quite overcome', wrote a fan from Bristol:

> It was almost too beautiful to be borne – so pitiful so young so carefree and then so agonized and helpless, and you look so lovely throughout. Too lovely to be real dear! I found myself with such a hatred and horror in my heart at her betrayal and anguish and shame (the effect of shame was wonderful) that I had to really shake myself to realize it was not actually taking place. You were so fine in the part and on the Saturday when those beasts dragged you away, a man in the audience cried out with such a horror; that it gave me the shivers – With all truth and sincerity I say that I shall never see a more perfect performance, or a more lovely vision, of personal beauty on any stage.[1] (Figure 4.1.)

Countless devotees felt the same, as the Vivien Leigh and Laurence Olivier archives prove. There were a few newspaper critics, too, who were willing to acquiesce in Brook's vision. For Philip Hope-Wallace, 'even lopped Lavinia, most ghastly of spectacles, "thou map of woe", was made a memorable picture of silent reproach – Vivien Leigh making a marvellous grieving Christian martyr of her from some morbid Veronese canvas' (Hope-Wallace, 1955: 1074). Nevertheless, as was usually the case with Leigh, there was little unanimity. For neither

Figure 4.1   Leigh and Olivier in *Titus Andronicus*, Shakespeare Memorial Theatre, 1955, by Angus McBean.

the first nor the last time Kenneth Tynan seized an opportunity to pounce:

> As Lavinia, Vivien Leigh receives the news that she is about to be ravished on her husband's corpse with little more the mild annoyance of one who would have preferred foam rubber. (Tynan, 1955 c: 11)

If similes could kill, Leigh's career would have ended much earlier than it did. Fortunately not everyone felt the same as Tynan. When Evelyn Waugh reviewed *Titus* he managed to persuade himself that the actress was caught up in 'a private rite of enchantment' so that members of the audience, including himself, were invited to be complicit with her performance.

> When she left us to collect a basin full of blood she mimed a demure Victorian bride. When she mewed over the bookshelves, when she raised her paws to enumerate her ravishers, she just hinted an affinity with Dick Whittington's cat. She wrote in the sand with endearing nonchalance. When she was dragged off to her horrible fate she ventured a tiny impudent, barely perceptible roll of the eyes, as who should say: 'My word! What next?' She established complete confidence between the audience and the production. 'We aren't trying to take you in,' she seemed to say. 'You're too clever, and we are too clever. Just enjoy yourselves'.[2] (Waugh, 1955: 300–301)

Waugh's tribute reminds the historian not to expect consistency in audience response. No other twentieth-century actress came close to Vivien Leigh for stirring up such divergent views. It might seem unlikely, and certainly very distant from the director's intention, that Leigh would have asked her audience to delight in what amounted to a send-up of Shakespeare's bloody tragedy. Yet, we do know that she liked to joke with Noël Coward about this, her most grisly, role (Dent, 1969: 62).

We can infer even more about her wholeheartedly professional attitude to her work, which certainly didn't preclude an amused distance, from a letter about Lavinia that Leigh sent to her friend Meriel (Mu) Richardson:

> I have never enjoyed or perhaps 'enjoyed' is not the word – let's say been so interested in a part before. It is quite extraordinary to be tongueless and handless – to say nothing of raped (though that is the least of the apparent fortunes) on the stage for quite [ever?] and how it means one really has to act with one's thoughts and has taught me more than anything I have ever done.[3]

To 'act with one's thoughts' – by the 1950s this had become the overriding goal of an actress whom audiences had initially acclaimed for her theatrical presence.

Personality

When the critic and author Caryl Brahms reviewed *Titus Andronicus* she made an intriguing comparison and came up with an unusual metaphor.

To say that Miss Leigh is at her most moving when her Lavinia cannot speak is only to remind the reader that she is, as it were, the Fonteyn of Drama, taking direction as a river takes rain and so absorbing it into her art that who is to know what she found in herself and what she has been lent.[4]

This was a discreet way not only of hinting at the weakness of the actress's voice, her compensating elegance of movement, but of acknowledging her dependence upon external influence. Throughout her career Leigh saw herself primarily as an actress and had few, if any, directorial ambitions. Yet, although she tended to be guided by men, her professional relationships were not at all like that between Svengali and Trilby. She seems to have maintained good relations with one mentor even as she moved on to another. Nor did the guidance of directors, friends and agents necessarily determine the final outcome. Although she often sought out advice, we also know from her dealings with film directors such as Elia Kazan that she was quite capable of insisting on her own interpretation.

In her very early days she had been introduced to the French tradition. As a schoolgirl in her mid to late teens, she had been drilled by an actress from the Comédie Française in 'elocution and deportment' (Walker, 1987: 37) and, according to one account, had participated in a performance of Victor Hugo's *Ruy Blas* – a cornerstone of Sarah Bernhardt's nineteenth-century repertoire.[5] At RADA she sought out the French actress and teacher Alice Gachet, who rehearsed students in the language. It seems reasonable to assume that Gachet's emphasis would have been on projection rather than on motivation, on precision of gesture and correct rhythmic stress and – a resource Leigh would sometimes rely upon later – the ability to deliver lines at an exceptionally rapid rate. These techniques were certainly still emphasised at the Comédie Française and the Conservatoire well into the twentieth century.

Soon after leaving RADA, two important mentors entered her professional life: the agent John Gliddon and Sydney W. Carroll, the critic and producer who first picked her out. Having started out as an actor, Carroll was theatre critic for the *Sunday Times* between 1918 and 1923 as well as setting himself up as a producer. He now seems an interesting intermediary, a mixture of the entirely conventional and the intellectually enquiring. Like many of his contemporaries, he looked back to a Victorian and Edwardian past while showing some curiosity about recent continental experiment, writing, for instance, about Max Reinhardt. Leigh may have benefitted from Carroll's experience; more to the point, she already possessed some of the qualities that he admired. A 1923 collection of essays and reviews entitled *Some Dramatic*

Opinions contains 'A Plea for the Beautiful' which asks for a Ruskinian revival of aesthetic values from elocution to movement. Nevertheless,

> In making this appeal for beauty I am sensible of the fact that we have some very beautiful actresses. The stage is crowded with professional beauties, yet nevertheless is full of ugliness. Beautiful women do not, however numerically strong, make beautiful plays, though beautiful frocks may go far towards making a woman look beautiful. The beautiful actress is mainly engaged in showing her tragic inanity or fatal fascination. (Carroll, 1923: 36)

Something else was needed for artistic success and it had a name: 'personality'. Carroll's book contains a whole chapter entitled 'Personality and the Stage' (ibid: 100–107) in which he concedes 'that the first essential thing in an actress is to be interesting. I admit that no amount of plasticity will help the performer who is handicapped by an unattractive or unsympathetic stage personality' (ibid: 103).

'Personality' does more than simply give meaning to physicality. In a later book, *Acting for the Stage*, published in 1938 only three years after Leigh's initial success, Carroll amplifies the idea that while theatre depends on beauty, beauty benefits from theatre, by allowing that 'occasionally, intelligence and a lovely or handsome appearance are combined in a remarkable way' (Carroll, 1938: 5).

There was an obvious example to hand:

> I had the fortune to encounter Miss Leigh on the threshold of her career, a young girl whose mental balance equalled her physical poise, one who brought a divine sense of humour to meet the many vicissitudes and setbacks of the acting business, a girl of singular beauty and rare personality. (Ibid: 32)

The most important word is the last. 'Personality', Carroll had announced early on, is 'that essential asset for a stage career' (ibid: 3).

Although often treated as if it were some magical gift from the gods, 'personality', then as now, is one of several words we use to indicate a quality that is indefinable not because it lies beyond the reach of understanding but because it embraces energy and contradiction. For performers, 'personality', paradoxically, is the element of personal uniqueness that permeates impersonation. In the 1920s – just before Leigh's emergence – the equivalent word was 'It', and Joseph Roach has written at length about the idea of 'Itness', tracing the history back to the seventeenth century (Roach, 2007). Like today's related terms, 'celebrity' and 'presence', 'personality' is both an abstract and a personal noun – a quality and an identity. 'Personality' is like 'It' as defined by Roach: 'the power of apparently effortless embodiment of contradictory qualities simultaneously: strength *and* vulnerability, innocence *and* experience, and singularity *and* typicality among them' (ibid: 8). At the moment of performance the effect is dynamic: 'the opposite motions instigated by the contradictory forces ... drawing toward the charismatic figure as *attraction*; radiating away from him or her as broadcast *aura*' (ibid: 7).

In the 1920s and 1930s, some of the most powerful theatrical contraries embraced tradition and modernity, the advanced and the conventional. Vivien Leigh emerged in and through this climate making her, in another set of contraries, both typical and singular. Complicating matters even further, as her screen career got underway, she became both physical and transcendent, absent and present. But, generically and on stage, the most frequent of female opposites remained innocence and experience, the traditional contraries of the *coquette*.

In 1935, having made a modest début in *The Green Sash*, a play set in fifteenth-century Florence, Leigh appeared in another historical drama, *The Mask of Virtue*, an adaptation by Ashley Dukes of a German play based on a story by Diderot and set in eighteenth-century Paris. An aristocratic libertine is duped by his ex-lover into marrying an apparently virginal young girl who is, in fact, a prostitute. When the trick is discovered and the girl repents her deception, the couple stay together. As a melodramatic comedy, the moral point is to show that a fallen woman can remain fundamentally pure and be rewarded. More immediately, it offered scope for Leigh to demonstrate her gracefully erotic style. An astonishingly effusive reception led to the famous film contract with Alexander Korda.[6]

The challenge to develop as a stage actress remained, however, depending upon the availability of parts. Although Leigh probably wasn't to read him until later (Funke and Booth, 1961: 239), it is clear that ideas superficially similar to those put forward by Stanislavski were afloat in Europe and America in the 1920s and 1930s. For all his belief in the importance of 'personality' even Sydney Carroll, for one, had allowed that this fundamental quality could sometimes become ingratiating and over-indulged at the expense of identification with another:

> You will see Miss Jones playing Miss Jones; Mr Smith playing Mr Smith; and in every part, in every play, you will find personality fitted into character, instead of the assumption and development of character through personality. (Carroll, 1923: 100)

By contrast, ideal acting,

> should be a complete projection of oneself into the soul and body of someone else with the object of exactly portraying that someone else. Such acting seems to me an accomplishment on a much higher plane than the subordination of a part to one's own personality. (Ibid: 102–103)

Consequently,

> These players with marked personalities interest me enormously, quite as much as they do the general play-going public; but I am an enthusiast for the real actor, the man who can be something other than himself, who can show you that there are no boundaries to the imagination. (Ibid: 105–106)

Although now signed up for films, Leigh was still intent on becoming a 'real' actress in Carroll's sense, which is to say a stage actress. In the year after *The Mask of Virtue*, with Ivor Novello, she played Lady Anne in *Richard II*, an OUDS (Oxford University Dramatic Society) production directed by John Gielgud; a child-like ingénue in *The Happy Hypocrite*, a musical adaptation by Clemence Dane and Richard Addinsell of a Regency fantasy by Max Beerbohm; and Anne Boleyn in Shakespeare's *Henry VIII* at the Regent's Park Open Air Theatre. In 1937 she appeared in *Bats in the Belfry*, a Wildean farce; played Ophelia to Oliver's Hamlet at a rain-soaked Elsinore; and Titania in Tyrone Guthrie's Victorian fairy-tale staging of *A Midsummer Night's Dream*. By the early 1940s, though her film career was now paramount, she took on the major role of Jennifer Dubedat in Shaw's *The Doctor's Dilemma* (1942). The range of stage plays was deliberately disparate; the evidence suggests that the actress was consciously trying to broaden her experience and her appeal. 'When an actor or actress has had a certain amount of experience on the stage, and perhaps, a little success,' she noted at the time of *The Doctor's Dilemma*, 'it becomes increasingly important and difficult to choose the right part and the right play. The audience expect more and they want to see new facets of an actor's art, new sides to his or her personality and, quite rightly, they become more critical and on their guard against unreasoning praise.'[7]

Nevertheless, the reviews of her performances up until this point are in many ways strikingly consistent: awestruck acknowledgement of her beauty and her handling of period costume, reservations about her delivery, particularly of verse. Reviewing her Titania, the *Evening Standard* said that she 'glimmers through the forest like a star, and speaks her lines with a starry beauty which however does not always suggest a heartfelt appreciation of them'.[8] While James Agate suggested that she spoke 'a lucid prose' in the part.[9]

In 1945 – after *Gone With The Wind* and war-time tours entertaining the troops – Leigh returned to the theatre in Olivier's production of Thornton Wilder's *The Skin of Our Teeth* (1942). The play, rarely revived these days, is the history of the human race told in what Olivier recognised as a popular 'cartoon' mode. A suburban couple relive the Biblical flood and various historical crises to emerge by the 'skin of their teeth', making it an ideal post-war play. Formally it was a lightweight version of Pirandello, arguably a forerunner of 'the absurd'; its near contemporaries were the Marx Brothers' films and the 1941 movie *Hellzapoppin'*. There are many moments when the fourth wall illusion is broken by direct address to the audience. In order to play the part of 'Sabina', who effectively directs the show on stage, Leigh was required to be lively and commanding. Scantily dressed, she embodied both the 'eternal feminine' and an erotic modern woman. Much later, in 1959, Leigh chose the play for her first venture into the medium of TV. Throughout the live broadcast, which has survived in a recording, she displays enormous confidence, and the alienation devices – peering into the camera and so on – give a sense of comic rapport with an audience while reinforcing the contraries of intimacy and distance that had originally marked her out as a 'personality'[10] (Figure 4.2).

Early in 1949, the Oliviers, by now the most celebrated theatrical couple in the country, appeared at the New Theatre in three plays: *Richard III* (Leigh as Lady Anne), *The School for Scandal* (Leigh as Lady Teazle) and, most significantly, *Antigone*, a translation of Anouilh's

Figure 4.2   Vivien Leigh as Sabina in *The Skin of Our Teeth*.

version of Sophocles with Leigh in the name part. In France in 1944 the play had been seen as an ambiguous comment on the Occupation; in London five years later it was open to less contentious interpretations. The setting was restrained. Olivier in evening clothes played the Chorus, allowing Leigh to move into the centre stage, quite literally. Her dark hair cut close, her features pale, her eyes wild and staring, her body remained intensely still. To those accustomed to Leigh's fluid grace this really was a surprise. She had, said *The Times*, 'the appeal of an exquisitely carved statuette'.[11] Even more surprising, and noted by several but not all, was the fact that she had learned how to lower her voice to give it a new authority. Intensive work with Elsie Fogerty, teacher of speech and founder of the Central School, much respected by Olivier, was beginning to show results. As Sydney Carroll wrote to his former 'discovery':

> I tell you honestly that it's the finest thing that you have done. It combines the chiselled clear-cut classicism of the Greek with the passionately moving impulses of the modern.[12]

Although his letter was intended as consolation for some of the less than convinced reviews, Carroll recognised that the role marked an advance. Recasting Greek tragedy in present-day circumstance is a French tradition dating back to the seventeenth century, but Carroll's combination of ancient and modern had particular relevance to Leigh at this moment, and would help her to bring a contemporary sensibility to some monumental roles (Figure 4.3).

Antigone was immediately followed by the most morally controversial production of the post-war years: Tennessee Williams's *A Streetcar Named Desire*, in which Leigh challenged her own legend and brought the *coquette* up to date by embodying her decline. Harold Hobson, critic of *The Sunday Times*, came closest to foretelling the ways in which Leigh's subsequent performances would develop in the 1950s. Describing her as 'more fatiguedly beautiful than ever' he first of all wrote of her performance that it 'mitigates nothing of the horror and the evil terror of Blanche DuBois's moral and physical collapse'. Initially finding her 'too restless, too distracted', he succumbed completely 'to the overwhelming power of her final scene when she loses her fragile hold on reason and frantic fear gives way to a trust, even more frightening, in the asylum attendants who lead her off the stage'. It was, he concluded, 'an impressive performance, casting out pity with terror' (Hobson, 1949a: 2). In November, Hobson, who had been in correspondence with Olivier, revisited the production:[13] 'I said a month ago that this performance casts out pity with terror. I was wrong. The balance and the struggle with the woman medical attendant chills the

Figure 4.3   Vivien Leigh as *Antigone*, by Angus McBean.

spine, but the pity is overwhelming' (Hobson, 1949 b: 2). Leigh's extraordinary representation of a female psyche under stress had tipped the balance of Aristotelian tragedy in a new and disturbing direction that required technical solutions to match psychological insight. Later on, about to start working on the film version, Leigh wrote to the director Elia Kazan:

> I may be totally wrong but having tried a number of different things over the last 9 months, I am sure it is desperately important to get as much variety and as little monotony into BLANCHE'S sudden flights, fancies, terrors and what have you's, as possible. What I'm trying to express very badly is that the running, clutching, brittle, jumpy exposition of BLANCHE'S nervosity quickly becomes tedious, and one must find as many different ways as possible of expressing her neurasthenia.[14]

Playing Blanche had encouraged her to think more probingly about characterisation and the roots of emotion. She told an interviewer that before the stage production Tennessee Williams had explained to her

> how he had traced the journeys of his two leading characters. Blanche passes from delicacy to decadence and her brother-in-law from simplicity

to brutality. When she comes to stay under his roof in New Orleans their paths cross and tragedy is inevitable. Their story is an eloquent plea for tolerance and understanding.

It followed that

Far from being an evil character, Blanche is simply a sensitive young girl who, at the age of 16, faced the horrifying disillusionment of having married a handsome degenerate.

On no account was Blanche to be viewed as a prostitute (a topic of much discussion at the time), but rather as 'a pitiful soul who is the unfortunate victim of loneliness'.[15] This concern with Blanche's past history is equally apparent in remarks Leigh made much later:

I tried in *Streetcar* to let people see what Blanche was like when she was in love with her young husband when she was seventeen or eighteen. That was awfully important, because Blanche, who needn't necessarily have been a beautiful person but she – you should have been able to see what she was like, and how this gradually had happened to her ... you should have to evoke this whole creature when she was young and when she was tender and trusting, as opposed to what she had become – cynical and hard, mad, and distressed and distraught. (Funke and Booth, 1961: 244)

Probably as a result of a number of factors – her experience in films working with a range of directors, the influence of her husband and, above all, the demands made upon her by great roles – from this point on, if not before, Leigh developed the preparatory habit of imagining the previous lives of the women that she played and, quite specifically, of treating this imagined evidence as a clue to their mature relationships with men.

Histories

The few recordings available are of limited help in understanding Leigh's accomplishments as a Shakespearean. Narrow vowels, swooping tones, the sense of special occasion that she brought to the delivery of famous lines are as likely to alienate as to persuade today's listener. There has been more than one revolution in verse speaking since her time and there's no easy way back, except through sympathetic acts of the historical imagination and careful reconstruction.

Already, by 1951, Kenneth Tynan was claiming to hear in her voice a kind of fastidious gentility – though few in her audience seem to have responded with quite his anger. The more fundamental questions were to do with her representation of femininity, its nature, its function and its power. The qualities of 'incisiveness, *retenue*, and obvious intelligence' (Agate, 1935) that, in the words of James Agate, had first marked her out as special, were no longer sufficient in themselves, certainly not in the roles to which she now aspired.

As their contribution to the Festival of Britain in 1951, the Oliviers presented Shaw's *Caesar and Cleopatra* together with Shakespeare's *Antony and Cleopatra*, both directed by Michael Benthall. Leigh scored well in the Shaw, which she had filmed in 1944, finding that it suited her light comedy approach; the Shakespeare was more difficult. Shaw's heroine is effectively little more than a teenage girl; Shakespeare's a middle-aged woman. The most obvious technical challenge for the actress would be to age between the two plays. In preparation, Leigh carried out research into the historical Cleopatra. She read Plutarch and other works that dealt with events that lay beyond those outlined in the play. These included a novel by Emil Ludwig which began with Cleopatra's girlhood and, although they were not to meet again for thirteen years, continued with her first encounter with Antony when she was 14 and he 27.

> There they sat at table, an Aphrodite bright as the crescent moon, a merry Hercules with youthful features, both far enough from the mature divinities whom they would one day mime and represent; a tender Greek virgin, a Roman officer, Antony and Cleopatra. (Ludwig, 1937: 27)

Early stress on her virginity prepares the way for Cleopatra's eventual discovery of the sexual passion that dominates the remainder of the book in a lurid and highly physical way. Cleopatra repeatedly 'flings' herself at her lover, is possessed by 'a torrent of physical force' (ibid: 172), moves 'like a young animal' (ibid: 178) and expresses 'Bacchic' feelings (ibid: 215). A more recent fiction offered additional insights. Leigh's friend Thornton Wilder gave her proofs of his epistolary novel *The Ides of March* (1949) which she had specially bound.[16] This is a fictional account of intertwined lives in the years 46–45 BC. Like Emil Ludwig, Wilder stresses Cleopatra's girlhood as preparation for a future in which she will become equal to men.[17]

Current academic scholarship was at least as important – not only for Leigh but for Olivier and Benthall as well. In the previous year, John Dover Wilson had published his edition of *Antony* for the New Cambridge Shakespeare and in his introduction (Shakespeare, 1950: xvii) had adjudicated between the views of A.C. Bradley, who had dealt with Cleopatra in his *Oxford Lectures on Poetry* (Bradley, 1950: 279 308) by calling her the 'courtesan of genius', and those of Lord David Cecil in his *Antony and Cleopatra* (Cecil, 1944), who saw the play as an historical and political drama. Despite their academic disagreements, all three critics adopted an essentially character-based approach that worked well with the primary concerns of the actors as they went into rehearsal. For all her obsessive concern with costume and appearance, Leigh was never simply interested in effect. Cause was more important. What did a character bring to the play in which she appeared? Invariably this meant: what does she bring to emotional and sexual relationships?

When Dover Wilson wrote to Olivier asking if he could set aside tickets, Oliver took the opportunity to ask for comments about the shortened performance text that he and Benthall had created.[18] Worried about playing time, Olivier admitted that he couldn't 'really arrive at the true reason for the length of the play after Antony's death, and as the part of Cleopatra was written for a boy of 14, I can't quite believe that all the various vicissitudes of character attributed to Cleopatra by many purists can really have been intended.'[19]

As a follow-up the actor sent Dover Wilson a full list of cuts. Most of these, he said, were merely functional – until Act Four:

> Going straight on, we merely cut Scene 11; and now we do something which I fear may shock your Shakespearian scholarship, and that is to cut Act 4, Scene 13, Cleopatra: 'Help me, my women, etc.'
>
> I know of certainly one famous Cleopatra who has never failed to get an unfortunate laugh in this scene and, apart from that, I do believe that to a modern audience the absolute knowledge that Antony's grief was all for nothing does not so much stir their sympathy as their irritation, as to the present day mind sheer futility is no longer tragic and detracts very much from the emotion that should be inspired by 'Where souls do couch on flowers etc.'[20]

The scene in question is extremely short, a dozen or so lines in which Cleopatra and her attendants plan to fool Antony by claiming that she has committed suicide. Omitting the scene not only sped up the action but ensured that Cleopatra emerged as considerably less devious than might otherwise have been the case, and that the passionate feelings between the two lovers epitomised in the lines that follow Antony's 'Where souls do couch on flowers' were thrown into greater relief. In his reply, Dover Wilson was sanguine: 'though the cut of 4.13 took breath away at first, and will certainly bring the professors down upon you, this old prof. is content to wait and see how it works!!'[21] In the event, he was full of praise for all concerned, especially Leigh.[22]

Occasionally mentioned in the more searching reviews, Olivier's editorial interventions do, indeed, seem to have worked well. For all the unease that greeted Leigh's representation overall, few spectators could resist the stripped-down intensity of her closing moments. Only one or two, such as T.C. Worsley, stood out for their refusal to be persuaded.[23] Tynan, characteristically, went much further than anyone and seized the opportunity of his new commission at the *Evening Standard* to launch a full- scale critique under the heading 'How Great is Vivien Leigh?':

> there is in Miss Leigh's Cleopatra an arresting streak of Jane Austen. She picks at the part with the daintiness of a debutante called upon to dismember a stag, and her manners are first-rate ... Miss Leigh's piercing, candid blankness is superbly pretty; and for some years to come it will not be easy to refrain from wishfully equating her prettiness with greatness (Tynan, 1951: 9).[24] (Figure 4.4.)

The fact that Tynan's attacks were so sustained invites speculation as to what lay behind them. A frequent explanation is that the critic believed that Olivier, his great hero, was obliged to hold back his full range of artillery so that Leigh's relative frailty wouldn't be shown up. This is quite likely. But Tynan also knew full well that beauty was Leigh's unquestioned possession. By treating her immaculate surface as frigid essence, his criticisms became a form of abuse. This was more than the evaluation of a performance – the critic's task – it denied all possibility of personal development – which was otiose. It's noticeable, for instance, that he was considerably less vicious, though still harsh on occasion, when writing about Peggy Ashcroft.

A more constructive response came from the director Glen Byam Shaw who, invited to comment on the two productions (perhaps because he had directed the Shakespeare himself in 1946, and was also a long-term acquaintance of Leigh's), delivered in a letter to Leigh what, despite his protestations, was obviously a carefully considered reply.[25] *Caesar and Cleopatra* passed muster, especially the comedy, although Byam Shaw did hint at what was to come when he wrote: 'You act with your whole body in the most delightful way, & the way that the character matures during the performance is wonderfully true and effective. There is also an animal quality in it which is very thrilling and very Eastern.' As he moved on to the Shakespeare he became more involved and the matter of 'animal quality' even more pertinent:

> Don't hate me when I say that to me you didn't really get started until the scene with the messenger, but from then on it was magnificent & absolutely right in scale.

He then went through Act One. The very first scene was

> To me not voluptuous enough. They seem to be married & happily so. There is no smouldering fire, no strange and almost frightening sensuality ... The lusts of the flesh are too delicately or politely indicated. It should be sexually exciting to watch. To me both you & Larry are far too discreet. I can't see the bellows & the fan cooling a gypsy's lust.

Figure 4.4   *Antony and Cleopatra*, by Angus McBean.

Accordingly, the next scene, though short and lacking Antony,

> should also provide evidence of just how much in love Cleopatra is with
> him:
>> It's the start of the fight between her and Rome. We should see all her
>> Eastern intuition, suspicion & jealousy at work in her.

Byam Shaw was nevertheless convinced that 'You can teach your audience much more about life and love than you do at present'. Repeatedly

he stressed the erotic, commenting on the lines 'Noblest of men, woo't die?/ Hast thou no care of me':

> The way you said that was sublime. I shall never forget it. Yes, the tears jerked out of my eyes but that is nothing much; what you did for me is to make me realise that the love between a man and a woman can be more important than anything else in the world and that is something far beyond tears or sobs, but darling, you must act Scene III with the same amount of truth, humanity and depth although the circumstances are entirely different.

When it came to Act One, Scene Five:

> Forgive me for saying this but the whole scene should, as it were, be played below the waist. – It is sexual from beginning to end ... Sex, sex, sex. It is animal, primitive & restively unsatisfied.
>
> Again you seem to me too cultured, too much in control. Not enough like the woman who envies the horse that bears the weight of her lover's body.
>
> After that you seem to throw away all care, consideration and discretion and play the part as though you were, in fact, Cleopatra. The result was what one had dreamed of.

Byam Shaw was known to be a highly controlling director who tended to arrive at rehearsals with a carefully plotted promptbook – and his chance to rectify Leigh's 'too cultured' manner, to lead her even more deeply into the realm of the 'human', was to come in the summer of 1955, when he directed the Oliviers in *Macbeth* as part of a season including John Gielgud's *Twelfth Night* and Brook's *Titus*.[26] Rehearsals for *Twelfth Night*, which was to open, were fractious, with severe disparities between Gielgud's romantic approach and Olivier's determination to play Malvolio as the embittered victim of social prejudice. Leigh, cast as Viola, prepared by reading the Victorian Mary Cowden Clarke, whose series *The Girlhood of Shakespeare's Heroines in A Series of Tales* had first appeared in the 1850s. In a series of 'prequels' Cowden Clarke imagined events prior to those covered in the plays themselves. Obviously the genre was most compelling when – unlike Cleopatra – there was little or no historical evidence upon which the character could have been based. As Leigh later recalled, Cowden Clarke's 'Viola, for instance, was very helpful to me because there was the whole of Viola's life before the play starts, and the fact that she'd seen Orsino when she was a small girl, so when she saw him suddenly at court – when she comes to Illyria – she's already in love with him, which starts her on the right foot' (Funke and Booth, 1961: 254–255). Cowden Clarke does indeed stress Orsino's youthful good looks: Viola's father describes 'his frank, yet refined beauty; the poetical look that beamed in his earnest eyes, and animated his handsome, intelligent countenance' (Cowden Clarke, 1892, vol. 5: 144). Once seen by Viola, Orsino 'became the object of her fond contemplation, her romantic regard, and filled her mind to the exclusion of any other man's idea as a lover' (ibid: 232).

Gielgud's *Twelfth Night* was to be followed by Byam Shaw's *Macbeth*, and Leigh again found some biographical hints in Cowden Clarke. She told an interviewer later on that 'there's marvellous account of Lady Macbeth before *Macbeth* starts, about how Macbeth rode up to the castle when she was a young woman and how she fell in love with him. Because, to me, "Macbeth" is a great love story and I'd never found Lady Macbeth a monster. I think she's a perfectly understandable human being and I adored playing it. It's one of my favourite roles' (Funke and Booth, 1961: 255).

Cowden Clarke's 'The Thane's Daughter', is long and full of incident, a complete novel in itself (Cowden Clarke, 1892, vol. 1: 116–202). It supplies a number of possible reasons for Lady Macbeth turning out as she does: her mother is disappointed at her being female rather than male and dies young, the girl is devoted to her father, she is innately cruel and even as a baby manages to kill a moth; she is beautiful but interested in masculine pursuits. Her marriage to Macbeth nevertheless brings together two people who have much to give one another and, despite the death of their son from an unspecified illness, this is still the case at the time when Shakespeare's play begins:

> There is a plenitude of feminine charm in the delicate features and figure that satisfies his inclination for that which is in contrast with his own manhood of strength and vigorous proportion; while in the marked decision, self-possessed manner, and confirmed opinion, that distinguish her character, there is that which he feels supplies well the defects in his own nature of which he is perhaps half conscious … Proud were they of and in each other; and joyfully did they link their lives in one, accepting a joint fate from that time forth. (Ibid: 162)

As Gail Marshall has explained, Cowden Clarke's narratives, with their emphasis on 'parental influence' and 'family dynamics', belong in the 'world of nineteenth-century fiction' (Marshall, 2012: 110). For a mid twentieth-century actress, however, the prequels suggested the grounds for psychological motivation, a way of thinking about relationships between men and women, about similarities and difference, and what can develop when mutual attraction coalesces into a single intent. From Leigh's perspective, characters behave as they do for reasons located in a distant past that may not be immediately referred to in the text. She disinters and reimagines a specifically female conditioning, looks to establish the origins of what we would now term gender identity in early manifestations of sexual desire.

In his review of Margaret Leighton's performance at Stratford in 1952 Tynan had protested, with all the perversity that made him such an effective *provocateur*, that 'it is probably a mistake to cast a woman at all, since Lady Macbeth offers none of the openings for nostalgia, yearning, and haggard glamour which attach to every other great female part, from Cleopatra to Blanche DuBois. No, Lady Macbeth is basically a man's role ...' (Tynan, 1952: 9). It was surely no accident that his two examples of 'haggard glamour' should have been career-defining roles for Leigh. There was certainly nothing unprepared about his single, spectacularly dismissive, sentence about her Lady Macbeth:

> Vivien Leigh's Lady Macbeth is more niminy-piminy than thundery-blundery, more viper than anaconda, but still quite competent in its small way. (Tynan, 1955b: 6) (Figure 4.5.)

When it comes to theatre reviewing, the size of the reference usually reflects the scale of the performance, as Tynan was very much aware. Many years later, when he was involved with the notably sexy Roman Polanski film of *Macbeth*, he told another critic, John Russell Taylor, that 'he thought that was one of the worst errors of judgment he had ever made. In retrospect the combination of Olivier and Vivien, with its emphasis on the way Macbeth is held in sexual thrall by his lady and so will do anything to please her, made more sense of the play than any other reading he had seen, unconventional though it was in terms of the usual battle-axe interpretation of Lady M' (Russell Taylor, 1984: 99). But even Tynan's wife at the time of the Stratford season, Elaine Dundy, thought 'Ken was completely off base, as did not only other critics and theatregoers but her theatrical peers'. For Dundy, Leigh 'was the best Lady Macbeth I have ever seen, perhaps because, for once, Lady Macbeth was *married* to Macbeth both off and on the stage' (Dundy, 2002: 197–198). Dundy was not alone in recognising the double act as the portrait of a marriage, perhaps of <u>any</u> marriage. For Harold Hobson, 'Miss Vivien Leigh's pale and exquisitely lovely Lady Macbeth does at least explain why Macbeth married her, a mystery too many Lady Macbeths leave unelucidated' (Hobson, 1955: 4). There was much more to Leigh's understanding of the role than Tynan could initially acknowledge. Her expression of sexual love gained in power not simply because of her own predilections and experience (not our concern here), but because they were backed up by her preliminary research and by a post-war culture in which the woman's place in heterosexual marriage was both sacrosanct and increasingly under

Figure 4.5   Lady Macbeth, 1955, by Angus McBean.

scrutiny (see Stokes, 2007). For a would-be classical actress it was a remarkably modern reading – which makes it all the more regrettable that the 1955 Stratford and London seasons and the international tours that followed should, despite her being offered in 1958 Portia at the Old Vic, have turned out to be the culmination of Leigh's Shakespearean career. As Viola, Lady Macbeth and Lavinia she had enthralled some and disappointed others. Her ambition, integrity and determination to improve must sometimes have been undermined not only by her mental fragility but by the increasingly unreasonable and old-fashioned demands made upon her maturing 'personality'.

Longevity

Unless they are prepared to make a feature of their own changing appearance, actors, especially female ones, are rarely allowed to grow old in the same way and at the same rate as the rest of us. Not only must they endure close physical scrutiny, the gap between the declared or apparent age of a character and the perceived or known age of the performer, though flexible, risks becoming part of the show. Sometimes audiences find this fascinating, even heroic, more often they raise a collective eyebrow. What is true of physical beauty is equally true of a quality such as 'personality'. As times change and the dialectics of attraction shift, so characteristics once respected may come to seem outdated. In the late 1950s and early 1960s, often ill, her marriage under intolerable strain, Leigh faced the continuing problem of whether a romantic presence, a 'personality' established in the 1930s and refined through constant effort in the post-war years, could be further reconceived in the light of middle age. Given the scale of the prejudice and the lack of parts for older women, it is remarkable that she succeeded to the extent that she did.

She even took on new technical challenges such as the musical *Tovarich*, for which she won a Tony award, which required singing and dancing lessons and was relatively well reviewed when it opened in the US in 1963. Nevertheless, continuing a longstanding habit, Leigh and her advisors still tended to look across the channel for inspiration. *Duel of Angels* (1963), Christopher Fry's adaptation of Giraudoux's *Pour Lucrèce*, was a commercial and, to an extent, critical success, although significantly, and perhaps ominously, it drew upon past traditions and theatrical legends (Stokes, 2005: 176–178). Following on from *Streetcar* there had been mention of *La Dame aux Camélias* – a personal favourite of Blanche DuBois – and Leigh did, indeed, tour the Antipodes in a version in the early 1960s. (Plans for a production on America TV never came to anything.) *Diane de Lys* by Dumas fils, *Le lys rouge* by Anatole France, a version of Daudet's *Sapho*, were all considered and rejected.[27] A seeming anomaly such as *Look after Lulu*, Noel Coward's adaptation of an ancient Feydeau farce at the radical Royal Court in 1959, can be explained not only as an attempt to raise cash (which, despite a transfer to the West End, it failed to do) but as an instance of late Francophilia. George Devine, Artistic Director, had known the

Oliviers since the 1930s, his enthusiasm for the French canon was long established and he had appeared happily alongside Leigh in *The Skin of our Teeth*. *Lulu* featured fishnet stockings and tight garments much as Wilder's play had done earlier. It took another Francophile, Harold Hobson, to identify a fundamental problem: Leigh 'does not as Feydeau intended, look ridiculous, absurd, grotesque. On the contrary she looks ravishing for she cannot look anything else' (Hobson, 1959: 15).

The name of Ibsen sometimes came up in discussion. The actress herself rejected Michael Meyer's translation of *The Lady from the Sea*,[28] but she did show interest when, in August 1964, Michael Redgrave suggested she play Hedda Gabler and Natalya in Turgenev's *A Month in the Country* at the new Yvonne Arnaud Theatre in Guildford.[29] Chekhov, too, had his appeal and Leigh did reasonably well, though often in poor health, in an American run of *Ivanov* directed by Gielgud in 1966. She knew that tastes were changing – her personal investment in new plays such as Brendan Behan's *The Hostage* makes that clear – but it can't have been easy to see where she might fit in. Despite Tynan's malevolent over-statement, it's true that she was associated to a damaging degree with theatrical status and social 'breeding'. Just how desperate the situation sometimes felt is demonstrated by the strange idea that she might assume a rubber mask in order to play Archie Rice's dowdy and put-upon wife in John Osborne's *The Entertainer* (Wardle, 1978: 213). Fortunately, American writers offered less class-bound roles. In 1966, she worked on Edward Albee's A *Delicate Balance*, potentially a very appropriate choice, hoping to open the following year.

A 'great career' is not only a matter of financial success and critical acclaim, but also the result of applied intelligence and the kind of professional acumen that is prepared to adapt, to exploit and, when necessary, to lie low. Back in the 1930s, Sydney Carroll, Leigh's mentor, had written on the basis of her début that 'It is grand to think that old England can turn out all promising material out of which we hope to see emerge the Bernhardts and the Duses of the future' (Carroll, 1938: 33).

He was writing when the legendary continental divas were still present in living memory. Bernhardt had died in 1923 aged 79; Duse in 1924 aged 66. Their survival had become a measure of their greatness. For Vivien Leigh, who was to die at the age of 53, survival, sadly, wasn't to be an option. For some she remained the over-indulged subordinate of a very great actor; for others, a vast number of committed followers, her looks were only the premise, the beginning rather than the end. For them she had revealed in her finest work beauty of a more thoughtful and, occasionally, a more terrible kind.

Notes

1 Letter from 'Carmen', to Vivien Leigh, 11 July 1957, Laurence Olivier Archive, Add MS 80627.

2 Evelyn Waugh, 'Titus with a Grain of Salt', *The Spectator*, 2 September 1955, pp. 300–301.

3 Vivien Leigh, to Meriel Richardson, Ralph Richardson Archive, Add MS 82044.

4 Caryl Brahms, '*Titus Andronicus*', *Plays and Players*, August 1957, p. 11.

5 Cutting from an interview attributed to *Women's Wear Daily*, 13 May 1963, n. p. Vivien Leigh Archive, THM/433/4/2/10.

6 See Kate Dorney's Chapter 2.

7 Typescript, 'An Actress's Dilemma', Vivien Leigh Archive, THM/ 433/9/11.

8 'S.W.', 'A Faintly Precious Atmosphere', *Evening Standard*, 28 December 1937, p. 10.

9 James Agate, 'Elizabeth or Victoria?', *The Sunday Times*, 2 January 1938, p. 4.

10 A collection of reviews and material relating to the TV broadcast is housed in the Laurence Olivier Archive, Add MS 80683.

11 'New Theatre', *The Times*, 11 February 1949, p. 2.

12 Sydney Carroll, to Vivien Leigh, 11 February 1949, Vivien Leigh Archive, THM/433/2/3.

13 Olivier's side of the exchange with Hobson is in the Vivien Leigh Archive, THM/433/4/3/11.

14 Photocopy of a letter from Leigh, to Elia Kazan, Vivien Leigh Archive, THM/ 433/4/3/11.

15 'Who's Right about A Streetcar? Vivien Leigh's Point of View.' *The Stage*, 27 October 1949, p. 1.

16 'Dottie' Welford, to Vivien Leigh, 31 January 1953, Vivien Leigh Archive, THM/433/2/23.

17 Another contemporary work, probably known to Leigh, offered a multiple perspective on the Egyptian queen, based not on supposed historical evidence but on literary and dramatic interpretations: Oliver C. de C. Ellis, *Cleopatra in the Tide of Time* (Ellis, 1947).

18 John Dover Wilson, to Laurence Olivier, 27 February 1951, Laurence Olivier Archive, Add MS 80049.

19 Laurence Olivier, to John Dover Wilson, 28 February 1951, Laurence Olivier Archive, Add MS 80049.

20 Laurence Olivier, to John Dover Wilson, 5 March 1951, Laurence Olivier Archive, Add MS 80049.

21 John Dover Wilson, to Laurence Olivier, 8 March 1951, Laurence Olivier Archive, Add MS 80049.

22 John Dover Wilson, to Laurence Olivier, 22 May 1951, Laurence Olivier Archive, Add MS 80049.

23 See T.C. Worsley, 'The World Well Lost', *New Statesman*, 19 May 1951, pp. 559–560.

24 Tynan repeated some of these damning phrases in an otherwise more moderate account in 'Festival in the Theatre', *Harpers Bazaar*, July 1951, pp. 50–53, 78–80 (79).

25 Glen Byam Shaw, to Vivien Leigh, 11 July 1951, Vivien Leigh Archive, THM/433/2/2.
26 For detailed analyses of the 1955 *Macbeth*, see Bartholomeusz (1978); Mullin (1976); Rosenberg (1978).
27 See Arnaud Duprat de Montero's Chapter 6.
28 Add MS 80631.
29 Letters from Michael Redgrave to Vivien Leigh, Vivien Leigh Archive, THM/433/2/18. These letters show that there been talk in the 1950s of Leigh starring in a film of *Hedda Gabler* to be directed by Redgrave.

References and bibliography

Agate, James (1935) 'The Mask of Virtue', *Sunday Times*, 19 May, p. 6.

Barber, John (1955) 'What I Thought of his "Macbeth" Last Night', *Daily Express*, 8 June, p. 4.

Bartholomeusz, Dennis (1978) *Macbeth and the Players*, Cambridge: Cambridge University Press.

Bradley, A.C. (1950) 'Shakespeare's Antony and Cleopatra' in *Oxford Lectures on Poetry*, London: Macmillan and Co., pp. 279–308.

Brook, Peter (2013) *The Quality of Mercy. Reflections on Shakespeare*, London: Nick Hern Books.

Carroll, Sydney W. (1923) *Some Dramatic Opinions*, London: F.V. White & Co.

———— (1935) 'Stage "Discoveries" ', *Daily Telegraph*, 23 May, p. 20.

———— (1938) *Acting for the Stage*, London: Sir Isaac Pitman and Sons Ltd.

Cecil, David (1944) *Antony and Cleopatra. The Fourth W.P. Ker Memorial Lecture*, Glasgow: Jackson, Son and Company.

Cowden Clarke, Mary (1892) 5 vols. *The Girlhood of Shakespeare's Heroines in A Series of Tales*, London: Hutchinson & Co.

Dent, Alan (1969) *Vivien Leigh. A Bouquet*, London: Hamish Hamilton.

Dundy, Elaine (2002) *Life Itself*, London: Vintage.

Edwards, Anne (1977) *Vivien Leigh. A Biography*, London: W.H. Allen.

Ellis, Oliver C. de C. (1947) *Cleopatra in the Tide of Time*, London: Williams and Norgate Ltd.

Funke, Lewis and John E. Booth (1961) *Actors Talk About Acting*, New York: Random House.

Hobson, Harold (1949a) 'Too Much Wit', *The Sunday Times*, 16 October, p. 2.

———— (1949b) 'Miss Vivien Leigh', *The Sunday Times*, 13 November, p. 2.

———— (1955) 'Nonpareil', *The Sunday Times*, 12 June, p. 4.

———— (1959) 'Calculated Frisks', *The Sunday Times*, 2 August, p. 15.

Hope-Wallace, Philip (1955) 'Stratford-on-Avon', *Time and Tide*, 9 April, p. 494.

Ludwig, Emil (1937) trans. by Bernard Miall, *Cleopatra. The Story of a Queen*, London: George Allen and Unwin Ltd.

Marshall, Gail (2012) 'Shakespeare and Fiction' in *Shakespeare in the Nineteenth Century*, Cambridge: Cambridge University Press, pp. 96–112.

Mullin, Michael ed. (1976) *An Annotated Facsimile of Glen Byam Shaw's 1955 Promptbook*, Columbia and London; University of Missouri Press.

Olivier, Laurence (1986) *On Acting*, London: Weidenfeld and Nicolson.

Roach, Joseph (2007) *It*, Ann Arbor: University of Michigan Press.

Rosenberg, Marvin (1978) *The Masks of Macbeth*, Berkeley, Los Angeles, London: University of California Press.

Russell Taylor, John (1984) *Vivien Leigh*, London: Elm Tree Books.

Shakespeare, William (1950) *Antony and Cleopatra*, ed. by John Dover Wilson, Cambridge: Cambridge University Press.

Shulman, Milton (1955) 'Sir Laurence Lets Restraint Run Riot', *Evening Standard*, 26 April, p. 6.

Stokes, John (2005) *The French Actress and her English Audience*, Cambridge: Cambridge University Press.

———— (2007) 'Out of the Ordinary: Exercising Restraint in the Post-war Years' in *The Cambridge Companion to the Actress*, ed. Maggie B. Gale and John Stokes, Cambridge: Cambridge University Press, pp. 116–133.

'S.W.' (1937) 'A Faintly Precious Atmosphere', *Evening Standard*, 28 December, p. 10.

Tynan, Kathleen (1987) *The Life of Kenneth Tynan*, London: Weidenfeld and Nicolson.

Tynan, Kenneth (1950) *He That Plays The King. A View of the Theatre*, London: Longmans, Green and Co.

———— (1951) 'How Great is Vivien Leigh?', *Evening Standard*, 9 July 1951, 9. Repr. *Curtains*, p. 9–10.

———— (1952) 'Sir Ralph Does it all by Numbers', *Evening Standard*, 13 June 1952, 9. Repr. *Curtains*, p. 26.

———— (1955 a) 'Arrivals & Departures', *Observer*, 24 April, p. 11.

———— (1955 b) 'Fate and Furies', *Observer*, 12 June, 6. Repr. *Curtains*, p. 98–99.

———— (1955 c) 'Chamber of Horrors', *Observer*, 21 August, 11. Repr. *Curtains*, p. 103–105.

———— (1961) *Curtains. A Critic's View of Plays, Players and Theatrical Events 1950–1960*, London: Longmans, Green and Co. Ltd.

Walker, Alexander (1987) *Vivien: The Life of Vivien Leigh*, London: Weidenfeld and Nicolson.

Wardle, Irving (1978) *The Theatres of George Devine*, London: Jonathan Cape.

Waugh, Evelyn (1955) 'Titus with a Grain of Salt', *The Spectator*, 2 September, 300–301.

Wilder, Thornton (1942) *The Skin of Our Teeth*, New York; London: Harper and Bros.

———— (1949) *The Ides of March*, London: Longmans, Green and Co.

Worsley, T.C. (1952) *The Fugitive Art. Dramatic Commentaries 1947–1951*, London: John Lehmann.

———— (1955) 'The Dark and the Dreadful', *New Statesman*, 18 June, p. 840.

Archives

British Library: Laurence Olivier Archive (1794 –1999) (Add MS 79766 – 80750)
Victoria and Albert Museum: Vivien Leigh Archive THM/433.

5

Film performance and Vivien Leigh: from starlet to Scarlett, and Blanche DuBois to Mrs Stone

Lucy Bolton

Was Vivien Leigh an actress or a film star? This is a question about which Leigh herself had an opinion: 'I'm not a film star, I'm an actress. Being a film star is such a false life, lived for fake values and publicity.'[1] Her denigration of film stardom is an attitude that can be seen to permeate her acting career, as she repeatedly returned to the stage between her select film roles. Leigh stated that she did not prefer the stage to the screen, saying 'both are exciting. I love my profession in any form.'[2] It seems, however, that she chose not to capitalise on her two Academy Awards to develop a more consistent film career following other acclaimed actresses of her era such as Deborah Kerr or Merle Oberon.[3] The dismissal of film stardom as something divorced from hard work, talent, skill or achievement is an attitude that is often applied to film actresses celebrated for their physical attributes. Karen Hollinger describes how actresses 'are most often characterised not as skilled craftswomen, but rather as screen goddesses naturally gifted with the beauty and charisma that has made them stars' (Hollinger, 2006: 4). As Helen Taylor observes, 'Until recent scholarship unveiled new information from the Laurence Olivier and Vivien Leigh Archives, Leigh was represented in biographical and popular discourse as vulnerable, needy, neurotic – her performances often judged in that light, as if she were playing herself rather than performing' (Taylor, 2015: 61). Taylor identifies the allegation so frequently levelled at film stars: that they are simply playing themselves. For many fans, however, Leigh as Scarlett O'Hara, in the arms of Clark Gable's Rhett Butler, epitomises the zenith of Hollywood stardom in its romance, beauty and longevity. As Blanche DuBois, opposite the brooding young hero of 'the Method', Marlon Brando, Leigh's performance encapsulates intensity and fragility in her second Oscar-winning role. She is indeed a legendary British *and* Hollywood film star, despite her protestations, as well as an actress who cut her teeth on the London stage and in British 'quota quickies' in the early 1930s.

In this chapter, rather than re-tread the familiar ground of Scarlett and Blanche (although the fame surrounding these roles is testament itself to the international impact of Leigh as a film actress), I investigate the ways in which Leigh developed as a performer across her nineteen film roles between 1935 and 1961. The exploration of the range of her film roles and their transformation over time resists the stereotypes and dismissals, and creates a framework for understanding her individuality as a film actress with a distinctive body of work. This entails confronting the challenge of looking at her films beyond her 'physical perfection', which, as Laura Thompson argues, 'could irradiate a load of old hokum' (Thompson, 2013: 1). Leigh may have been a great beauty, whose looks were the usual starting point of any piece of criticism or journalism, but her celebrated screen acting demands a fuller appreciation than a superficial concentration on her appearance. Also, her film roles run across her life, from her early 20s to her early 50s, and so call for analysis in light of the changes and development in her performances and screen persona. There are three clearly discernible phases to her screen career and persona: the mischievous girl, the strong maturing woman and the ageing beauty. They are not necessarily sharply delineated, but they are distinct, and analysing them in detail helps us to both understand the range of performance characteristics that Leigh developed as she matured, and to appreciate the variety she displayed in her film performances from a young actress in British cinema to a Hollywood Academy Award winner and beyond.

The young British actress

In her first film roles, Leigh played largely insubstantial parts that enabled her to forge the beginnings of her career and to meet some industry players, but which did not serve her particularly well in other ways. As an uncredited but chirpy schoolgirl in *Things are Looking Up* (Albert de Courville, 1935), Leigh is one of a group of young female pupils, but she is the focus of attention in a couple of scenes. In one, she sticks out her tongue in a pesky display of childlike defiance as the grumpy schoolmistress leaves her dormitory. In another, Leigh is in the centre of a group of schoolgirls framed by a window, which draws attention to her smiling face. Leigh is the focus of these scenes by reason of her looks, but also her lively, mischievous screen personality.

Early films like this, such as *The Village Squire* (Reginald Denham, 1935) and *Gentlemen's Agreement* (George Pearson, 1935), were typical 'quota quickies': low budget and low profile, but they were a way in to the film industry.[4] As John Russell Taylor explains, 'each was made in less than a week, and neither received much notice of any kind, but at least the pay was improving' (Russell Taylor, 1984: 38). Her experience on *Look Up and Laugh* (Basil Dean, 1935) was not a happy one, as director Dean was not terribly impressed with Leigh and 'did not spare this unimportant new girl the lash of his tongue' (Russell Taylor, 1984: 40). Alan Dent writes that she 'seldom referred to these earliest films, though she once told me how severe was Basil Dean in the direction of this particular one, and how kind was the star, Gracie Fields, who once said to her after a bout of directorial severity: "Don't worry, love – you've *got* something!"' (Dent, 1969: 109).

Producer Anthony Havelock-Allan told Alexander Korda's biographer Charles Drazin what he looked for when casting these films:

> First, you look around for faces that are remarkably pretty if they're women, or if they're men, that are remarkably good looking, and then if they're acting or wish to act, you then eventually try to find out if they are unselfconscious enough, or in control enough to have a modicum of talent for acting. Only a modicum for films. All they have to do is to remember where they are told to look and to remember their lines, and to say their lines as if they mean something. (Drazin: 2000, n.p.)

He continued, about Leigh in particular:

> Now Vivien started with the first prerequisite of those things. She was immensely pretty, and she was pretty in a way which indicated that she would certainly look pretty in the camera: she did not have too big a nose, she did not have any of those things that the camera might find out ... she had the perfect photographic face, small features. So having got that, I and subsequently Alex [Korda], thought this woman, if she's got any talent, could be a star. It depends whether she's got any personality or not ... she must have a reasonable voice, which she certainly had, in other words, she was photogenic and obviously would sound all right. She was very bright, well educated, spoke very good French. So there was a good chance that unless she was an absolutely duff actress and couldn't remember lines or couldn't make herself anything but stiff and unnatural that she was going to be something ... Alex was in a position to put her in a play to see what sort of audience reaction she got, *The Mask of Virtue*, which he financed to put on at the Ambassadors Theatre, which ran there for about six months ... She got nice notices ... and then the greatest piece of luck was that she got the part in *Gone with the Wind* that was exactly her. This was what made her. (Drazin, 2000: n.p.)

This rather perfunctory and workmanlike description of casting Leigh is at odds with the usual discourse of film stardom, that of the 'star is born' moment. Leigh certainly has one of these in her life story, but it was not on screen. Her first appearance on the London stage in *The Mask of Virtue* in 1935 was met with ecstatic reviews that declared her to be a great new discovery, but the event was also a hugely significant milestone in her film career. Legend goes that film producer Alexander Korda, described by biographer Charles Drazin as 'Britain's Only Movie Mogul' (Drazin, 2011), was in the audience that night and was so impressed by Leigh's abilities and potential that he offered her a £50,000 movie contract. This was reported widely and with excitement in the press, such as in the *Bulletin*: ' "Fame in a Night" Girl's £50,000 Film Contract, Follows Success in New Play';[5] or the *News of the World*'s report that 'far too glibly we write the time honoured phrase "Fame in a night" but in all sincerity now we can apply it to Vivien Leigh'.[6]

Havelock-Allan claims that Korda placed her in the play in order to assess her abilities and potential as a future investment. In any event, in the words of Hugo Vickers, 'Vivien became an instant star' (Vickers, 1988: 54), which contrasts with Drazin's observation that 'she was less a jewel discovered than one painstakingly moulded in Pygmalion fashion' (Drazin, 2011: 160). Most importantly, the contract brought Leigh under Korda's sponsorship and he proceeded to be hugely influential on the development of her screen career. The potential spotted by Havelock-Allan was beginning to bear fruit. She made three films for Korda in 1937, which served to establish her career and attract good notices for her screen acting. She was described in *Film Weekly* as 'one of Britain's most dazzling film discoveries'.[7] The first was *Fire Over England* (William K. Howard, 1937), starring Flora Robson as Queen Elizabeth I, and Laurence Olivier as Leigh's love interest. Leigh plays Cynthia, the Queen's lady-in-waiting. The film brought Olivier and Leigh together for the first time onscreen and this enabled Korda to pitch the film as a passionate story of young love in Elizabeth's court.[8] Michael Newton observes, 'Leigh had little to do but run about or pine, a petulant source of frustrated energy' (Newton, 2013: n.p.). Petulance is a characteristic that Leigh played well in these early years, and which would clearly form a large part of her performance as Scarlett O'Hara. Max Breen wrote how 'Vivien's chief business was to look "period" and heartbroken. She did that all right, without it imposing any terrific strain on her considerable acting ability' (Breen, 1938: 10). Although not terribly challenging as a role, this film marks a development in Leigh's film performance style. It shows her as a more relaxed and dramatically invested performer, displaying more emotional realism than in her previous roles and also a looser style of physical activity. There is an observable shift away from the stiffness and formality of her earlier performances, into a more fully fledged performance of a role in a less parochial story. In keeping with so many other 'quota quickies', Leigh's previous films had concerned fairly quotidian stories, such as the closure of a market or staffing trouble at a girls' school, whereas *Fire Over England* was a tale of international politics, dramatic passions and royal intrigue. This was Leigh's first significant international role, and reception of her performance was notable for the way in which it did not always focus exclusively on her looks:

> A new English Star rises with *Fire Over England*. Her name is Vivien Leigh. Dark, glamorous, with features that photograph perfectly, Miss Leigh is an actress, not merely a decoration.[9]

The *Sunday Times* critic was more specific still:

> The expression of a spiritual grace and a refinement as rare upon the screen as it is refreshing. Her voice seems to me to have improved in strength, her delivery has become clearer and bolder.[10]

This fuller, stronger, screen persona marked a further shift from mischievous girl to strong young woman. In the four films that followed, Leigh portrayed young women in the world of work, in sexual relationships, local politics and international espionage. Her onscreen image was developing into that of a woman of some sophistication, who wears designer clothes beautifully, conducts lively flirtations with the opposite sex and is an intelligent, independent-minded young woman. This is a clear development from the more conventional roles of the early films, and enabled Leigh to play opposite some of the most high-profile leading men in British and Hollywood cinema: Rex Harrison, Charles Laughton, Robert Taylor and Conrad Veidt.

In *Dark Journey* (Victor Saville, 1937), Leigh plays the owner of a designer dress shop, who has been recruited to the war effort. She appears, in Breen's words, 'sombre and inscrutable' (Breen, 1938: 11). Vickers describes her as 'demure and beautiful in mink, asking "what are my orders?" and when investigating an enemy spy, "Who's the head of section 8?"' (Vickers, 1988: 77). Leigh enjoyed making *Dark Journey*, despite confessing 'I don't really understand what it is all about' (Vickers, 1988: 76)[11] (Figure 5.1).

The young girl about town

Storm in a Teacup (Ian Dalrymple, 1937) pairs Leigh with Rex Harrison in a comedy in which she demonstrates her verbal dexterity and onscreen chemistry with her co-star. Breen describes how here she mainly had to be indignant, and 'appear sufficiently attractive to make her seem a prize worth winning' (Breen, 1938: 11). As Victoria Gow, Leigh embodies a modern young woman, from a well-to-do family,

Figure 5.1   Vivien Leigh (as fashionable spy Madeleine Goddard) in *Dark Journey* (1937).

who is returning home from urban adventures to support her father in his political career. The film opens with Victoria arriving at the rural Scottish port, and appearing more sophisticated than her surroundings. As in *Look Up and Laugh*, Leigh plays the daughter of a local dignitary, so while from a higher class than some of the locals, she is not strictly upper class. Rex Harrison plays Frank, the principled young reporter assigned to cover the Provost's political campaigns, but who becomes more interested in his determination to see that a local woman's dog is put to sleep for her failure to pay the license fee, while falling in love with the Provost's daughter. There is a marked contrast between the scene in which Victoria and Frank meet – where Leigh is literally the butt of the joke as a child's ice lolly gets stuck to her skirt – and the scenes towards the end of the film where Victoria comes to Frank's rescue in court by falsely claiming in the witness box that they are married. In Leigh's early scenes she appears stiff and self-conscious, occasionally seeming to look straight into the camera lens. As she makes her entrance into the village and at her father's home, her appearances are more presentations than performance; she seems contrived, and there are numerous close-ups on her facial expressions, her eyes conveying exaggerated expressions of surprise.

Leigh's voice is 'terribly cut-glass' English, and her costumes are more akin to a parade of suitable fashions on a comely mannequin – including a sporty golfing ensemble – than a contribution to the development of her character. Victoria relates how she has been to a finishing school, and the film affords Leigh the opportunity to demonstrate her French in a somewhat forced exchange with her father. There is a stiffness and superiority to her bearing, especially in her exchanges with the maid, although her character emerges as strong and determined, and ultimately she is happy to lie for Frank in the witness box to save the day. She 'warms up' onscreen as the film proceeds, so that her eyes become increasingly full of meaning, suggestive of growing involvement in the film's activities and Frank's predicament. When Frank confesses the personal reasons why he feels compelled to stand up to bullies, Victoria's face, in close-up, registers empathetic emotion and admiration. Dent notes that Leigh 'was able to bring so much charm and humour to match the urbanity of Rex Harrison that people began to talk about them as an ideal light-comedy team'(Dent, 1969: 111).

Roles such as Victoria Gow did not enable Leigh to demonstrate, or perhaps develop, the emotional range that she demonstrated in films to come, but, as Thompson observes:

> Leigh was always more interesting, in fact, than the pretty-girl roles she was given in films such as *A Yank at Oxford* or *A Fire Over England*. Her demure porcelain face was full of latent vitality; her smile had a quality of perverse intrigue, like a Siamese cat pondering how to strike against a bird. (Thompson, 2013: 2)

This quality begins to emerge onscreen in Leigh's character as *Storm in a Teacup* progresses; a thoughtfulness and confidence that indicated the maturity on the horizon.

In the next film for Korda, *21 Days* (Basil Dean, 1940), Leigh plays a woman whose lover (Olivier) murders her ex-husband.[12] In this peculiarly amoral film, Leigh's performance is more redolent of the early films as she expresses wide-eyed love and anguish. Leigh was not happy with the film at all. Alan Dent writes how he was not allowed to see it: 'the Oliviers themselves forbade me ever to see this film and I never did. They themselves only saw "about a third of it" at a public showing in New York' (Dent, 1969: 113).

After this, Leigh made three films for three different companies. Her part in *A Yank at Oxford* (dir. Jack Conway, 1938) was a role that Leigh secured amid tough competition, and which therefore attracted a good deal of publicity for her. The film placed her alongside old school friend Maureen O'Sullivan and Hollywood heartthrob Robert Taylor. On loan to Michael Balcon at MGM British, Leigh played a more vampish woman than previously. As the young wife of an older man who runs a bookshop in the university town, Leigh's Elsa Craddock is predatory and sexually bold in her interactions with Robert Taylor's American jock Lee Sheridan. She is more lively and cheeky than in *Storm in a Teacup*, engaging in eyelid-fluttering flirtation with Taylor and carrying off risqué innuendo convincingly. When Elsa and Sheridan meet, her first appraisal of him is shown in a tight close-up on her face as her eyes run up and down his form. Her lively eyes, and appreciative, saucy, smile, display her spotting a new object for her amorous attentions. Sexual connotation is overt as Sheridan pumps up his bicycle tyre with vigour while not being able to take his eyes off her: Elsa encourages him with faux coquettishness mingled with seduction. Breen describes Elsa as Leigh's first 'vamp' role, and adds that 'it may be regarded as her first "character" part (as distinct from juvenile leads) and, as such, it paved the way for her current effort, which is likely to be of utmost importance to her career' (Breen 1938: 11).

That 'current effort' was *St Martin's Lane* (1938), in which Leigh plays an ambitious street performer, demonstrating her physical skills in dancing and singing, but also following a strong character arc from down-at-heel busker to cabaret star, leaving emotional casualties in the wake of her ascent. This film marks a significant step up in the complexity of Leigh's onscreen persona, as she plays a:

> substantial and multi-layered character ... A self-assured pickpocket with dreams of one day rising out of the gutter, Libby is coquettish, petulant, mean, and unscrupulous as she casts aside Charles and her adoptive family of buskers in order to see her name up in lights at the Holborn Empire. (Bean, 2013 a: n.p.)

There are flashes of Scarlett O'Hara to come in Leigh's facial expressions, which convey quicksilver thinking, fickle changes in speech and demeanour to suit her ends, and a wildness conveyed by her unkempt hair and confident, loose, capable physicality. Breen comments that she 'has suddenly become vivid' and wonders whether George Cukor shouldn't reconsider Leigh for the role of Scarlett on the basis of her performance, having previously felt that she 'seemed to be a little static' and 'not quite sufficiently temperamental for such a fiery role' (Breen, 1938: 11). Michael Newton considers 'there are signs of greatness' in this performance, despite her less than convincing cockney accent (Newton, 2013: n.p.). *Film Weekly* considered that Leigh 'shows herself to be an actress of character with a fine sense of the complexity of human nature, and a real gift for creating a true pattern of its lights and shadows' (Anon, 1938: n.p.).

In *A Yank at Oxford* and *St Martin's Lane*, Leigh's persona had developed to display an element of steely determination: whether to capture the hearts of attractive young male students or the rewards of having her name in lights. Leigh had demonstrated the ability, then, to move from sophisticated and superior young lady to determined and devious woman. These qualities would all be called upon in her creation of her next, iconic, role: that of Scarlett O'Hara.

The Hollywood leading lady

The ways in which Leigh expressed her devotion to playing the role of Scarlett, and indeed how she obtained the part, are now the stuff of legend.[13] As reported widely at the time, many of the leading actresses in Hollywood were under consideration for the role, and it is indeed remarkable that Leigh, little known outside of Britain, would land the part. What is important to note is the dedication Leigh displayed to getting this role, believing herself to be perfect to play it, and also the work that went into the crafting of Scarlett: the convincing screen tests, the creation of the Southern accent, and the determination required to complete the shoot despite the changes in director and hardships on set.[14] The experience of playing Scarlett does not appear to have been a happy one, but Leigh was certainly thrust into the world of Hollywood stardom with all of the media exposure that entailed. As Kendra Bean notes, 'With a single performance she achieved a level of cultural significance that would not be reached by any other British actress of her generation.' She became, 'the most sought-after actress in Hollywood' (Bean, 2013b: 66).

In her next film, *Waterloo Bridge* (Mervyn LeRoy, 1940), Leigh plays Myra, the object of Roy Cronin's (Robert Taylor) obsession, and in this role she displays both girlish charm and an ability to perform ballet, living through passionate love and desperate loss.[15] In one particular scene, Myra does not react to Roy's mother's conversational gambits because she believes the man they both love to be dead. Leigh displays a restrained tragic countenance, demonstrating the antithesis of the 'chirpy gal' evident from the quota quickies, and the sprightly fighting spirit of Scarlett. The film then, as a doomed romance, displays a further element of Leigh's film persona, that of sustained resignation and disappointment sufficient for this tragic role. Significantly, now, Leigh had demonstrated the ability to convey a woman's story over a period of years, and to mature into a complex and multi-layered adult with a deep emotional register. Archer Winsten in the *New York Post* wrote that 'she shows her fine sense of camera acting as well as her pert and saucy beauty.'[16]

Figure 5.2   Vivien Leigh and Robert Taylor (as doomed lovers Myra and Roy Cronin) in *Waterloo Bridge* (1940).

Lee Mortimer in the *Daily Mail* writes that 'Miss Leigh, in her first American film since *Gone with the Wind* not only lives up to the high premise (*sic*) shown in that achievement but actually in a part wholly unlike that of Scarlett surpasses her former performance'[17] (Figure 5.2).

Maturing on screen

Leigh's next three films develop this idea of maturing onscreen as she plays three iconic women: Emma Hamilton, Cleopatra and Anna Karenina. In the playing of these roles, Leigh demonstrates that her screen persona has developed to the extent that she can inhabit such roles but not at the expense of her individuality. This is indicative of her star status by this stage in her career. Thompson writes:

> stars are both more, and less, than actors. They carry into every role a vast shimmering weight of themselves, their own personality, above all their vulnerability. That was Vivien Leigh, a British girl whose image conquered the world, and whose desire to transcend that image made it all the more persistently fascinating. (Thompson, 2013: 3)

These female characters are incarnated as the star Vivien Leigh, reflected in her top billing in the credits above Olivier, Claude Rains and Ralph Richardson respectively.

In *That Hamilton Woman* (dir. Alexander Korda, 1941) Leigh plays society beauty Emma Hamilton in a loveless marriage, with a passionate love for Nelson (played by Olivier). The film begins with a destitute Emma being locked up in debtors' prison, weak, drunken and aged, with dark circles under her eyes, ravaged with wrinkles and barely able to raise her voice above a whisper. Her voice is deep; she embodies dejection and resignation with her lot. Encouraged by a fellow cellmate, she looks back over her life, beginning when she was 18, when her unbelievable beauty matches that of her likeness captured and admired in a portrait. Arriving at Naples as socialite Emma Hart in anticipation of marrying Charles Greville, she affects a more upperclass voice, manners and conversational style in order to impress his uncle, Sir William Hamilton (Alan Mowbray). Accompanied by her chatterbox mother (Sara Allgood), Emma is affecting a style she believes to be ladylike. When telling her mother about Vesuvius, she says: 'it's knowing little things like that that make you a lady'. This performance as put on by Emma, enables Leigh to create a multi-layered character who can be preposterously vain (she repeatedly states 'wasn't I wonderful?' after every party she throws), endearingly childlike – she echoes 'boom' after Nelson's canon's fire and grabs Sir William's spyglass as if she were his child – and endearingly loyal to her socially gauche mother. When meeting Nelson, Emma is initially her most frivolous, party-planning self, but when talk of war becomes inevitable and she is expected to leave, her voice drops, her attitude becomes knowing and intelligent, and she observes, 'is it as wicked as all that?' When they next meet, five years later, Emma has matured, and is more subdued and watchful of Nelson. Leigh's performance as Emma plays on many facets of her own star persona at this point in her career, embodying the wit and charm of the socialite, the social ease of the Lady and the passion and devotion of the woman head-over-heels in love. As Emma, walking into a room and taking control, Leigh's voice is strong and commanding; her gestures are grand, theatrical and confident; her posture and gait are self-assured, her bearing becomes more mature and stable, and she is aware of her charms and how she might use them. She changes from self-centredness to selfless love: Nelson and Emma acknowledge their love for each other, and Emma cries into his shoulder in close-up 'I would have died if you'd left me here'. Her emotion is palpably strong and overwhelming for her.

When Emma meets Lady Nelson (played by Gladys Cooper) for the first time, Leigh demonstrates her ability to convey many emotions at once. Not expecting Lady Nelson to be there, Emma is at first exhila-rated by the crowd's adulation of Nelson; there is slight start and pause as she realises the identity of the other woman in the room, a quick appraisal of her and a deflation in the presence of the woman married to the man she loves, before civility kicks in and she introduces herself. The gamut of emotion – from elation to stark realisation – is conveyed without any more words than her name. Leigh's body, stance, expres-sion and posture convey the magnitude of this moment, in all its complexity and intensity.

The loss of her status as Lady Hamilton following the death of her husband and her continued relationship with Nelson is conveyed through her costume, hair and manner, as she is seen in simple clothes, with more softly styled hair, and a more relaxed, less affected style of speech. Her idyllic life with Nelson is ruined once again by his being called away to war, and when Hardy brings the news of his death this signals the end of her life too. She continues her embroidery urgently, breathing heavily, while waiting for Hardy to pluck up the courage to say the words. A close-up on Emma's face as Hardy strug-gles to tell her before breaking down is a portrait of terror, then horror, then paralysis, as she hears the words that tear her world apart. With dark circles under her eyes, no lip colour, staring eyes and heaving chest, Leigh conveys the magnitude of Emma's collapse with emo-tional intensity and physical commitment. Bosley Crowther described how 'Vivien Leigh's entire performance ... is delightful to behold. All of the charm and grace and spirit which Miss Leigh contains is beauti-fully put to use to capture the subtle spell which Emma most assuredly must have weaved'[18] (Figure 5.3).

In the film of Shaw's *Caesar and Cleopatra* (Gabriel Pascal, 1945), at the age of 30, Leigh plays the Egyptian queen as childlike and uppity, with an indulgent, amused Caesar played by Claude Rains. Crowther describes her here as 'timid and electric as a girl and drenched with a hot, aggressive nature as the woman who Caesar inspires'.[19] Leigh's next role, as *Anna Karenina* in 1948 (Julien Duvivier), signalled a move towards the figure of the tragic woman with which she would now become closely associated. At the moment when Anna first meets Vronsky, Leigh's performance registers both the attraction and the inevitability of the complications that will follow, through the spark of life in her eye and the slight deflation of her shoulders and torso. Her performance is that of a woman who knows her actions will leave her a vulnerable outcast, but who is driven to do them anyway. The dra-matic death, as Anna throws herself under the steam train, can be seen to mark Leigh's entry into what might be considered a darker phase of her film career.

Figure 5.3 Vivien Leigh (as the elegant and confident Emma Hamilton) in *That Hamilton Woman* (1941).

The darker phase

Leigh had played the role of Blanche DuBois in the 1949 stage production of Tennessee Williams' *A Streetcar Named Desire* on the London stage, in which she was directed by Olivier, and letters in her archive reveal the detail of the discussions with Elia Kazan and others about the making of a screen production of the play.[20] Kazan described difficulties at the beginning of the shoot because Leigh did not really get on with the rest of the cast, until 'I saw her courage and the way she worked, her candour, I began to like her a lot. Everyone was touched and moved by her will to be good' (Young, 1999: 86). As Kazan and others have observed, Leigh's outsider status contributed to her performance as outsider Blanche. Linda Constanzo Cahir goes so far as to say, in relation to Blanche's 'ever shifting façade', that 'in paradox, Leigh's classical acting, thought to be inappropriate, speaks to the essence of Blanche Dubois, and in this odd circumstance could be argued to constitute a form of method acting' (Cahir, 1994: 73). Leigh expressed her own thinking about 'the Method' after she had made *Streetcar*: 'it seems to me that the Method is: if you say something, you've got to mean it, and you've got to say it as interestingly as possible. But that applies to life – and acting is life, to me, and should be' (Funke and Booth, 1961: 199). Leigh described how she tried:

> to let people see what Blanche was like when she was in love with her young husband when she was seventeen or eighteen ... to evoke this whole creature when she was young and when she was tender and trusting, as opposed to what she had become – cynical and hard, mad, and distressed, and distraught. (Ibid: 204)

Her performance as Blanche is one of completely exhausting tension and nerviness: never relaxed, always concerned about what people think of her, while wrestling with her own demons and horrors. For Newton, Leigh's Blanche 'is simply one of the greatest pieces of acting in any American film' (Newton, 2013: n.p.). Many others agree. Walker considered that she embodied Blanche's madness brilliantly (Walker, 1994: 276), and Cahir considers that 'what makes Leigh's performance so powerful ... is that we see Blanche, drawn and tired from the years of laborious performance, make a last ditch effort to find the role of a lifetime' (Cahir, 1994: 74). It certainly showed Leigh portraying a degree of neuroses, and a fear of ageing, hitherto unseen in her performances, and ushered in the final phase of her screen career as a tragic middle-aged beauty (Figure 5.4).

Following her second Oscar for the leading actress role, Leigh went on to play three more roles directly concerned with the vulnerabilities of ageing women. In *The Deep Blue Sea* (Anatole Litvak, 1955) she plays Hester, obsessed with young pilot Freddy (Kenneth More). Leigh has a natural look of refined glamour in this film, her dark hair is fairly short and styled quite simply. It is the first time Leigh has looked like a more sedately middle-aged woman on-screen. Leigh is in her early 40s, playing a woman in her 40s, and certainly not attempting to look younger than she is. She evokes desperation and loneliness in a relationship where Hester has no power other than the constant threat of committing suicide. Crowther described how 'Her eyes often tend to

Figure 5.4   The exposure of Blanche's age and fragility: Vivien Leigh in *A Streetcar Named Desire* (1951).

abstract wandering. Her mind seems perpetually involved. And now and again, her physical movements have a peculiarly volcanic force' (Crowther, 1955: n.p.). The tragedy of the film is that Freddie does not seem to care at all for Hester, and yet she is willing to stoop so low to keep him. This is a brave and stark performance by Leigh, which Josephine Botting considers has been underrated, with critics failing,

> to perceive the subtlety and restraint of her performance, which so well suits the character of Hester, a woman emotionally exhausted after her dramatic rejection of convention and the respectability of marriage. (Botting, 2013: 3)

Botting makes an insightful observation about Leigh's appearance and her skill:

> While undeniably beautiful, especially seen in colour, Leigh was always in complete control of her looks, manipulating her appearance as required for each role. Hence, in 1944 at the age of 30, she was utterly convincing as the teenage Cleopatra in *Caesar and Cleopatra*, while six years later she transformed into fading Southern belle Blanche DuBois in *A Streetcar Named Desire*. As Richard Stirling observed on stage in his introduction to the BFI's current Vivien Leigh retrospective 'her beauty should be counted

as one of the actress's talents, a tool for crafting her dramatis personae rather than just a passive, physical trait. (Botting, 2013: 4)

This is particularly significant in relation to *The Deep Blue Sea*, as the Rattigan play makes clear that Hester is supposed to be a plain woman, in thrall to this younger man who has revealed the pleasures of sex to her. Botting tells how Rattigan and co-star Kenneth More thought Leigh was too beautiful for the role of Hester, which had been played on stage by the less glamorous Peggy Ashcroft (ibid). This links back to my initial comments about beautiful star actresses being considered to be simply playing themselves. Acknowledging the degree of labour and skill involved in crafting appearance and physicality is a significant element of studying a star's performances, and of doing justice to the work of the individual actress, rather than portraying them as moulded by Svengali figures or simply showing natural talent.[21] As Crowther describes, in *The Deep Blue Sea*, 'Miss Leigh's strangely tense and fierce performing seems to indicate a depth charge set to go' (Crowther, 1955: 35).

In her next film, *The Roman Spring of Mrs Stone* (José Quintero, 1961), Leigh gives an unflinching portrayal of a woman who feels she has nothing to lose. This is a further move along the trajectory of Leigh's career into the stark engagement with the issue of being an ageing beauty and the effects of age on a woman's career and personal life (Figure 5.5).

In the film, Leigh is made up to look older, which brings its own challenges for an actress celebrated for her youthful beauty. For any actress, however, this role is a brave challenge, tackling as it does the idea that an actress can be too old to play some roles convincingly. The opening scenes confront this not only through the reactions of the audience to Karen Stone's performance as Rosalind in *As You Like It*, but also because of her appearance in the costumes in which we see her; cleverly designed to look like pantomime costumes of a princess and a principal boy, Leigh looks quite clearly too old for both. Depressed by this experience, she calls off the play, and is then soon widowed, leaving her to face up to the realities of her age in her personal and her professional life before the opening credits roll. Leigh was 48 when she made this film, and Stone is said to be 'approaching 50'. In the pre-credit sequence, Leigh looks thin, small, and pale, with ashen clothes, hair and face. When we next see Karen in her apartment in Rome, she is smartly dressed, with set hair, full makeup, pearls, jewellery, and manicure, idly flicking through a magazine as the voiceover says that 'self-knowledge is something Karen Stone had always been able to avoid'. When the Contessa and Paolo come to call, Karen pays

Figure 5.5   Vivien Leigh (as the vulnerable Karen Stone) in *The Roman Spring of Mrs Stone* (1961).

little attention to Paolo, saying she is 'drifting'. She looks disengaged, superior and dismissive, and she is difficult to engage in conversation. When Paolo manages to track her down while she is horse riding – ably, it should be noted – Karen walks in a very composed manner, meeting his attention with a steady gaze. But Paolo's invitation to dinner unnerves her, and she suddenly looks wary and vulnerable. In this moment, cracks begin to show in Karen's composure; cracks which develop over dinner, when she appears slightly shy, but picks up interest at the possibility of being understood by Paolo. In a delicate but affective moment, Paolo observes that 'your hand is a fist', drawing attention to Karen's tension; even though her hand is gloved, she is still shy to open the hand at Paolo's touch, indicating her repression and physical isolation.

Leigh's physicality in this film is unlike any role played previously. Her character is wealthy and aimless, so she wears expensive clothes and has the slow walk of a drifter, rather than the assertive strut of young Victoria Gow or the commanding glide of Emma Hamilton. Karen Stone is past her breaking point, and masks her vulnerability with wariness and social ease until Paolo breaks through her veneer.

Once exposed, however, we see Karen's susceptibility to his fickle attentions. She becomes slightly more joyful as she entertains the possibility he might be attracted to her. When he suggests that she is 'frightened of her feelings', and leaves her tantalisingly on her doorstep, we see her gaze longingly after him, until she inevitably relents and admits him to her apartment. After they have spent the night together, we see Karen excited and giddy having had her hair cut into a shorter style, accompanied by light, hopeful, non-diegetic music. In a moment of wild irresponsibility, she lies to some old friends, saying that the reason for her reclusiveness is the diagnosis of a fatal illness, and then giggles to herself in the back of the taxi home. She cries when she holds Paolo, as she confesses 'I'm so happy'. In these scenes she appears rejuvenated, and is lighter and more joyful than at any point in the film so far.

Looking bright in a vibrant blue suit, Karen tells her friend Meg that she's in love with Paolo, who is busily flirting with a young girl at another table in the restaurant. As Meg tries to convince her of her vanity and silliness, Karen is wholly distracted by the sight of Paolo, and her face saddens as her mood darkens, until she leaves the restaurant unable to face what she can see, which accords with her friend's analysis of the situation. There is great tension between Karen and Paolo at home that evening as Paolo has invited people over to see their home movies, including the young actress, Miss Bingham (Jill St John) who he is hoping to seduce. As Karen is on screen playfully throwing a cushion at Paolo behind the camera, he is out on the terrace making romantic arrangements with Miss Bingham. Karen's eyes are wet with tears, her mascara running down her face, and the tension builds until she explodes, has a fight with Paolo on the terrace, and asks everyone to leave. Her face is wrought with disappointment, but it is a desperate disappointment, not a shock: Leigh catches this nuance perfectly, as her furious emotion overwhelms any sense of pride or decorum she may have had left.

There is an extra-textual poignancy in the moment when Leigh as Karen sits in the darkness, deserted and in tears, as the film reel has come to an end. Karen's final humiliation is yet to come, however, as she follows Paolo and sees him go into Miss Bingham's hotel. This is enough for her to throw her keys to the vagabond boy who has been following her throughout the film. This is clearly an act of self-abandonment, but she sits and waits for him in her apartment with no fear on her face. Rather there is preparedness for what is to come, albeit that her chest rises and falls rather heavily as she sits opposite the door and lights a cigarette.

Leigh's performance as Karen Stone is unlike anything she had done previously in her career, with her superior demeanour undercut by her sexual vulnerability, through a journey from resignation to ecstasy and ending in dejection. She seems to physically shrink at the sleights of Paolo's rejections, her eyes registering the wounds and disappointments, and yet there is strength and determination in her final perverse decision. Alexander Walker wrote: 'I report, with my heart leaping up in admiration, that her brutally candid, immensely skilled performance makes her comeback a triumph',[22] and Felix Barker described it as 'the best thing this still beautiful actress has ever done on the screen'.[23]

In her final film, *Ship of Fools* (Stanley Kramer, 1965), Leigh plays Mary, an ageing, heavily made-up divorcee who is flirting with casual encounters and testing her sexual attractiveness. In a disturbingly brutal scene, when Mary realises that Bill (Lee Marvin) has stumbled into her room by mistake rather than intention, Mary is disappointed not to have been sexually assaulted by him and attacks him viciously, hitting him with her shoes. Leigh worked hard to perfect the Virginian accent, which she said was 'a bit difficult to capture; its somewhere midway between Southern and British'.[24] Her performance was highly praised. David Lewin wrote that 'this film face can give Vivien her third Oscar', and praised the bravery of her performance, saying 'Miss Leigh has always had courage – and to spare'.[25]

Star quality

There are several occasions where Leigh has reflected on her screen career, but in general she is not a reflexive or forthcoming interviewee. One of her most open interviews is with Robert Ottaway in 1965. Here she says that she has always distrusted what people have said about her: 'there is a difference between what an artist knows she has done, and what outsiders, however knowledgeable, claim for her. I have never wanted to be known as a film star, partly for that reason. It is too difficult and unrewarding to hand over responsibility for one's career to circumstances and that is what most film contracts demand.'[26] Observing that Leigh relishes change and chooses 'against the grain' parts, Ottaway concludes 'her seeming fragility is her most misleading characteristic'.[27]

The popular perception of Leigh's film stardom is clearly bookended by Scarlett and Blanche, as two vastly different Southern belles, but there is an array of complex and challenging performances around those roles. As Ottaway writes: 'Her career cannot be graphed. It seems to wander from peak to peak, with no path to connect them.'[28] And

Plate 1   Vivien Leigh with David O. Selznick, Orry-Kelly and Robert Helpmann in George Cukor's garden, 1960.

Plate 2 Vivien Leigh's cloak from *Antony and Cleopatra* (1951), designed by Audrey Cruddas.

Plate 3   Vivien Leigh and Marlon Brando in *A Streetcar Named Desire* (1951), costume designer Lucinda Ballard.

Plate 4 The curtain dress from *Gone With The* Wind on display in the
Victoria and Albert exhibition 'Hollywood Costume', 2012.

Plate 5 *Picture Play*, May 1940.

Plate 6 Vivien Leigh photographed by Madame Yevonde, 1936.

Plate 7 Vivien Leigh in the dressing room of the Huntington Hartford Theatre. Photo by John Merivale, 1960.

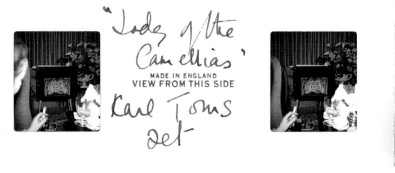

Plate 8 Leigh inspects *The Lady of the Camellias* set, Eaton Square (1961).

Plate 9 'The Oliviers Off Stage', *House and Garden* (May 1958).

yet, Leigh remains a high-profile film star, whose work was the subject of a British Film Institute retrospective season in 2013 and who is still considered to be 'one of Britain's few genuine woman "movie stars" ' (Newton, 2013). Richard Dyer writes of how stars reconcile contradictions or tensions, such as innocence and sexuality in Monroe, and coolness and heat in Grace Kelly (Dyer, 1998: 64), but with Leigh it is impossible to pick just two. Certainly there is the British theatrical tradition, alongside the twice-Oscar winning Queen of Hollywood; there is refinement and mischievousness; beauty and character; intelligence and vitality; sensitivity and strength. For Molly Haskell, Leigh was one of a few actresses 'who crossed back and forth, who were sweetness and light one minute and devils incarnate the next, suggesting that their innocence was sheer hypocrisy. Or that their sensuality was' (Haskell, 1987: 193).

Leigh's persona is certainly transatlantic, and the Britishness of her early films is very different from the Hollywood gloss of others. Uniting them all from *St Martin's Lane* onwards is an intelligent, cerebral quality: she appears thoughtful and knowing, as if reflecting upon the other people in the scene, or indeed her character herself. To return to Helen Taylor's observation that it is often implied that her two most celebrated roles reflect the divided self that was Vivien Leigh the woman, this assumption can either be shored up or debunked by an analysis of Leigh's career as a whole. In other words, it can be argued that the range and complexity of characterisations that Leigh demonstrates in many of her roles, including Scarlett and Blanche, marks out her performances as skilled, rich and multifarious; or each film could be mapped onto a stage of Leigh's life, picking out the biographical resonances and drawing parallels between on and off screen lives. Certainly Scarlett and Blanche are 'perfect fits' for Leigh's star image: mischievous young woman and tragic, ageing beauty. These two roles, however, are award-winning points in a film career that mark Leigh's progression onscreen from 'pesky young gal', to a woman maturing and coping with love and loss, and to a defiant figure of ageing beauty, railing against the cultural expectations of middle-aged women. These performances draw on the complexity in Leigh's star persona, constituted as it is out of physical characteristics, personality traits, performance styles, vocal range and intonation, and above all sheer ability, hard work and charisma as an actress to convey that multiplicity, veering from vulnerability to steeliness, naked honesty to conniving duplicity, joyous playfulness to desperate misery.

Her obituary in the *Observer* noted that 'Above all she had the star's quality of glamour. No one could capture like her the dissolute romance of beauty, abandoned, ageing and betrayed. Posterity may forget her performances, but it will remember her face.'[29] This prediction has proven incorrect: her film performances are precisely the means through which she is experienced in popular culture. In an unattributed article on *St Martin's Lane* entitled 'Why Vivien Leigh is Great', the following observation is made:

> As Vivien shows in *Gone with the Wind*, she has no rival on the screen for her type of greatness. In the right roles, she is sure to remain, and to be recognized as, the top tough-but-lovely lady of the screen – the most incendiary actress of our times.[30]

When discussing 'star acting', Charles Affron writes that 'the prime function of certain stars is their incarnation of superficiality. They are totems whose mystery is either too impenetrable for interpretation or (more likely) simply absent' (Affron, 1977: 3). This description could not be farther from Leigh's function as a star actress. It is precisely the complex, mercurial and fiery strength embodied in a delicate physique and fine-boned face that defines the Vivien Leigh star image as 'tough-but-lovely': and not too lovely at that.

Notes

1 David Lewin, 'Vivien Tells', *Daily Express*, August 17 1960.
2 'The Twenty Questions Everyone is Asking about Vivien Leigh – Answered by Herself', *Picturegoer*, 26 November 1955.
3 Leigh differed from both these film actresses, with whom she is sometimes compared, due to the success and longevity of her theatrical career. For further analysis of Oberon, see Drazin (2011: 128–134). Leigh's theatre work is discussed in John Stokes's Chapter 4 in this volume.
4 This term is used to describe the films that were made following the passing of the 1927 Cinematographic Films Act, with the purpose of supporting the British Film Industry by obliging exhibitors to play a certain number of British films. These films were made quickly and on low budgets, and many do not survive. For further information, see Steve Chibnall (2007).
5 '"Fame-in-a-Night" Girl's £50,000 Film Contract', *Bulletin*, 18 May 1935. Vivien Leigh Biographical File, V&A.
6 'Fame in a Night and £10,000 a Year', *News of the World*, 19 May 1935. Vivien Leigh Biographical File, V&A.
7 John K. Newnham, 'Vivien Leigh's Strange Career', *Film Weekly*, 1937, p. 11. Vivien Leigh Archive, THM/433/4/2/7.
8 For more on this, and Robson's disgruntlement, see Drazin (2011: 161–163).
9 Review of *Fire over England*, *Evening Standard*, 27 February 1937. Laurence Olivier Archive, Vivien Leigh Papers, Add MS 80668.
10 Sydney W. Carroll, Review of *Fire Over England*, *Sunday Times*, 28 February 1937. Laurence Olivier Archive, Vivien Leigh Papers, Add MS 80668.

11 Here Hugo Vickers is citing correspondence between Leigh and her first husband Leigh Holman, from the papers of Leigh's daughter Suzanne, which he references 'V.L. to L.H. 31 August 1936 (SFP)'.

12 The film was not released until 1939, after Leigh's contract for *Gone With The Wind* had been signed: see Drazin (2011: 165).

13 For a succinct account of the casting, production and reception of *Gone With The Wind*, see Helen Taylor's BFI Contemporary Classic on the film.

14 Again, all well documented in many of the biographies and accounts of the making of the film: see Bean (2013 a: 45–68).

15 Leigh undertook ballet lessons in preparation for a dancing scene in the film. Vickers quotes her as saying in a letter to Leigh Holman that she asked 'to be between two strong girls who can prop me up' (Vickers, 1988: 131).

16 Archer Winsten, 'Waterloo Bridge' at Capitol Theatre, *New York Post*, 17 May 1940. Vivien Leigh Archive, THM/433/4/2/5.

17 Lee Mortimer, 'Waterloo Bridge in Prize-Winning Class', *Daily Mirror*, 17 May 1940. Vivien Leigh Archive, THM/433/4/2/5.

18 Bosley Crowther, '*That Hamilton Woman*, The Story of a Historic Love Affair', *New York Times*, 4 April 1941. www.nytimes.com/movie/review?res=9C07E6 DE1E3BE33BBC4C53DFB266838A659EDE, accessed 4 March 2016.

19 Bosley Crowther, 'Shaw's Caesar and Cleopatra', *New York Times*, 6 September 1946. www.nytimes.com/movie/review?res=9802EFD91439E731A25755C 0A96F9C946793D6CF, accessed 25 June 2016.

20 Letters between Leigh and Kazan are particularly concerned with how Blanche should look, as considered by Keith Lodwick in Chapter 8 in this volume.

21 Melanie Bell explored this issue recently in relation to Julie Christie, discussing how female stars are often portrayed as 'Galatea figures' (Bell, 2016: 28–29).

22 Alexander Walker, 'Such courage, Miss Leigh, – and What a Triumph!', unknown publication, 1961. V&A Vivien Leigh Archive, THM/433/4/2/10.

23 Felix Barker, 'A Warning to Women ... and a Triumph for Vivien Leigh', unknown publication, 15 February 1962. Vivien Leigh Archive, THM/433/ 4/2/10.

24 B. Thomas, 'As Southern Gal – Vivien Leigh Back for Another Movie'. *LA Journal*, 23 June 1964. Vivien Leigh Archive, THM/433/4/2/15.

25 David Lewin, 'This Film Face Can Give Vivien her Third Oscar', unknown publication, 14 May 1965. Vivien Leigh Archive, THM/433/4/2/11.

26 Ottaway (1965).

27 Ibid.

28 Ibid.

29 *Observer*, 9 July 1967. Laurence Olivier Archive, Vivien Leigh Papers, Add Ms 80644.

30 'Why Vivien Leigh is Great'. Vivien Leigh Archive, THM/433/4/2/5.

References and bibliography

Affron, Charles (1977) *Star Acting: Gish, Garbo, Davis*, New York: E.P. Dutton.

Anon (1937) Review, 27 February, *Fire Over England, Evening Standard*, Laurence Olivier Archive, Add MS 80668.

———— (1938) Review, *St Martin's Lane, Film Weekly*.

———— (1967) *Observer*, 9 July Obituary.

Bean, Kendra (2013 a) 'Before Scarlett', Booklet Essay for *The Vivien Leigh Anniversary Collection*, Cohen Film Collection and British Film Institute.

———— (2013 b) *Vivien Leigh: An Intimate Portrait*, Philadelphia and London: Running Press.

Bell, Melanie (2016) *Julie Christie*, London: BFI Palgrave.

Botting, Jo (2013) 'Vivien Leigh adrift: *The Deep Blue Sea*', British Film Institute Features, www.bfi.org.uk/news-opinion/news-bfi/features/vivien-leigh-adrift-deep-blue-sea, accessed 15 April 2016.

Breen, Max (1938) 'A Vamp at Oxford', *Picturegoer Weekly*, pp. 10–11.

Cahir, Linda Costanzo (1994) 'The artful rerouting of *A Streetcar Named Desire*', *Literature/Film Quarterly*, 22:2, pp. 72–77.

Chibnall, Steve (2007) *Quota Quickies: The Birth of the British 'B' Film*, London: British Film Institute.

Crowther, Bosley (1955) 'Vivien Leigh Exquisite in "The Deep Blue Sea" ', *Screen: Woman's Choice, New York Times*, 13 October, p. 35.

Dent, Alan (1969) *Vivien Leigh: A Bouquet*, London: Hamish Hamilton.

Drazin, Charles (2000) 'Interview with Anthony Havelock-Allan', courtesy of Charles Drazin, Private Collection.

———— (2011) *Korda: Britain's Only Movie Mogul*, London: I.B. Tauris.

Dyer, Richard (1998) *Stars*, London: BFI Publishing.

Funke, Lewis and John E. Boothe (1961) *Actors Talk about Acting: Nine Actors Discuss their Art*, New York: Random House, Inc.

Haskell, Molly (1987) *From Reverence to Rape: The Treatment of Women in the Movies* (2nd edition), Chicago and London: University of Chicago Press.

Hollinger, Karen (2006) *The Actress: Hollywood Acting and the Female Star* (1st edition), New York: Taylor & Francis.

Newton, Michael (2013) 'Vivien Leigh – A Life on Screen', *The Guardian* www.theguardian.com/film/2013/nov/22/vivien-leigh-life-on-screen, accessed 14 April 2016.

Ottaway, Robert (1965), 'Vivien Leigh: The Mask Behind the Face', *Queen*, 10 March 1965. Vivien Leigh Biographical File, V&A.

Russell Taylor, John (1984) *Vivien Leigh*, London: Elm Tree Books.

Taylor, Helen (2015) *Gone With the Wind*. London: BFI/Palgrave.

Thompson, Laura (2013) 'Vivien Leigh: A Star, Pure and Simple', *The Telegraph* 15 November.

Vickers, Hugo (1988) *Vivien Leigh*, London: Hamish Hamilton.

Walker, Alexander (1994) *Vivien: The Life of Vivien Leigh*, London: Orion.

Young, Jeff (1999) *Kazan on Kazan*, London: Faber and Faber.

Filmography

21 Days (1940), dir. Basil Dean, London Film Productions, UK.

Anna Karenina (1948), dir. Julien Duvivier, London Film Productions, UK.

A Streetcar Named Desire (1951), dir. Elia Kazan, Charles K. Feldman Group, Warner Brothers, USA.

A Yank at Oxford (1938), dir Jack Conway, Metro-Goldwyn-Mayer British Studios, UK.

Caesar and Cleopatra (1945), dir. Gabriel Pascal, Gabriel Pascal Productions, for Independent Producers, UK.

Dark Journey (1937), dir. Victor Saville, London Film Productions, UK.

Fire Over England (1937), dir. William K. Howard, London Film Corporations, UK.

Gentlemen's Agreement (1935), dir. George Pearson, British & Dominions Film Corporation, UK.

Gone With The Wind (1939), dir. Victor Fleming (and George Cukor, Sam Wood, uncredited), Selznick International Pictures, Metro Goldwyn Mayer, USA.

Look Up and Laugh (1935) dir. Basil Dean, Associated Talking Pictures, UK.

Ship of Fools (1961), dir. Stanley Kramer, Stanley Kramer Productions, USA.

St Martin's Lane (aka *Sidewalks of London*) (1938), dir. Tim Whelan, Mayflower Pictures Corporation, UK.

Storm in a Teacup (1937), dir. Ian Dalrymple, Victor Saville, Victor Saville Productions, London Film Productions, UK.

That Hamilton Woman (1941) dir. Alexander Korda, Alexander Korda Films, London Film Productions, UK.

The Deep Blue Sea (1955), dir. Anatole Litvak, London Film Productions.

The Roman Spring of Mrs Stone (1961) dir. José Quintero, Seven Arts Pictures, USA.

Things are Looking Up (1935) dir. Albert de Courville, Gaumont British Picture Corporation, UK.

The Village Squire (1935) dir. Reginald Denham, British and Dominions Film Corporation, UK.

Waterloo Bridge (1940), dir. Mervyn LeRoy, Metro-Goldwyn-Mayer, USA.

6

Vivien Leigh and her French collaborations: a rethinking of her art

Arnaud Duprat de Montero

(Translated from the French by Matthew Cast)

Many biographers have noted that Vivien Leigh was both a francophone and a Francophile. Having mastered the language of Molière as a teenager, her life featured frequent visits to Paris, Brittany, the Basque Country and the Mediterranean coast. She expressed her enthusiasm for French films on many occasions, both during the period of Poetic Realism and later on during the New Wave. Throughout her professional life, Leigh crossed paths with some of the great names in French culture, such as Jean-Louis Barrault, Jean-Pierre Aumont and Simone Signoret; she was awarded the Legion of Honour,[1] performed in Shakespeare's *Titus Andronicus* in Paris and played Anna Karenina, directed by Julien Duvivier. However, all of these collaborations occurred within anglophone productions, while *Titus Andronicus* was a restaging – in English – of Peter Brook's production which was crafted on the London stage.[2] While other European actresses who were also great Hollywood stars gave distinguished performances in French films and theatre – such as Ingrid Bergman or Marlene Dietrich – it is a legitimate source of regret that Vivien Leigh never had the opportunity to perform in French on stage and/or in French films.[3] But should we conclude from this that the relationship between Vivien Leigh and French culture constitutes a missed opportunity? Is the lack of French works on the list of films and plays Leigh performed in simply due to unfortunate circumstance, paths which did not cross at the right moment, or could it be the consequence – given that Vivien Leigh was in frequent contact with French artists – of an incompatibility concerning the very conception of dramatic art? In order to answer this question, which implies a new reading of her career, it is important to assess the position and significance of French culture in Vivien Leigh's development as an artist, as well as in her work in cinema and theatre, and thereby to evaluate any possible divergence between the way she exercised her profession and practices in France. These divergences and the description of her relationships with other artists like Barrault or Aumont open up a different way of understanding her own conception of her achievements and limitations as an actress. This line of thinking then extends into an examination of the highly positive way her cinema work – despite these artistic divergences – was received by French critics and film viewers. Her films were, for historical reasons, only revealed to and watched by a wider French audience in the late 1940s and early 1950s. Finally, this chapter focuses on the film directed by Julien Duvivier, which was made in the middle of these 'golden years'. Although it is a British film, *Anna Karenina* (1948) can almost be viewed as the 'French' film in Vivien Leigh's cinematographic history because the key creative personnel – Jean Anouilh, who wrote the film, Henri Alekan the cinematographer and Duvivier – were all French. Despite the famous conflict between the filmmaker and the actress, which sheds welcome light upon the relationship between the actress, her art and the heroine she played, we will see that the themes closest to Duvivier's heart, and Alekan's lighting, are in tune with both Leigh's persona as well as her creative universe, making this film a necessary step towards the accomplishment of both in *A Streetcar Named Desire* (1951).

Vivien Leigh and the French arts: an acting incompatibility?

France was an integral part of Leigh's education: the Catholic school – the Convent of the Sacred Heart in Roehampton – in which her parents enrolled her in 1920, and where she remained until July 1927, was one of a French-based group of schools which also included establishments across Europe. Along with English but also foreign girls, she received her first French lessons at this school (Edwards, 2013: 21). However, it was from 1927, when her parents decided that her education should be completed on the Continent, that Leigh really perfected her command of French.[4] Having spent the 1927–1928 school year in Dinard on the Brittany coast in a Sacred Heart Order school,[5] she visited Biarritz during the summer of 1928. In 1929, following a year in another establishment in San Remo, Italy, she proceeded to study mainly French literature and language in the Villa Sainte-Monique school in Paris. The drama lessons which she received there provided her with the opportunity to meet Mademoiselle Antoine, an actress who, as Leigh recalled, performed for the Comédie-Française.[6] Although she had already taken to the stage at Roehampton and had yet to devote her life to the dramatic arts,[7] Leigh remembered

Mademoiselle Antoine many years later as the first person who had encouraged her to take up such a career:

> She was a most inspiring teacher, and I owe a great deal to her care in correcting my diction and to her encouragement.
> 'I believe you have a future in the theatre, *mon enfant*,' she told me, 'but you must go back to England and work ... work ... work. If you do that I shall see the name Vivien Hartley in big letters outside a London theatre one day. I promise you'. (Vickers, 1988: 24)

It was in Paris that Leigh began to diligently frequent various theatres, particularly the Comédie-Française, sometimes with Antoine. And from this period onwards her interest in the French language and in French culture never diminished. The actress loved to be surrounded by Renoir or Degas paintings even when travelling,[8] and wore, in town as well as on stage, clothing by Dior – for example, the costumes in *Duel of Angels* (1958) – Chanel or Balmain – in *The Roman Spring of Mrs Stone* (1961) among others. She was also a long-term friend of the director of the latter – Ginette Spanier. French culture was a recurring element of her career in the theatre, from her first great success in *The Mask of Virtue* by the German playwright Carl Sternheim (1935), inspired by Diderot,[9] to the penultimate play she ever performed in, *La contessa* by Paul Osborn (1965), adapted from Maurice Druon's novel *La volupté d'être* (1954). Leigh trod the boards in Georges Feydeau's *Occupe-toi d'Amélie* (1908) translated by Noël Coward and entitled *Look After Lulu* (1959); played Marguerite Gautier in 1961–1962, the heroine created by Alexandre Dumas *fils*, in *La dame aux camélias* (1852); and most of all created *Pour Lucrèce* by Jean Giraudoux (1953) in England – *Duel of Angels*, in an adaptation by Christopher Fry (1958) – and *Antigone* by Jean Anouilh (1944), translated by Lewis Galantiere (1949).

Onscreen, Leigh displayed on several occasions, each time in just a few lines, her command of French.[10] Her heroines often spend time in France – *Storm in a Teacup* (1937), *Dark Journey* (1937), *Lady Hamilton* (1941) – and embrace their French heritage, be it recent or distant – *Dark Journey* (1937), *A Streetcar Named Desire* (1951), and *Gone With The Wind* (1939). This phenomenon appears to shed light on Leigh's taste for French cinema. Indeed, in 1941 she placed French cinema, along with Russian cinema, higher than American cinema.[11] A few years later, she saw *Les enfants du paradis* (Marcel Carné, 1945) in which Jean-Louis Barrault, whom Laurence Olivier had just met in Paris, starred (Robyns, 1968: 89).[12] Similarly, she expressed her admiration for François Truffaut's *Les 400 coups* (1959) in the 1960s (Robyns, 1968: 210). In 1949, she shared the character of Blanche DuBois with Arletty

– the actress from *Les enfants du paradis* who was playing in Tennessee Williams's play in Paris, in an adaptation by Jean Cocteau and directed by Raymond Rouleau, at the same time as Leigh was performing in it in London – as well as sharing a billing with Simone Signoret in her last film, *Ship of Fools* (1965). Although Vivien Leigh did not exchange any lines with these two actresses, they were nevertheless highly generous in their praise of her performances. Arletty made the most of a day off to travel to London and see Laurence Olivier's staging of the play: 'Vivian [sic] Leigh, an extraordinary Blanche' (Arletty, 1971: 188) 'she looked like a fallen Lady' (Demonpion, 1996: 354). The two actresses met following this performance. Simone Signoret wrote in her autobiography: '*Ship of Fools* was her last film and she was tremendous in it' (Signoret, 1976: 300).[13]

On the other hand, Vivien Leigh played on stage alongside Jean-Pierre Aumont – *Tovarich* (1963) – and under the direction of Barrault in *Duel of Angels*, created by the latter in Paris; with Madeleine Renaud and Edwige Feuillère in the role of Paola that was subsequently played by Leigh. The accounts provided by these two men offer an excellent insight allowing us to understand Leigh's approach to acting.

Barrault wrote: 'Vivien Leigh's face! ... what a "person"! And how well we got on! ... when, some years later, her death was announced on the radio, I could not believe that such a captivating creature, so irresistible, like the most devilish of all the angels, could have gone. Madeleine [Renaud] and I felt profound heartache' (Barrault, 1972: 348–349). Despite his admiration for Leigh, he expressed his surprise at the way she approached the heroine: 'She worked on her role all the while hating her character – namely, on this occasion, Paola. She attacked her. She continually sought reasons to dislike her. So I had to stick up for Paola. She approached the character by provoking antipathy. It was only when she had run out of reasons to hate Paola that she accepted her' (Barrault, 1972: 348–349). This approach, which could potentially damage any empathy between the character, the performer and the viewer, perhaps explains this somewhat lukewarm comment by Jean-Louis Barrault when comparing Vivien Leigh to Edwige Feuillère: 'She [Vivien Leigh] is more comical, although she has less strength than Edwige Feuillère' (Mignon, 1999: 242).

Aumont's recollections shed further light on this phenomenon. He was complimentary to the actress: 'I observed Vivien with delight every evening. She only had to enter, to move, to come and go with such royal ease ... to conquer all hearts. It mattered little whether she was the character or playing the situation, she created, by her very presence, a magic ... It was far more than a question of talent, grace or elegance. It was one of charm' (Aumont, 1976: 293). However, he bemoaned the fact that Leigh determined the way she would play a role very early on and stuck to it rigidly despite the appeals of her acting partners:

> For me although like many I was far from insensible to her charms, having played evening after evening alongside her I could not help but regret that she never varied her portrayal. She had decided once and for all at the first rehearsal that she would say a certain line in a certain way, with a certain rhythm and with a certain gesture: the earth could have collapsed beneath her but nothing was going to make her change her mind.
>
> Strange actress ... Sublime onscreen ... but far less free on stage. Quick, insolent, fast in delivery of her lines, she appears lost when it is her partner's turn to speak. (Aumont, 1976: 294)

The discussions the two actors had upon this subject reveal two diametrically opposed conceptions of acting:

> Little by little ... I began to alter my intonations, to accelerate or slow down the tempo, in such a way as to surprise her, with the aim of fighting against the routine that we were slipping into and rediscovering invention, spontaneity, the freshness we had at the beginning. But Vivien refused to follow my lead.
>
> Every evening, after the show ... we would talk about ... our different conceptions. To try and convince her I told her about my early experiences playing in *La machine infernale* [by Jean Cocteau], where I had gradually altered [Louis] Jouvet's staging (which was certainly a more serious affair than altering an intonation!) and that Jouvet, far from blaming me actually congratulated me. Vivien was irritated and included Jouvet in her condemnation.
>
> 'Ah! these French types are all the same! Jouvet, Chanel, de Gaulle, and you, all amateurs ...'
>
> By chance I happened upon an article written by Laurence Olivier for *Life Magazine*. In it he confirmed that the only way for an actor to preserve spontaneity was to vary his intentions and every evening to find some new element to provide the show with a lifelike element of improvisation, so that the lines burst forth as if they had just been made up.
>
> I put ... Larry's article on Vivien's makeup table. She never mentioned it, but from that day onwards she never again called me an amateur. (Aumont, 1976: 294–295)

Aumont's observations chime with those of Bernard Braden, a Canadian actor who played Mitch opposite Leigh in the London version of *A Streetcar Named Desire*. He concluded that Vivien Leigh was not an 'instinctive actress', which, according to him, she perceived as a 'limitation'[14] (Robyns, 1968: 136–137).

Did Leigh stick to this rigorous approach because she did not feel capable of spontaneity or improvised inventiveness? Did she aspire to a greater degree of freedom in her art, a free-ranging liberty, and did she recognise and appreciate this capacity in French actors and artists, despite calling them amateurs, an epithet which was tinged with a degree of 'bad faith' as Aumont points out (Aumont, 1976: 293)? While a certain emancipation with regard to academic rules became emblematic of 1960s French cinema and of the New Wave – notably with the actors of this period refuting an academic way of acting as a means of gaining authenticity – Leigh spoke of *Les 400 coups* in meaningful terms, as recalled by Bob Webb, a publicist she met during the filming of *Ship of Fools*:

> One day I plucked up courage to sit beside her and she told me she had been to see François Truffaut's *Four Hundred Blows* the night before. She was so excited about it and explained that it was a completely new concept of picture making:
> 'Oh how I wish they'd offer me a part in one of these new-wave pictures,' she remarked sadly. (Robyns, 1968: 210)

Unfortunately, whereas many French artists of her generation admired her,[15] those of the New Wave ignored her. During the ceremony in Paris when Vivien Leigh received the *Étoile de cristal* award for *Ship of Fools*, the director Alain Resnais (*Hiroshima, mon amour* (1959); *L'année dernière à Marienbad* (1961)), the actors Maurice Ronet (*Ascenseur pour l'échafaud* (1958) and *Le feu follet* by Louis Malle (1963)), Anouk Aimée (*Lola* by Jacques Demy (1961)), and most particularly Brigitte Bardot, famed for her unrealistic, spontaneous and non-academic way of acting, were present.[16] However, despite the fact that Ginette Spanier persistently tried to get the two stars to converse, Bardot spent her evening avoiding Leigh, who remained on her own (Vickers, 1988: 321).

The French public and Vivien Leigh, the post-war foreign star

The way Leigh was treated by the proponents of the New Wave was connected to the fact that the French public was less than appreciative of her final films, despite the *Étoile de cristal* award she won in 1966 and the Legion of Honour she received in 1957. *The Deep Blue Sea* (released in France on 6 January 1956), *The Roman Spring of Mrs Stone* (16 May 1962) and *Ship of Fools* (1 October 1965) were commercial failures.[17]

However, from 1945 to 1952 Vivien Leigh experienced a golden period in France. Following four films which were released before the Second World War – *Fire Over England* (5 February 1937), *Dark Journey* (7 May 1937), *A Yank at Oxford* (28 October 1938) and *St Martin's Lane* (6 September 1939) – the French public had to wait until 1945 to fully discover her, due to the ban on American and British films by the Nazi occupiers and the Vichy regime. Thus, in France, *Lady Hamilton* was released on 20 December 1945, *Waterloo Bridge* on 11 April 1947, *Caesar and Cleopatra* on 3 May 1948, *Anna Karenina* on 25 May 1949, *Gone With The Wind* on 20 May 1950 and *A Streetcar Named Desire* on 28 March 1952. While the population of mainland France rose from 39,660,000 in 1945 to 42,460,000 in 1952, *Lady Hamilton* attracted 2,360,970 French viewers and *Waterloo Bridge*, with 3,946,313 tickets sold, took 11th place in that year's box-office hits.[18] *Anna Karenina* and *A Streetcar Named Desire*, with 1,692,414 and 1,571,713 viewers respectively, were also popular successes, albeit to a lesser extent. Unsurprisingly, *GWTW* was the biggest box-office success with 16,723,795 tickets sold.[19] Only *Caesar and Cleopatra* attracted fewer than a million viewers, 815,007 to be precise, and can only be considered a partial success. Due to her frequent presence on screen and her box-office figure, Leigh was during this period one of the most popular foreign stars in France.

The press reactions confirm this. While her films, aside from *Gone With The Wind*, were violently criticised – *Lady Hamilton, Caesar and Cleopatra, Anna Karenina* – or were given a lukewarm reception – *Waterloo Bridge, A Streetcar Named Desire* – Vivien Leigh herself was always spared and was the object of widespread veneration.[20]

After receiving praise for the pairing she formed with Laurence Olivier in the 'great historical machine' which was *Lady Hamilton*,[21] *Les Lettres Françaises* concluded that *Waterloo Bridge* was simply another melodrama 'but with Vivian [sic] Leigh' who was, 'radiant and pure, displaying a capacity to free her character from the straitjacket forced upon her and, via her accomplished acting, involves us in her character's misfortunes rather than leaving us to the simple role of viewers' (22 April 1947). Although *L'Aurore* viewed *Caesar and Cleopatra* as 'lousy', the newspaper spares Vivien Leigh who 'alone, would convince us to forgive the processions of the Roman legions' (21 January 1949). *Spectateur* also deems that 'Vivian [sic] Leigh and Claude Rains [...] are remarkable' (10 September 1946).

With regard to *Anna Karenina*, French critics, with the exception of André Bazin,[22] consider that Vivien Leigh emerges with glory from the inevitable comparisons with Greta Garbo. *Le soir* praised her 'sober and nuanced acting', adding 'it cannot be said that Vivian [sic] Leigh, with her soft, intelligent face which is at times so childlike and so serious at others, is in any way an inferior actress to her illustrious predecessor ... Her beauty is more human, more tender and more genuinely pitiable' (29 May 1949). As for *Franc-tireur*, the two actresses are judged to be equal, albeit with certain differences:

Stepping into Greta Garbo's shoes; now there is a risk everyone cannot take! But by tackling the risk head on Vivien Leigh knew that she was minimising it. They share few common characteristics indeed, not only regarding their temperament as artists but also as women. One was passion, lasciviousness, defiance. The other – the current actress – is fragility, sensitivity, freshness. And both of them render an eternal femininity which contains value, wealth and mystery. (28 May 1949)

This chorus of praise continued into the 1950s. About *Gone With The Wind, France Soir* spoke of 'a vivacious and marvellous performance. Vivien Leigh … is an incomparable actress, because she has an ability to hit every note, because she is without vanity and without weakness' (6 August 1955). Regarding *A Streetcar Named Desire, Les Lettres Françaises* concluded that 'Vivien Leigh is able to embody an Ophelia in her fifties with such skill that the viewer can only sense all the craft of a great Shakespearian [sic] actress' (April 20 1952) and *Les Cahiers du cinéma* praised 'Vivien Leigh, whose intelligence and finesse appear unsurpassable. This masterful transformation which she puts herself through, this febrile, crumpled appearance, which she forces upon herself, which she adds to via a build-up of details, each being a masterpiece in itself, and which she crowns at the end with her terrible heartbreak and the cries of a dying animal, inspire admiration' (May 1952). In 1956, when *The Deep Blue Sea* was released, *Le Film français* rejoiced at 'the return of the moving Vivien Leigh to the screen', as she 'was the only one who could make this Esther, who is fascinated with the absolute, sensitive and bring her close to the viewer, a kind of English "Bovary" and her charm is extremely lively' (20 January 1956), whereas *Radio Cinéma* stated that 'Vivien Leigh plays Esther with a talent which is reserved to very few actresses' (22 January 1956).

Before the future directors of the New Wave developed their famous Auteur theory and attributed the director the exclusive title of the creator of a film, there existed in France, from the end of the 1940s, a genuine interest in actors among cinema lovers (De Baecque, 2001). This phenomenon can be observed with Leigh, not only in the many articles full of lyrical praise for her but also by the fact that certain critics did not hesitate to credit her with creative responsibility for her cinematographic works. Thus we may read in *L'Aurore* that '*Anna Karenina* is Vivien Leigh's film; it is not, unfortunately, that of Mr Duvivier' (27 May 1949). A year later, *Le Monde* stated that '*Gone With The Wind* is not the film of a director but is that of the reality and the presence of one actress, Vivian [sic] Leigh' (20 May 1950).

However, the perception of Leigh as an actress of such talent that she could accede to the status of an actress-creator, building up an *œuvre* over many films, did not withstand the advent of Auteur theory.

Accordingly, it is significant that the commendatory article published by *Les Cahiers du cinéma* reviewing *The Roman Spring of Mrs Stone*, does not allude to the actors and concludes with the words: 'The success of this film is the success of its direction' (July 1962), in much the same way that upon the release of *Ship of Fools*, the unanimous praise for Leigh's performance was limited to a few flattering words with little genuine substance.[23]

The state of grace from 1945 to 1952 which Leigh experienced in France is therefore remarkable with regard to this perception of her as an actress-creator. She was not the only one, of course, but this way of thinking was essentially founded at the time upon American actors. This was the case of the future directors of the New Wave, who were critics at the time and who were fascinated by Humphrey Bogart, and then subsequently by actors hailing from the Actors' Studio, like James Dean, Marlon Brando or Montgomery Clift. Apart from the collection of books entitled 'Masques et visages',[24] which focused on French actors of the previous generation, actresses were very much margin-alised in this line of thought and were often greeted, especially in the case of these new critics, with fetish-like or even erotic praise which forced their acting and artistic approach into the background (De Baecque, 2001: 124–129).

Yet in Leigh's case, although her beauty is frequently emphasised, it is her dramatic talent which is praised. Furthermore, we should note that in the two articles which evoke her as the genuine creator of *Anna Karenina* and of *GWTW*, note is also taken of a confrontation with the director on each occasion. This is particularly interesting in the case of *Anna Karenina* – *GWTW*, with its multiple directors, has always been viewed as a producers' film – because the director of this film, Duvivier, was a great figure of French cinema. Given that Leigh's per-formance in the role of Anna was far better received in France than in Great Britain, it would appear that the subjectivity and the artistic approach that the actress brought to the film conformed to the French school of thought about screen actors, thereby distancing this work from its nationality and bringing into relief its French origins. At the same time, this creative phenomenon guaranteed that *Anna Karenina* would hold a key role in Leigh's filmography.

Anna Karenina, a French film *by* Vivien Leigh?

Anna Karenina was released in Great Britain at a time when dramas dominated screens and the theatrical scene was, according to John Stokes and using the terms employed by Celia Johnson, 'ordinary, suburban, rather dull' (Stokes, 2007: 116). The author evokes this period by elaborating on the film *Brief Encounter* (David Lean, 1945) and the play *The Deep Blue Sea* (Terence Rattigan, 1952), two stories of adultery. After the Second World War, which was marked by 'considerable sexual freedom' (Stokes, 2007: 117), the post-war period saw an 'attempt to draw a line under what had gone on immediately before and to resume that idealised "normality" [of the period between the wars]'. The Archbishop of Canterbury himself exhorted the British people in 1945 to 'reject "wartime morality" and to return to Christian lives!' (ibid: 118). While the tragic destiny of the Russian heroine could easily be used as a moralising example, Duvivier's film contains a distinction in that Anna, unlike Laura – *Brief Encounter* – and Hester – *The Deep Blue Sea* – does not resign herself to solitude at the end of the film. In addition, as Stokes points out, the feeling of guilt, which is very much present for Anna, is notable by its absence in the other cases:

> Hester never apologizes for following her sexual impulses even if she finds them hard to explain, and Laura would surely have slept with her doctor companion if they hadn't been interrupted by the return of the friend who had let them a flat. Both women are isolated, already emotionally alienated from their formal male partners, their husbands. They are psychologically on their own – and in neither case are female friends or children much consolation. (Ibid: 120)

These heroines are not 'hysterical because that would pathologise her', Stokes specifies, basing his analysis on Richard Dyer (ibid: 118), contrary to Anna who, beyond her suicide, is the most neurotic of all the Anna Kareninas portrayed on film due to her hallucinations, her delirium when suffering and the fact that the film resorts to voiceover in the final scenes. Whereas it is noteworthy in *Brief Encounter* or *The Deep Blue Sea* that the 'public protestations of essential decency muffle the deeper resonances that films and plays had for performers and audiences alike' (Stokes, 2007: 116), Duvivier's film appears to avoid this fact.

The establishment of this distance from the British moral context of the time could, of course, spring from the very origins of Jean Anouilh's screenplay[25] which, before the intervention of Guy Morgan (ordered by Alexander Korda), had transferred, with Jean Duvivier's assistance, Tolstoy's novel to France – where heroines in films at this time often met with death during the finale.[26] Due to this, and following the framework of previous adaptations of this Russian work, the screenplay focuses on Anna's adultery and leaves the other protagonist of the literary text, Levine, somewhat on the sidelines.

After spending several years in Hollywood, including an initial collaboration with Alexander Korda – *Lydia* (1941) – Duvivier was in negotiations for several months with the producer and Leigh with a view to making a film together. The first possibility was an adaptation of Enid Bagnold's play, *Lottie Dundass*, and filming should have commenced in July 1945. The cancellation of this project due to Leigh's fragile health allowed the filmmaker to direct *Panique* (1946) in France, with Michel Simon and Viviane Romance, often considered one of his best films. In early 1947, an adaptation of Mary Webb's novel, *Gone to Earth*, was mentioned. However, in the light of Leigh's 'absolute determination to play a great heroine' and the fact that she 'was haunted by the memory of Greta Garbo' according to Julien Duvivier (Bonnefille, 2002: 51), Korda proposed that they bring *Anna Karenina* to the screen.

The conflict between Duvivier and the crew involved in making the film has attracted much attention (Bonnefille, 2002: 52), and these tensions have often been attributed to conflict between the director and Leigh. Despite a certain number of clashes, Alekan nevertheless speaks of several dinners shared 'in little London bistros' where Leigh, Duvivier and himself met amicably after a day's work (Niogret, 2010: 56). The conflict was essentially artistic. Whereas Duvivier wanted to see a romantic and generous Anna, in order to chime with the filmgoing public's wishes, according to Kieron Moore, Leigh 'wanted to show the hard, driving nature of Anna's obsession ... the carnal appetite the lovers had for each other ... and the physical nature of love' (Walker, 1994: 253). This divergence led Duvivier to say that although 'Vivien Leigh was superior to Greta Garbo', 'she was not this character. Anna Karenina is woman who gives, Vivien Leigh is one who takes' (Niogret, 2010: 170). There is a visible disparity between the actress who seizes the character and stamps her subjectivity upon it – 'I know Anna. I was inside her. I know everything about her', said Leigh (Mafioly, 1990: 204) – and a filmmaker who, again according to Moore, 'didn't believe in any kind of love and certainly not the obsessive, destructive kind, but would be prepared to push the claims of romantic love in the interest of commercial success' (Walker, 1994: 254).

And yet we cannot conclude that *Anna Karenina* is a complete denial of Duvivier's cinematic universe. Cruelty, a theme he addressed at length in the films he co-wrote with Charles Spaak, is certainly present in the way that Anna is rejected by society. As for the cruelty of fate and the impossibility of escaping it, this can be found in the recurring image of the dead railway worker at the start of the film, which comes back to haunt the heroine's imagination. Yet where, according to Yves Derichard, 'the novel is a quest for God as well as a pantheistic ode', in the film 'this perversion of Tolstoy ... focuses the action on the nefarious trio of Anna/Vronsky/Karenin, sacrificing the dignified characters, Levine, Kitty' (Derichard, 2001: 64). The final sequence therefore avoids any facile pathos. Yves Derichard underlines the absence of music from it and evokes it as 'a long march towards death – nearly ten minutes – which reminds us of Duvivier's talent for this kind of scene (see also *Poil de carotte* or *Pépé le Moko*)' (Derichard, 2001: 55).

The tension between passion and the cruelty of fate is magnified, almost contrary to Duvivier's commercial ambitions, by Cecil Beaton's costumes and Alekan's photography: 'Anna's face is, for most of the time, in the light when she is with her husband, an accusatory light, whereas with Vronsky she is often found in a protecting shadow. This association of brightness with unhappiness and darker shades with passion is in large part to be found in Anna's dresses ... And accordingly when Anna's face is well-lit in a scene opposite Vronsky it is when the latter's feelings have weakened' (Derichard, 2001: 54–55).[27]

Alekan, who had been noted for *La bataille du rail* (René Clément, 1946) and especially *La belle et la bête* (Jean Cocteau, 1946), specified that Duvivier had 'allowed him to proceed with great freedom' and that 'in general, he was happy with what [he] had proposed' (Niogret, 2010: 56). The cinematographer recalls: 'I well remember spending whole Sundays, our day off, re-reading Tolstoy whose writing moved me greatly especially in the final chapters, to try and find any parallels I could draw between what was described in literary form and what the pictures would become, meaning the transposition which one could call cine-plastic' (ibid: 55). However, although 'the lighting must be meticulously linked to the subject matter' (ibid: 56), it also depends on the 'actor [who] enters, much like the space where he transforms himself, into a "lumino-spatial complex" which will match his verbal expressions and body language in order to affirm and exalt feelings, and lighting is a propagating element of these' (Alekan, 1991: 232–234). If these words are to be believed, then the lighting for the film sprang from Leigh and Alekan's fascination with her. Moreover, in his memoirs, the cinematographer evoked at length the productive and friendly collaboration he enjoyed with Leigh, before adding: 'Dear Vivien, you not only had beauty but also delicacy and humour. I was quite right to adore you' (Alekan, 1999: 65).

The intelligence of the work carried out by Alekan, who was attuned to Tolstoy's work but also to that of the director as well as the performance of the actress, allowed *Anna Karenina* to become an integral part of Duvivier's filmography, as we have seen, but also that of Leigh, where the heroines share a feeling of guilt, are faced with a moral dilemma and try to show, like Anna with her sister-in-law, that they are good women.[28] Henri Alekan's photography provides a sense of continuity after *Waterloo Bridge* where the love between Myra and Roy is born in the shadow of a restaurant in which the candles are being put out one by one and where the young woman's demise is played out under the raw light of a station café, before the ambulance head-lights of the suicide which foretells that of Anna.[29] Similarly, the dec-larations of love between Emma and Nelson in *Lady Hamilton* take place on sparsely lit terraces, whereas the exchanges with the husband take place indoors and are lit by many candles. This phenomenon reaches fulfilment in *A Streetcar Named Desire*, where Blanche has to dim the lights to live in a world of imaginary romances before being placed by Mitch under the aggressive lighting of a bulb which reveals her truth and plunges her into madness. It is also significant that Blanche appears at the start of the film on a station platform coming out of a luminous cloud of smoke, just as Anna had met her death at the end of the previous film.[30]

Conclusion

Unfortunately, Leigh never performed in French despite her command of the language and her interest in French culture. Is this because she viewed acting in France as more free and less constricted by rules than in Great Britain and that she, feeling herself incapable of acting instinc-tively, needed these rules to practise her art? The various statements and declarations quoted here suggest as much. It seems even more of a pity given that, as we have seen, her work in cinema was highly appreciated in France; indeed sometimes more than in her own country. It was not just a simple recognition of her talent, but more particularly that her approach to acting corresponded to a French school of thought at the time which underlined the creativity of film actors and their creative responsibilities in cinematic works. It has not escaped the attention of certain French cinema experts, especially during the period of *Anna Karenina* and *GWTW*, that Leigh's filmog-raphy can be viewed as an *oeuvre*, namely – and Auteur theory would do the same regarding directors – a canon with a line of thought running through it, manifested by recurring themes, a typical heroic profile which would determine its cinematographic writing. This French theoric focus allows us to view Vivien Leigh's career and the way she exercised her profession as a screen actress in a new light. This phenomenon is particularly evident in *Anna Karenina* where Jean Anouilh and Julien Duvivier's adaptation, Cecil Beaton's costumes and most of all Henri Alekan's photography, place this work firmly in the lineage of the actress's filmography and open the way to subsequent titles, with *A Streetcar Named Desire* first in line. Hence we cannot talk of a missed opportunity between Vivien Leigh and France, for *Anna*

Karenina constitutes a necessary pillar in her filmography – certainly to a greater extent than her previous English film, *Caesar and Cleopatra*. This is thanks to the contribution of the mainly French partners in this film, which certainly positions it as being contrary to the artistic and moral climate in Britain at the time, but also enables and guides the expression of Vivien Leigh's universe.

Notes

1 The Legion of Honour is the highest French honour. It was created by Napoleon in 1802 and rewards military or civil services to the French Nation.

2 This staging was created at the Shakespeare Memorial Theatre in Stratford-Upon-Avon on 16 August 1955 and toured from 6 May until 22 June 1957 in Paris, Venice, Belgrade, Vienna and Warsaw. The play was performed at the Théâtre Sarah Bernhardt during the Parisian leg from 15 May to 25, during which Vivien Leigh received the Legion of Honour.

3 Ingrid Bergman performed in the French film *Elena et les hommes* (Jean Renoir, 1956) and in the Franco-American film *Aimez-vous Brahms?* (Anatole Litvak, 1961), which was filmed in English but for which Bergman provided the dubbed French voice. At the theatre, she performed in *Tea and Sympathy* by Robert Anderson in a staging by Jean Mercure at the Théâtre de Paris (1956), then in *Hedda Gabbler* by Henrik Ibsen in a staging by Raymond Rouleau at the Théâtre Montparnasse (1962). Marlene Dietrich played in *Martin Roumagnac* (Georges Lacombe, 1946) alongside Jean Gabin, Daniel Gélin and Marcel Herrand.

4 Vivien Leigh stated that she essentially learned foreign languages when she was abroad. About the lessons she had in Roehampton, she wrote: 'I was allowed to specialise in history, literature, and music, and to study languages abroad' (Vickers, 1988: 16).

5 Although Alexander Walker implies that the actress stayed in Dinard for a year (Walker, 1994: 58), Hugo Vickers contends, although not categorically, that 'this can have been no more than a short holiday course' (Vickers, 1988: 22), thereby making the supposition that Vivien Leigh left Roehampton in 1928 in order to join the establishment in San Remo, Italy, for the start of the new school year.

6 Was Mademoiselle Antoine really an actress with the Comédie-Française? It must be specified that the institution's archives contain no record of an actress called Antoine during this period.

7 She had already played Mustardseed the fairy in *A Midsummer's Night Dream* in Roehampton and Miranda in *The Tempest*. She wrote: 'I can scarcely remember when I first thought of going on the stage, because it was such an accepted fact of my childhood. I never imagined myself in any other career' (Vickers, 1988: 16). According to Anne Edwards, Vivien Leigh, when only 7, stated to Maureen O'Sullivan, another Roehampton pupil, that she wanted to become an actress (Edwards, 2013: 20).

8 She said of her Renoir: 'I never travel without it. I like to have something pretty to look at when I'm on tour' (Vickers, 1988: 286).

9 Specifically, the episode of Mme de la Pommeraye in *Jacques le fataliste et son maître* (1796), which also inspired Robert Bresson's film, *Les dames du bois de Boulogne* (1945).

10 This can be heard in *A Storm in a Teacup* when she addresses a few words to her father, in *Waterloo Bridge* (1940) when she explains some figures from the ballet to Roy, in *Lady Hamilton*, notably during the opening scene when she steals a bottle of wine, in *Anna Karenina* when she reads a French hairdresser's advertisements, in *A Streetcar Named Desire* when, while flirting with Mitch, she states that he is Armand Duval and she is *la dame aux camélias*.

11 She wrote to Leigh Holman, on 5 November 1941, that *Citizen Kane* by Orson Welles was 'most original and interesting, though not such an advance on French and Russian pictures, as one was led to believe' (Vickers, 1988: 137).

12 After the 1945 Armistice, Laurence Olivier played in *Peer Gynt, Arms and the Man* and *Richard III* in Paris. Jean-Louis Barrault travelled to London afterwards with his wife, the actress Madeleine Renaud, to admire Laurence Olivier at the Old Vic. In 1946, the latter returned to Paris to attend a performance of *Hamlet* staged by Jean-Louis Barrault. In 1951, the French couple were invited by Laurence Olivier and Vivien Leigh to perform on the stage of the St James's Theatre in London.

13 Simone Signoret wrote also: 'In Hollywood, Vivien Leigh hosted dinner parties ... She was no longer Laurence Olivier's wife but she wanted to remain Lady Olivier ... At the end of the evening, the theme from *Gone With The Wind* was played, which made her sad but she did it on purpose. From one hour to the next she sparkled or was depressed. She was ill' (Signoret, 1976: 300).

14 Bernard Braden confided: 'Vivien Leigh was not an instinctive actress. She was not an actress in the way that Laurence Olivier, who is probably the most successful instinctive actor in the world, is.

Because she did not have this, Vivien had to work very hard and was conscious of the need for direction. She also became a perfectionist technically. For instance, she could never interrupt a thought of her own on stage other than mechanically. She would always do it on precisely the same syllable whereas if the instinctive actress is playing the same part every night she will feel the need to change it' (Robyns, 1968: 132). 'In my view no one was more aware of her own limitations than she was – no one' (Robyns, 1968: 134). To read the actor's full declaration, see Robyns (1968: 132–138).

15 With the exception of Edwige Feuillère who asked, during the premiere of *Titus Andronicus* on 15 May 1957 at the Théâtre Sarah Bernhardt: 'What can the English see in her?' (Vickers, 1988: 242).

16 The ceremony took place on 2 November 1966. The cinema academy jury, presided over by Georges Auric, awarded the *grand prix* to *La guerre est finie* by Alain Resnais, the prize for Best French Actress to Brigitte Bardot for *Viva Maria* by Louis Malle, for Best French Actor to Yves Montand for *La guerre est finie*, for Best Foreign Actor to Oscar Werner for *Ship of Fools* and for Best Foreign Actress to Vivien Leigh. Although Leigh appeared in most of the photographs which accompanied articles about the ceremony, the headlines gave all the importance to Yves Montand and especially to Brigitte Bardot.

17 *The Deep Blue Sea* only totalled 248,510 viewers, *The Roman Spring of Mrs Stone* 106,962 and *Ship of Fools* 99,456. For reference, the French population

was about 46 million people in 1960. The figures of more than 500,000 are provided by Simsi (2000). Many thanks to Didier Trevisan, from Rentrak, for his valuable help in researching all figures below 500,000.

18 Alfred Hitchcock's *Rebecca* and *Casablanca* by Michael Curtiz, which were both released in 1947, reached 5,106,851 and 3,597,959 viewers respectively. In 1947, the market was divided with 43.5% going to American films and 44.5% to French cinema. In 1950, American cinema obtained 42.5% and in 1952 37.2%.

19 The two other most watched American films in France in 1950 were Walt Disney's *Cinderella* – 13,216,631 viewers – and *The Three Musketeers* by George Sidney – 4,362,068. It must be specified here that these figures are those for the initial release and any subsequent re-releases. While this way of counting does not bring about any major changes for Vivien Leigh's other films, regarding their audience figure for the first release, *Gone With The Wind* is a different case as it was re-released with great popular success in 1955, 1961, 1969, 1976 and 1981. In 1950, the film attracted about 5,000,000 French viewers.

20 The only negative reviews concerned *Caesar and Cleopatra*, when one reviewer bemoaned the fact that Vivien Leigh 'will never really stop being Scarlett from *Gone With The Wind*' (*Noir et blanc*, 2 February 1949), and *Anna Karenina*. *Les Lettres Françaises* concluded that 'Vivian [sic] Leigh is a highly disappointing Anna' (5 July 1949) and *Les Nouvelles littéraires* wrote that she 'makes a poor job of showing by her expressions the internal torment which leads Anna to commit suicide' (2 June 1949). *Ciné-miroir* concludes that she 'is not Anna Karenina. She is not Russian for a single second. She is not passionately in love or tortured for so much as a minute' (Bonnefille, 2002: 58). It may also be noted that *Les Cahiers du cinéma* declared, regarding *A Streetcar Named Desire*: 'that to see Tennessee Williams played as if it were Shakespeare, in Laurence Olivier's finest style, by Vivien Leigh, added nothing to our enjoyment' (*Cahiers du cinéma*, October-November 1951).

21 See the article by Philippe D'Hugues, 'Rule, Britannia!' (*Le Monde*, 23 August 2005), in which the journalist reviews the reception by the French press at the time.

22 André Bazin wrote: 'Vivien Leigh, whose acting is excellent, does not, unfortunately, possess that superhuman aura which was behind Garbo's great charm' (Bonnefille, 2002: 58).

23 Only *Combat* (4 October 1965) and *Télérama* (17 October 1965) stand out by comparing Mary Treadwell to Blanche DuBois.

24 This is a collection of books edited by Roger Gaillard for the publisher Calmann-Lévy, from 1951 to 1954. Of the twelve books which make up the series, seven are devoted to actresses: Sarah Bernhardt, Marguerite Jamois, Yvonne Printemps, Arletty, Maria Casarès, Gaby Morlay and Edwige Feuillère.

25 Jean Anouilh had already written five screenplays, dialogue for eight films and had directed a feature, *Le voyageur sans bagage* (1944), with Pierre Fresnay.

26 Such as Danielle Darrieux in *Bethsabée* (Léonide Moguy, 1947), Edwige Feuillère in *L'aigle à deux têtes* (Jean Cocteau, 1947) and Michèle Morgan in *La symphonie pastorale* (Jean Delannoy, 1946), for example.

27 It should be pointed out that the dramatisation of the light can also be found in other films by Julien Duvivier, such as his previous one, *Panique*. Whereas the humiliation of M. Hire during the funfair, and his death as brought about

by the residents of his neighbourhood, happen in broad daylight, the romantic encounters between Alice and her lover are filmed in a nocturnal half-light.

28 While Scarlett admits to Rhett that she would like to be as good a person as her mother, Myra proclaims her goodness to Kitty, just like Emma with Sir William Hamilton, or Blanche with Mitch and Stella.

29 Alan Dent sees the end of *Waterloo Bridge* 'as though Anna Karenina had fallen under the wheels of a Streetcar named Desire' (Dent, 1969: 123).

30 Finally, it should be noted that, from here onwards, their husbands are no help at all to the heroines, either because they are already dead at the beginning of the tale – *A Streetcar Named Desire*, *Ship of Fools* – meet death in the opening minutes – *The Roman Spring of Mrs Stone* – or are simply secondary characters – *The Deep Blue Sea*; whereas lovers confirm everything that Anna fears from Vronsky: abandonment. The heroines are thereby left to their solitude and their suicidal tendencies.

References and bibliography

Alekan, Henri (1991) *Des Lumières et des ombres*, Paris: Librairie du collectionneur.
———— (1999) *Le Vécu et l'imaginaire*, Paris: Source la Sirène.
Arletty (1971) *La Défense*, Paris: La table ronde.
Aumont, Jean-Pierre (1976) *Le Soleil et les ombres*, Paris: Robert Laffont.
Barrault, Jean-Louis (1972) *Souvenirs pour demain*, Paris: Seuil.
Bonnefille, Éric (2002) *Julien Duvivier, le mal aimant du cinéma français, Vol. 2: 1940–1967*, Paris: L'Harmattan.
De Baecque, Antoine (2001) 'La Cinéphilie a-t-elle aimé les acteurs?', in Farçy, G-D and Prédal, R. (eds) *Brûler les planches, crever l'écran*, Saint-Jean-De-Védas: L'entretemps éditions, pp. 115–130.
Demonpion, Denis (1996) *Arletty*, Paris: Flammarion.
Dent, Alan (1969) *Vivien Leigh: A Bouquet*, London: Hamish Hamilton.
Derichard, Yves (2001) *Julien Duvivier*, Paris, Courbevoie: BiFi, Durante.
Edwards, Anne (2013) *Vivien Leigh: A Biography*, Lanham, New York, Boulder, Toronto, Plymouth: Taylor Trade Publishing.
Mafioly, Serge (1990) *Vivien Leigh, d'air et de feu*, Paris: Henri Veyrier.
Mignon, Paul-Louis (1999) *Jean-Louis Barrault*, Monaco: Rocher.
Niogret, Hubert (2010) *Julien Duvivier, 50 ans de cinéma*, Paris: Bazaar & co.
Robyns, Gwen (1968) *Light of a Star: The Career of Vivien Leigh*, New York: A.S. Barnes and Company.
Signoret, Simone (1976) *La Nostalgie n'est plus ce qu'elle était*, Paris: Seuil.
Simsi, Simon (2000) *Ciné-passion*, Paris: Dixit.
Stokes, John (2007) 'Out of the Ordinary: Exercising Restraint in the Post-war Years', in Gale, Maggie B., Stokes, J. (eds) *The Cambridge Companion to the Actress*, Cambridge: Cambridge University Press, pp. 116–133.
Vickers, Hugo (1988) *Vivien Leigh*, Boston, Toronto, London: Little, Brown and Company.
Walker, Alexander (1994) *Vivien: The Life of Vivien Leigh*, London: Orion.

PART III

Constructed identities

7

From the fans
Kendra Bean

Amongst the many, many letters you must receive, I suppose one does not generally differ from another. An adoring member of the public is always the same, ever voluble, unreasonable, sometimes hysterical and more often childish. But they cannot really be blamed since to them, little stars, only one of millions, traveling their confined orbit, the glory and brilliance of a planet is intoxicating.

John F. Hufcoop to Vivien Leigh, 16 June 1951[1]

My own experience as a Vivien Leigh fan began in the summer of 2002. I was 18 and heading off to college having just read the novel *Gone With The Wind* for the first time. It had quickly earned pride of place on my mental shelf of favourites. Margaret Mitchell's vivid imagery of a volatile time in American history, as well as the depth she gave her two anti-heroes, moved me in a way few books before or since have managed to do. This feeling of awe was compounded when I watched the 1939 film adaptation, and I remember being struck most by how much Clark Gable and Leigh resembled the Rhett Butler and Scarlett O'Hara of my imagination.

There are many reasons why Leigh fascinates me. Her beauty; her screen presence and naturalness on film; the dynamics and cultural resonance of her relationship with second husband Sir Laurence Olivier; her determination to be seen as more than a film star and a pretty face; even her valiant struggle with mental illness, or what David Niven described as her 'toughness in the face of adversity' (Dent, 1969: 83). All of these elements are intriguing and admirable, to my mind. Initially, it was her association with Scarlett O'Hara, a character I admired as a teenager on the cusp of womanhood, that appealed to me. But the more I learned about Leigh as an actress and as a woman, the more I felt that it was she, not Scarlett, that I really connected with.

By the time Leigh began her acting career in the mid 1930s, Hollywood studio executives had perfected a formula for manufacturing stars to such a degree that producers in other countries were copying this model. In Britain, Alexander Korda created his own star system under the banner of London Films Productions, headquartered at Denham Studios in Buckinghamshire. On Korda's instruction, his publicity man John Myers planted stories about contracted actors, Leigh included, in newspapers and fan magazines such as *Picturegoer* and *Film Weekly*. The information released to the public – whether true or fabricated or a mixture of both – contributed to stars' images and informed fans' perceptions of the people they saw on screen.

The Vivien Leigh Archive at the Victoria & Albert Museum (V&A) and the Laurence Olivier archive at the British Library are full of fan letters to Leigh, dating from around 1939 to her death in 1967.[2] Written by film and theatre goers from the US, Spain, Japan, Australia, Turkey, India, Argentina and many places in between, the high volume of correspondence attests to both the widespread impact Leigh had as an actress and public figure, and to the degree to which fans appear to have found her accessible. While many wrote asking for signed photographs or personal meetings backstage or at her home, others put pen to paper to tell her how much her work affected them. Some carried on extended correspondence and felt that she was not just a celebrity but a friend. Perhaps Leigh's accessibility is not surprising. She knew firsthand the obsessive nature of fandom. Comedian George Robey and silent film star Ramón Novarro had captured her interest as a girl (Vickers, 1988: 17–24). By her early 20s, Olivier had supplanted other actors to become number one in her affections. She saw him perform the title role in *Hamlet* at the Old Vic in 1937 more than a dozen times and had decisively concluded that she would one day marry him, which she did in 1940.[3] That Leigh kept these letters from her admirers suggests not only her appreciation for fan loyalty, but also her understanding of the important role fans played in the maintenance of her fame.

Who were these people that wrote to Leigh? How did they connect with her during her lifetime? In what ways did they engage in wider fan communities? And how does this relationship with Leigh continue today, fifty years after her death? Delving into this material has been comparable to looking through a window into the past and experiencing fandom through the eyes of the men and women – young and old – who paved the way for future fans like me. It has been an eye-opening experience, at times comforting and wholly relatable, at other times shocking, sad and wondrously strange.

Fans of *Gone With The Wind*

Leigh is most widely recognised today for her performance as South-ern belle Scarlett O'Hara in *Gone With The Wind*. This in itself is quite remarkable considering she only appeared in nineteen films throughout her long career. In spite of its success, Leigh appeared in only seven films after *Gone With The Wind* – a source of regret to the studios employing her and the fans who wanted to see more of her. 'I certainly wish your film work was more frequent,' wrote New York fan Camilla Koch, 'although I suppose the rarity of your appearances adds to the enjoyment of each work.'[4] It is difficult to name many actresses of Leigh's era who became entrenched in popular culture based on such a small cinematic output. The widespread popularity of Marga-ret Mitchell's novel, winner of the Pulitzer Prize for fiction in 1937, guaranteed fame for the actress chosen to play the story's heroine on screen. Producer David O. Selznick's widespread public search for the perfect Scarlett created ample room for filmgoers and fans of Mitch-ell's novel to weigh in with their opinions about the type of person who should or should not play the part. The choice of Leigh over estab-lished Hollywood names – not to mention hundreds of young women across the Southern US who had hoped for the chance to bring their heritage to life on screen – caused widespread derision at the outset. Selznick International publicity guru Russell Birdwell carefully con-trolled Leigh's 'official' image in the press, likening her appearance and life story to that of Scarlett's. But this did not stop fans and gossip columnists from chastising Selznick for not choosing a home-grown actress, or from speculating about how an unknown Briton who had never stepped foot in the South nor heard a Georgian accent could possibly do justice to this character. Gossip columnist Hedda Hopper published disparaging remarks in her syndicated column about how casting Leigh was downright un-American: 'All this time we've had 56 [actresses] working right here in the heart of Hollywood on American-ism ... And out of millions of American women [Selznick] couldn't find one to suit him. Which would seem to cast a reflection on every girl born here.'[5] In the same article, she added a response from an angry filmgoer who seems to have forgotten that *Gone With The Wind* was a work of fiction:

> Scarlett O'Hara is southern, old southern, with traditions and inborn instincts of the South. How in the name of common sense can an English actress possibly understand Scarlett, her times or the characterization is beyond a thinking American. It makes as much sense as if England had sent for Jack Oakie to play King George at the coronation. (Ibid)

It is difficult to imagine the amount of pressure that Leigh must have felt while making *Gone With The Wind*. It was the type of film that could make a career or leave it in ruins. Protected as she was by Selznick, it is still likely she would have had access to newspapers and would therefore have been aware of the premature judgements passed against her. Scarlett O'Hara was the biggest and most important role of her career to that date. The margin for error was practically non-existent.

The enthusiastic critical reception of the film's première negated earlier suspicions of Leigh's acting abilities, and its popular success meant that many people associated Leigh with her onscreen character, as illustrated by a letter sent by Atlanta resident Clinton C. Chamberlin. Chamberlin was in the audience for the 1961 Civil War centenary and renewed première of *GWTW*, which Leigh attended in person. 'There can be no question that you were the "most beautiful hussy who ever invaded the South" in *Gone With The Wind*,' he wrote after the screening. 'Scarlett (I mean, Miss Leigh) imagine – a damned beautiful hussy from England to play the part of Scarlett.'[6] Given Chamberlin's brazen choice of word to describe Leigh, it is perhaps not surprising that the letter continues with comments about Leigh's personal life, particularly concerning her second husband, from whom she divorced in 1960. 'I never could do a damned thing for Sir Laurence Olivier. He is of the opinion that he is God's gift to women, but he impresses me as an *egotistically homely* maniac.'[7] There is no evidence of a response among Leigh's papers.

Not everyone was universal in their praise of *Gone With The Wind*. Theatre director Glen Byam Shaw 'finally' saw the film in 1952 and recorded his thoughts in a letter to Leigh dated 14 October:

> This film seemed to me utterly dead & out-of-date, except for your performance which I thought was quite wonderful. Sensitive, true, human, so interesting & exciting as a lifetime. One sees the thoughts flickering through that exquisite little creature's brain.[8]

Like any famous and influential figure, Leigh had her fair share of sycophants and hangers-on but Byam Shaw was a friend and colleague with whom she had an extensive correspondence. They had known one another since 1936 when he directed her in an OUDS production of *Richard II*.[9] In 1955, he would direct Leigh and Laurence Olivier in an acclaimed production of *Macbeth* at Stratford-upon-Avon. His observations here appear to be measured and sincere: 'Dare I confess that it was the first time I had ever seen you on the films. Only because I hate them so'[10] (Figure 7.1).

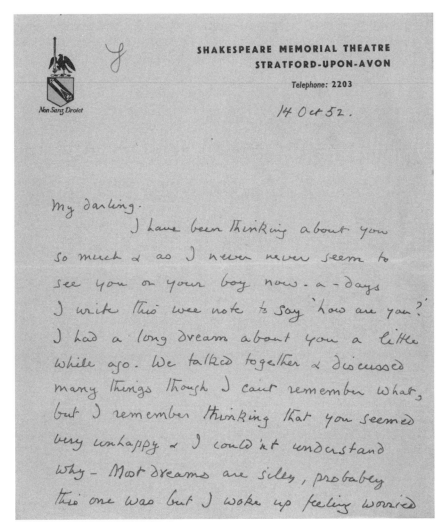

Figure 7.1   Letter from Glen Byam Shaw to Vivien Leigh about *Gone With The Wind*. 14 October 1952.

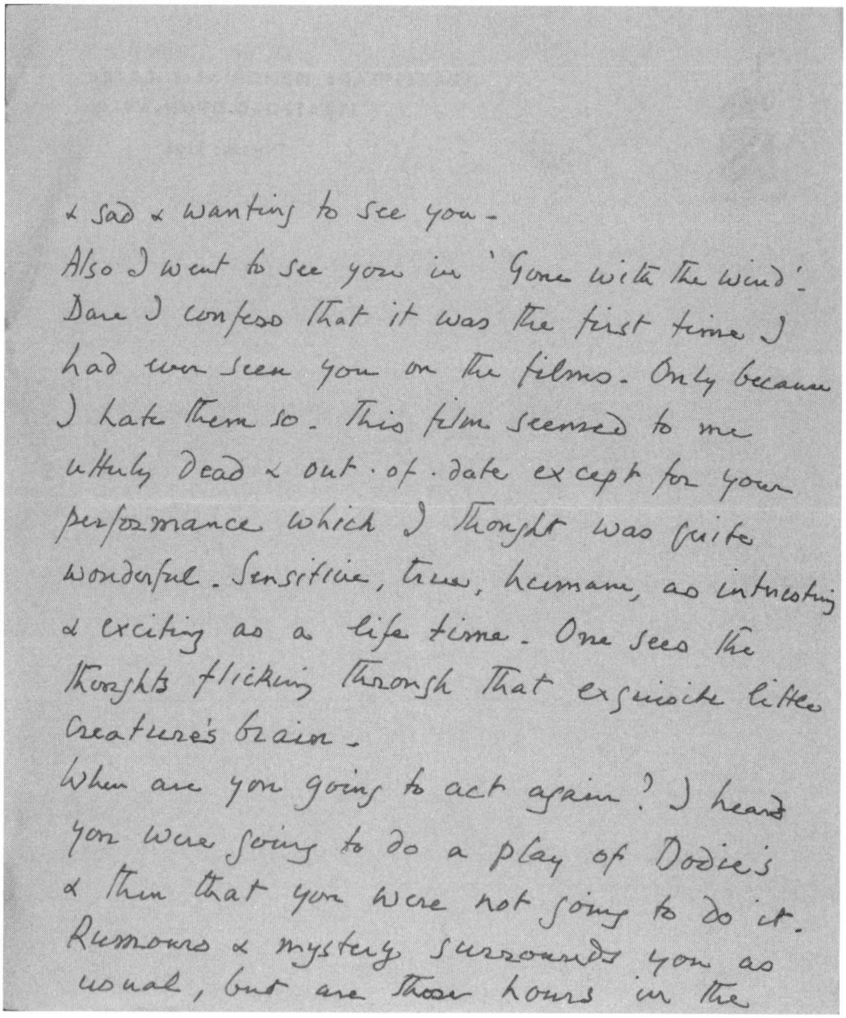

& sad & wanting to see you –

Also I went to see you in ' Gone with the Wind'. Dare I confess that it was the first time I had ever seen you on the films. Only because I hate them so. This film seemed to me utterly dead & out·of·date except for your performance which I thought was quite wonderful. Sensitive, true, humane, as interesting & exciting as a life time. One sees the thoughts flickering through that exquisite little Creature's brain –

When are you going to act again ? I heard you were going to do a play of Dodie's & then that you were not going to do it. Rumours & mystery surrounds you as usual, but are those hours in the

Figure 7.1   (Continued)

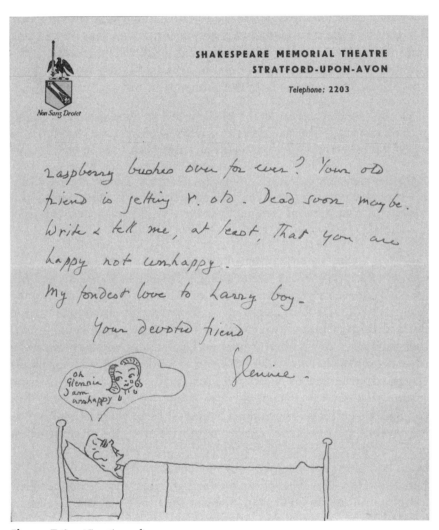

Figure 7.1   (Continued)

Since the end of the Depression when the film dominated screens across the US, *Gone With The Wind* has assumed iconic status in the annals of Hollywood history. Commemorative memorabilia, an authorised book sequel and two prequels, a West End musical, several academic studies, regular theatrical and home video re-releases and restorations have kept the story of Scarlett O'Hara – and Leigh – in the public consciousness. There is a certain sameness about the letters that mention the film, particularly among American fans: it was, and continues to be, a common point through which Leigh's work is discovered. A passionate letter penned in 1963 by Yvette Curran of Rego Park, New York, encapsulates the general sentiment:

> To me ... Scarlett, Rhett, all the people in the story, were as real – sometimes more so – than the people I knew. I was afraid to see the movie, for fear this little world would be shattered ... But when I saw it, Miss Leigh!!! Oh, when I saw it! You WERE Scarlett. You were the perfect Scarlett, the one and only possible Scarlett, the girl I had known she would be. How can I ever thank you for keeping intact all my most precious illusions? ... You were my heroine from then on, the only star I have ever admired.[11]

Curran is a wonderful example of a long-time fan who saw *Gone With The Wind* and proceeded to track Leigh's career in the years that followed. There are seventeen letters from Curran in Leigh's archive, the majority written when Leigh was performing on Broadway in the musical *Tovarich* (1963–1964). Curran had the privilege of being invited backstage after several performances. Leigh's kindness appears to be what prompted her to strike up a correspondence. 'I was absolutely staggered yesterday by your statement that you had been hunting around New York for a book for me!' she wrote in August 1963. 'But you have given me so much already that I'll be in your debt forever as it is: every time I ever saw you in the movies or on the stage or – best of all – in person, it has been a *priceless gift*, to cherish for a lifetime.'[12] Leigh had given her a signed copy of *Gone With The Wind*. The Korda film *That Hamilton Woman* (1941), starring Leigh and Olivier, also left a strong impression on Curran. She saw the film when it was released in 1941. Viewing it again in August 1963, she was compelled to tell Leigh how affected she remained by her performance: 'No other actress could ever be compared to you, not ever. Your acting simply transcends talent, it *[sic]* much more nearly genius. I have been going to the theater for years but I have never seen an actor or actress bring a part to life as completely as you do.' But *Gone With The Wind* appeared to remain Curran's favourite. 'Miss Leigh, if you want to see the greatest actress the world has ever known, all you have to do is look at each and every one of the pictures I have of you as Scarlett,' she wrote on 30 October 1964, long after Leigh had left *Tovarich* and returned to England. 'On not a single one is the facial expression the same as any other. The eyes speak, the whole face lives and tells the story. It passes belief ... Miss Leigh, I can look through my albums a thousand times and each time my heart catches with the beauty of your face and the truth of your performance, and now more than ever.'[13] Her collection of film stills topped a thousand, several of them having arrived from Leigh's MGM publicity agent at the actress's request.[14]

Fans of film

There were many people like Yvette Curran who discovered Leigh through *Gone With The Wind* but also took the time to share with Leigh their thoughts about her other film performances. After *Gone With The Wind*, Leigh's best-known film is Elia Kazan's screen adaptation of the Tennessee Williams play, *A Streetcar Named Desire*. Released in 1951 after successful runs on Broadway and in London's West End (where Leigh first played Blanche in 1949 under the direction of Olivier), *Streetcar*'s taboo themes of sexual promiscuity, homosexuality and rape courted controversy with the Catholic Legion of Decency, an agency heavily involved in Hollywood censorship.[15] Playing Williams' vulnerable butterfly Blanche DuBois was a strenuous experience, but one that really showcased Leigh's expertise before the camera perhaps more than any of her other screen performances. She saw Blanche as 'a pitiful soul who is the unfortunate victim of loneliness,' with a 'delicate and unstable make-up.'[16] She explained to readers of *The Stage*, 'When I first read the play I told Tennessee Williams that in Blanche he had written an "actor-killer" part. I have never tackled so physically exhausting a role.'[17] The film allowed Leigh to challenge what she perceived to be one of her biggest acting handicaps: her beauty. She emphasised to director Kazan her determination to do whatever was needed to look right for the part.[18] Through the use of heavy make-up and a messy blonde wig, she was able to physically transform herself into an ageing, debauched alcoholic, which added to the realism of her characterisation.

For some fans, like Curran, there was nothing Leigh could do to obscure her beauty:

> You are so beautiful that you couldn't help looking divine if you really set out to do it ... I think that would be the only thing you couldn't do. I saw you trying to do that in '*A Streetcar Named Desire*' and you were still as pretty as the angel on top of the Christmas tree.[19]

Others saw beyond the physical make-up to comment on the depth and emotional power of Leigh's performance. 'I know I have told you this before Miss Leigh, but of all the films & plays I have seen you in, your portrayal of Blanche just fascinates me,' enthused Joyce Attwood, a frequent correspondent from Melbourne, Australia. 'It is so different to what you are really like ... I felt after seeing it the first time as if I had just been through a ringer, in fact, I feel like that each time I see it.'[20]

Leigh won her second Academy Award for *Streetcar*. Accolades for her performance continued to pour in from various corners of the globe, including Kenji Honda in Chiba, Japan: 'I was deeply impressed by this film, and could not help tears flow in my eyes at [sic] last scene,' Honda wrote after a screening of *Streetcar* at his local cinema in May 1952. 'All audience also moved to tears even after the end of the picture and I did not want to stand up.'[21]

Both the Leigh and Olivier archives contain a significant amount of mail sent to Leigh from Japan. The post-war American occupation of the island nation brought with it significant Western influence, including the resumption of Hollywood film imports that had ceased during the war. It is likely that Leigh's films made between 1939 and 1945 were part of the backlog that built up in the Hollywood and British studios during the years of international conflict, which would explain why the earliest archived letters she received from Japanese fans date from around 1950. The new influx of American films also coincided with a productive period in Japanese cinema, with acclaimed directors releasing some of their best work – Akira Kurosawa: *Rashomon* (1950), *Seven Samurai* (1954); Kenji Mizoguchi: *Ugetsu* (1953), *Sansho the Bailiff* (1954); Yasujirō Ozu: *Tokyo Story* (1953). Cinemagoers had a rich selection to choose from.

Caesar and Cleopatra (1945) and *Waterloo Bridge* (1940) reached Japan before *Gone With The Wind* did, and it appears that both films had an impact on younger people. M. Soejima in Kanagawa Prefecture told Leigh he had seen *Waterloo Bridge* sixty-three times and had memorised all of the dialogue.[22] Seventeen-year-old Toshitake Fukomoro, in the 'quaint old large city of Osaka,' saw both films and described himself as Leigh's 'ardent fan'. In carefully printed English, using green ink, Fukomoro attempted to relate his admiration:

> I was completely charmed and fascinated by your talents, your beauty captures everyone's heart ... Many actors, singers, have visited our country since the end of the war, four years ago ... Oh, if only you could visit us, too. I will keep praying, so my dream may come true some day.[23]

These fans were not only eager to tell Leigh how much they appreciated her and her work, they were happy to share with her aspects of their own culture. Colourful cartoon sketches adorn corners of ageing paper; souvenirs and snapshot photographs are still tucked into yellowing envelopes. Tokens of appreciation that provided glimpses of life on the other side of the world.

Before the Leigh archive was made public at the V&A in 2015, much of the available information about the reception of her films came in the form of contemporary reviews. The archive reveals opinions of her lesser-known titles. There are several letters praising her performance in *The Roman Spring of Mrs Stone* (1961), for instance. Jeanne de Casalis, the South African actress and playwright who played the lead in Leigh's first West End play, *The Mask of Virtue*, commented on Leigh's 'beautiful & sincere, gay & lively performance' in *Fire Over England* (1937). 'Really and truly, darling, believe your old Jenny when she says that there's no one your age to touch you.'[24] Glowing accolades for Leigh's interpretation of Hester Collyer in the 1955 film *The Deep Blue Sea* came from Noël Coward's secretary Lorn 'Lornie' Loraine, who was particularly moved by Leigh's ability to shed genuine tears on camera.[25]

Letters pertaining to *Caesar and Cleopatra* (1945) are especially interesting. The film, which had been the most expensive made in England to that date, had promised to be the British film industry's answer to *Gone With The Wind* in cost and scale. Adapted from the George Bernard Shaw play, it was a film Leigh had been eager to make and she later recreated the role on stage opposite Olivier. However, despite being one of the most successful films of 1945 in terms of box office returns, it failed to turn a profit and the critical consensus was that the story and acting were overshadowed by Gabriel Pascal's heavy-handed direction (Bean, 2013: 92). Canadian author and actor Alexander Knox shared this sentiment. Then staying at the Sunset Towers in Hollywood, he was compelled to write after attending a screening in 1946:

> My impression of the picture has not been asked, but you're going to get it anyway. It was astounding that a brilliant script, played by such a brilliant cast, could be thwarted and tortured by ponderous and pedantic imitation Cecil B. DeMille direction. However, the script is still good, old man Shaw is still a giant, and when the actors are given a chance it comes beautifully to life.[26]

Roy Boulting and his twin brother John also felt that Pascal's direction had ruined an otherwise promising film. At the time they were just starting to make their own mark on British cinema as the Boulting

Brothers. Neither had worked with Leigh before but being in the same industry likely led to them crossing paths at some point. Roy's letter is worth quoting at length for its blunt insight:

> This morning John and I went to the press show of 'Caesar and Cleopatra'. Just in case the Doctor doesn't allow you to get up and see it for a while[27] – we both loved *your* performance, indeed, apart from Cecil Parker's Brittanus, the only consistently and truly Shavian performance in the entire film.
>
> I wish I could say that we enjoyed the whole as well as your part. Alas, it is a monumental bore – void of imagination, invention, or taste: and almost bare of Shaw's wit, so heavy has the Hungarian's imprint been.
>
> Why, oh why, didn't Larry do it? Why?
>
> If the film is a success G.P. should touch the ground before you with his forehead: nothing and no one else will have made it so!![28]

With a critical eye, one may discern that Leigh's films vary in quality (as indeed any actors do). However, the majority of letters in the Leigh archive suggest that even when a film did not work as a whole, many thought she transcended the surrounding material and stood out. While it may of course be that negative letters were not kept by Leigh, call it star power, charisma, presence – she had something people remembered when they exited the cinema.

Fans of theatre

Though her films are what have kept her alive in the public consciousness, Leigh always preferred the theatre. For those of us born after Leigh died, there exist small glimpses of what she must have been like on stage: an LP recording of her and Peter Finch reciting *Antony and Cleopatra* from 1964; digitised and abridged radio performances of her and Olivier in *Caesar and Cleopatra* (1950) and *Pygmalion* (1940); two acts of *The Skin of Our Teeth*, broadcast live on ITV in 1959. Unfortunately, none of her plays were filmed *in situ*, as Olivier's were in his National Theatre years. Critical reviews, photographs, mentions in diaries and letters are all that remain of this ephemeral aspect of Leigh's career.

There is not much difference between fans of Leigh's films and fans of her stage work except, perhaps, that there are a large amount of letters referring to the latter written by other members of the artistic community – possibly due to the lingering cultural attitude that theatre was superior to cinema. Harold Acton was moved by the way Leigh spoke her lines in the theatre. He gifted her a copy of his 1965 book *Old Lamps for New London* that included the following inscription: 'To the incomparable artist who can transform prose into poetry and clods into intellectuals, for you are unique and more beautiful with the passage of time. Your voice is magic.'[29] Another artist under Leigh's spell was the painter Alfred Kingsley Lawrence. In 1951, he saw Leigh perform in a double bill of *Caesar and Cleopatra* and *Antony and Cleopatra* at the St James's Theatre in Piccadilly, London, and thought her a moving success. 'You are great & therefore a rare artist – and you have the art which seems to me the perfection of art, in that you do create, and sustain, the illusion of reality,' he wrote on 25 August.[30] In another letter sent a week later, Lawrence put Leigh into perspective when he declared her adult Cleopatra in the Shakespeare play 'the most moving & beautiful, & memorable performance of any actress of my time, and I think I have seen most, if not all, the first rate actresses of my time (i.e. in their best roles)'.[31] Leigh's interpretation moved Lawrence so much that he requested, and was granted, permission to paint her portrait in character. It was not the first time he had immortalised Leigh on canvas. In 1949, he made a vibrant oil painting of her as Blanche DuBois, which held pride of place in Leigh's country home Tickerage Mill. She later gave it to the V&A and today it hangs in the reading room at Blythe House in London.

Leigh's films were available to a larger audience but she travelled widely during her career, performing in the US, UK and Europe, and leading two foreign tours with the Old Vic Company, the first of which she headlined with Olivier in Australia and New Zealand, where they represented the British Council. In 1962, she made several stops in South American countries as part of an Old Vic tour that she headlined herself, and this provided fans with not only a glimpse of Leigh in the flesh, but an opportunity to experience renowned English theatre. Both tours, and indeed most of the productions Leigh appeared in both domestically and abroad, were popular successes. During the 1950s, when she and Olivier were at the height of their partnership as a theatrical and married couple, Leigh occupied significant space in newspapers and magazines all over the world. Films like *Gone With The Wind* were also being distributed worldwide. She was an international celebrity, and this explains the warm reception she received from fans in far-flung cities like Zagreb, Warsaw, Caracas, Buenos Aires and Mexico City.

There does not appear to have been a typical audience for Leigh's stage performances. She received letters from both men and women, teenagers, housewives, soldiers, priests, the elderly. Out of this great variety of correspondence, one letter delights for its unexpectedness. On the afternoon of 31 March 1952, Leigh and Olivier took the stage at New York's Ziegfeld Theatre for a matinee of Shaw's *Caesar and Cleopatra*. In the audience were Helen Keller and her aide Polly

Thompson. Keller, whose story inspired the film and Broadway play *The Miracle Worker*, had been blind and deaf since childhood, but learned to communicate with the help of teacher Anne Sullivan, later mastering spoken and written language. In a typed letter, signed in squarehand, Keller related her enjoyment of the play, saying of Leigh's performance, 'So full were you of charm, "quips, becks, and nods" and the spirit of frolic, we could not think of the tragedy lowering over your head'[32] (Figure 7.2).

According to Jennifer Arnott, Research Librarian at the Perkins School for the Blind in Massachusetts, Keller was a voracious reader and 'was a fluent user of at least 5 different versions of braille,'[33] among other techniques. It is unclear whether Polly Thompson signed the dialogue or scenario of the play, but from the way she described her favourite scene ('The Pharos scene! – I shall remember its sparkle and roguish gaiety'),[34] Keller appears to have been familiar with the text. Leigh also took an interest in Keller's story. They were scheduled to meet again a few days after the performance and Keller signed a copy of her friend Nella Braddy Henney's biography of Anne Sullivan for Leigh. It was a mutually beneficial encounter.[35]

There are many letters in the archive that illustrate how the chance to see Leigh live solidified and even elevated fans' devotion. Take, for example, the letters of Nancy Abraham and Helene 'Henny' Sender, two New York high school students who, in 1963, went regularly to the Broadway Theatre in Manhattan to see Leigh dance and sing in the musical *Tovarich*. All told, they saw the production over forty times and considered themselves Leigh's 'most adoring admirers'.[36] Their letters make an interesting case study as they provide a glimpse of the way in which Leigh acted on and off stage, as well as how she interacted with her more passionate followers. With the unbridled enthusiasm of youth, the two friends lavished praise on the object of their affection, writing to Leigh regularly and even referring to her as their 'second mommy'. Each week, before going to the theatre, Abraham and Sender followed a particular routine that took them to the Seagram Building at 52nd and Park to throw pennies into the fountain ('all the wishes concern you in some way'),[37] before trekking to Leigh's rented home at 223 E. 52nd Street to try and catch a glimpse of her in the window. Abraham's father was a freelance archaeologist from Harvard who knew John F. Kennedy, so Abraham encouraged the President to see the show.[38] The girls' persistence and dedication eventually paid off (Figure 7.3). Leigh noticed their presence in the audience, even scolding them once for chattering during the play, which annoyed her. She invited them backstage for a personal meeting, sent them flowers and cigarettes, and once offered them a ride to the theatre in her

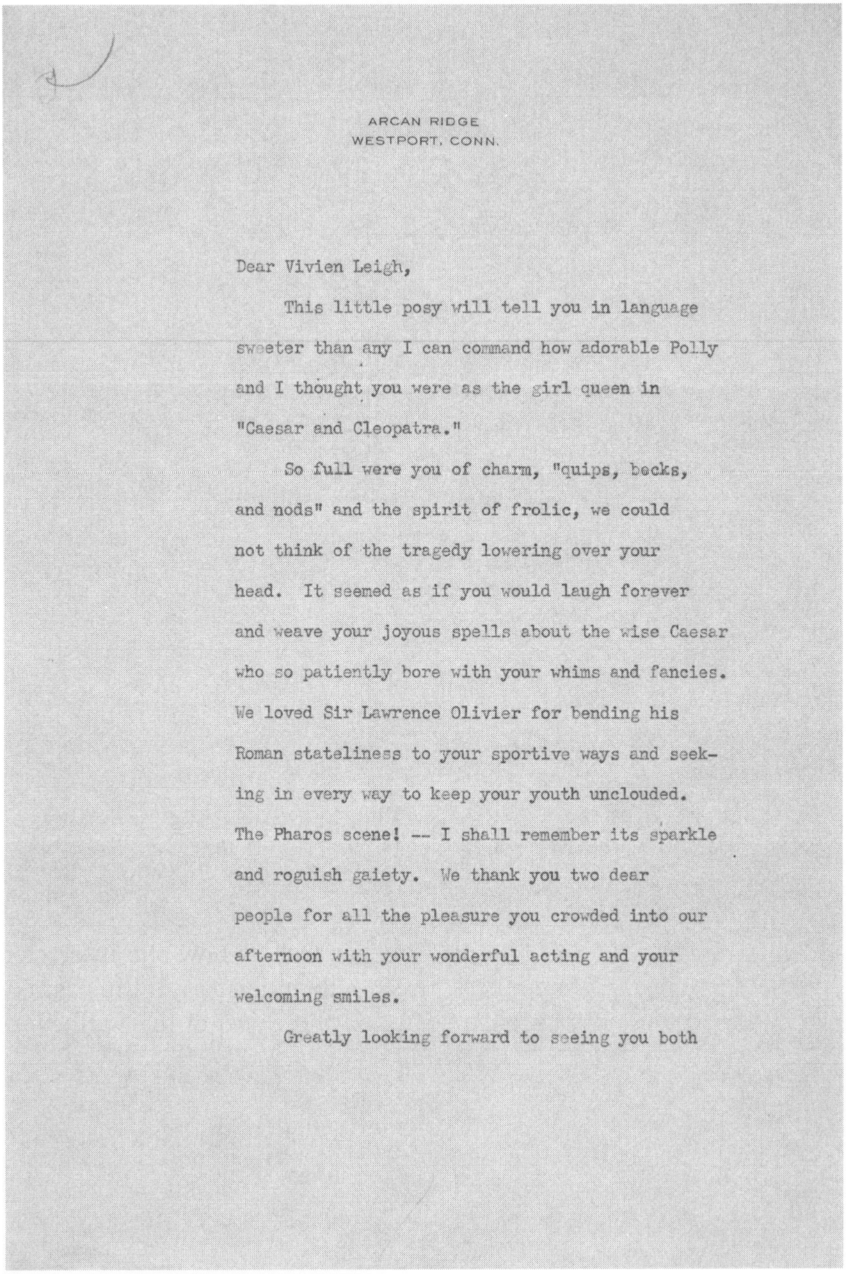

ARCAN RIDGE
WESTPORT, CONN.

Dear Vivien Leigh,

This little posy will tell you in language
sweeter than any I can command how adorable Polly
and I thought you were as the girl queen in
"Caesar and Cleopatra."

So full were you of charm, "quips, becks,
and nods" and the spirit of frolic, we could
not think of the tragedy lowering over your
head. It seemed as if you would laugh forever
and weave your joyous spells about the wise Caesar
who so patiently bore with your whims and fancies.
We loved Sir Lawrence Olivier for bending his
Roman stateliness to your sportive ways and seeking in every way to keep your youth unclouded.
The Pharos scene! -- I shall remember its sparkle
and roguish gaiety. We thank you two dear
people for all the pleasure you crowded into our
afternoon with your wonderful acting and your
welcoming smiles.

Greatly looking forward to seeing you both

Figure 7.2   Letter from Helen Keller to Vivien Leigh, 31 March 1952.

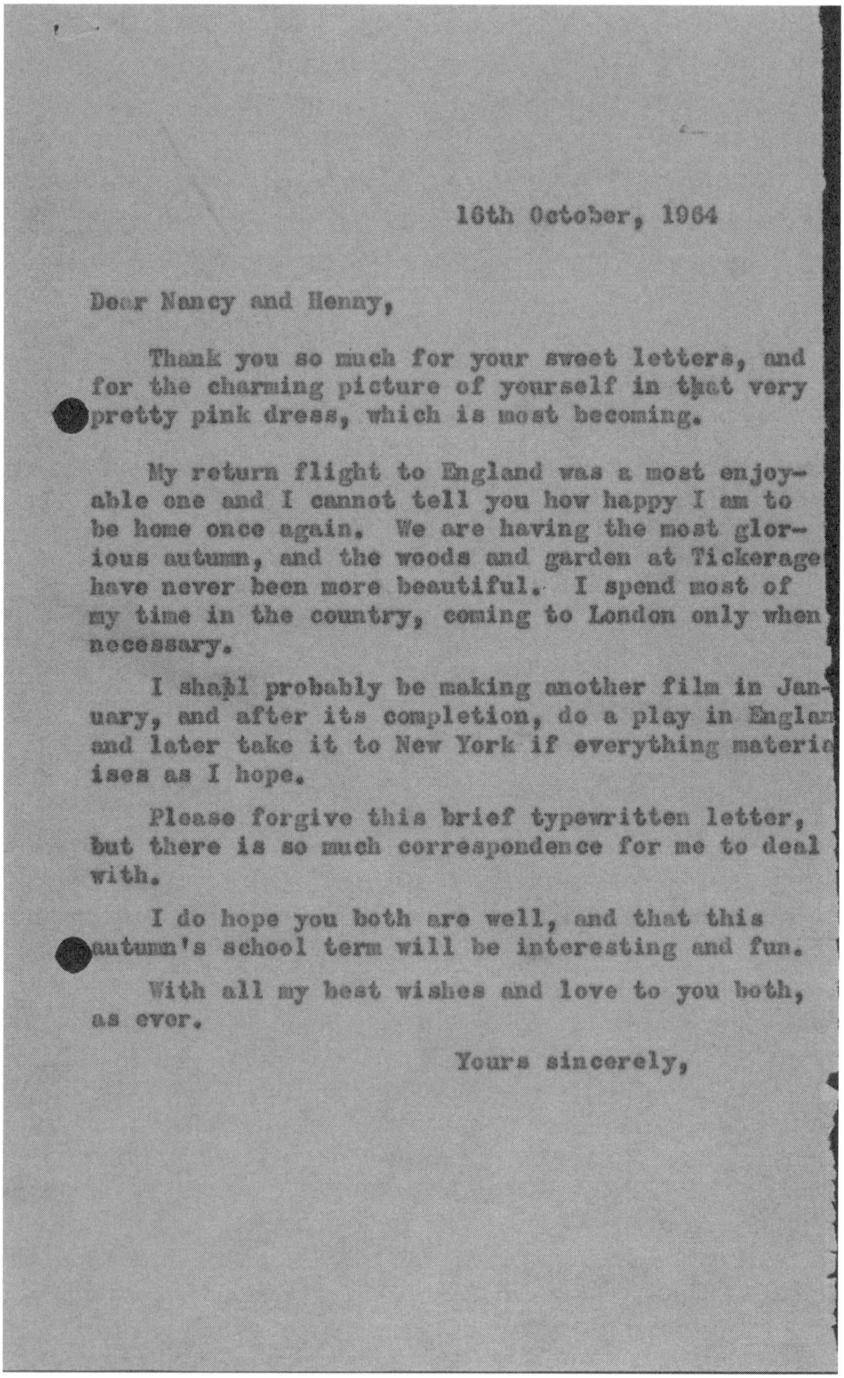

16th October, 1964

Dear Nancy and Henny,

Thank you so much for your sweet letters, and for the charming picture of yourself in that very pretty pink dress, which is most becoming.

My return flight to England was a most enjoyable one and I cannot tell you how happy I am to be home once again. We are having the most glorious autumn, and the woods and garden at Tickerage have never been more beautiful. I spend most of my time in the country, coming to London only when necessary.

I shall probably be making another film in January, and after its completion, do a play in England and later take it to New York if everything materialises as I hope.

Please forgive this brief typewritten letter, but there is so much correspondence for me to deal with.

I do hope you both are well, and that this autumn's school term will be interesting and fun.

With all my best wishes and love to you both, as ever.

                    Yours sincerely,

Figure 7.3 Facsimile of typed letter from Vivien Leigh to Nancy Abraham and Henny Sender, 16 October, 1964.

chauffeur-driven car. The attention Leigh paid to the girls made them feel like more than 'ordinary autograph seekers'.[39]

Their constant presence in the theatre allowed the two friends to observe and comment upon Leigh's acting technique. There was a sentiment among some of Leigh's theatrical colleagues that once Leigh decided how she would play a role, she stuck to that interpretation and never deviated. Abraham and Sender also noticed this trend, although the repetitiousness of Leigh's characterisation in *Tovarich* did not seem to bother them. Just being in Leigh's presence was enough. But when Leigh *did* add something different to her performance, it made their theatre-going experience all the more special. 'You were just adorable on Saturday,' they wrote on 16 October 1963. 'When you first came through the window we turned to each other simultaneously and commented on how differently you were saying your lines. It was such a treat for us as it felt just like seeing a completely different show, and after 44 times, it's fun to be so pleasantly surprised.'[40] The girls became so involved with their adoration for Leigh that they did not shy away from giving honest opinions about Leigh's career choices. It was difficult for popular stars, particularly females, to deviate from their established images. Leigh represented elegance and beauty, and when she attempted to obscure her looks or change her personality for a role, fans were not always accepting. While Leigh was doing *Tovarich*, the press announced that her next stage role would be that of an elderly woman in Paul Osborn's *La Contessa*. 'We beg you to *please* think carefully before you accept,' Abraham wrote on behalf of herself and Sender. 'Of course, you know you'd have *two* steady customers, but we'd rather see you as a duchess than as an old lady.'[41] Apparently others felt the same. *Tovarich* was a runaway hit, garnering Leigh a Tony Award for her performance. *La Contessa*, staged two years later, folded before the production made it to London.

That Leigh had a difficult time pleasing theatrical critics is well known. As Olivier told Melvyn Bragg long after Leigh's death, many people, 'particularly members of the critical faculty' were unable to take her seriously because of her great beauty. 'They didn't think *that* could nurse any talent.'[42] But while people like the *Observer's* Kenneth Tynan attempted to influence readers with disparaging remarks about Leigh's abilities and status (particularly in relation to her performances alongside Olivier), they did not succeed in influencing her loyal friends and fans. The Shakespeare Memorial Theatre production of *Macbeth* (1955) in Stratford-upon-Avon drew particularly harsh criticism from Tynan, at least when it came to assessing Leigh's performance (see John Stokes' Chapter 4). Actor Michael Denison, who was also targeted by Tynan's poisoned pen, described the failed actor-turned-critic as 'a revolutionary who in the early Fifties was still awaiting his revolution (signaled by *Look Back in Anger* in 1956) … he saw us and our life-style, and, by extension, our work-style as no more than objects of ridicule, unworthy of a place in his brave new world' (Denison, 1985: 40). Tynan's vitriolic insinuation that Leigh had no business acting opposite the great Olivier did not go unnoticed by her peers. Maxine Audley appeared as Lady Macduff in the Stratford production and wanted to let Leigh know how much she appreciated Leigh's Lady Macbeth: 'I think you show the rise and disintegration of her character completely, and with such immense and infinite variety, both in voice and in movement.' Audley also reassured Leigh that 'reporters' like Tynan were not worth worrying about. 'I think that they like to write unpleasant things about the great ones, because they like to think they have power to make or break people … it has nothing whatever to do with serious appraisal or criticism of a performance.' She added, 'So, to hell with all of them – you are a great actress and that's all that matters.'[43]

Leigh did not respond directly to critics' remarks in a public manner, but they did have an ill-effect on her confidence and mental wellbeing. For someone whose livelihood depended on putting her creativity on show for public consumption, it is understandable that Leigh, and likely other artists, felt vulnerable to criticism. However, as the letters in the archive reveal, for every biting review, there were numerous people who found enjoyment in her work and were happy to tell her so.

Fan clubs and communities

Though her fans may have been small marks on Leigh's radar, to receive a letter written in Leigh's own hand or, better yet, be invited backstage or to her home to meet her in person, meant something much more to the people she acknowledged. 'There was the feeling that while we were backstage, we had a connection,' says Michael Kerr, who was a teen when he and a friend were invited to meet Leigh after a performance of *Antony and Cleopatra* in London in 1951. Her way of clearing out the dressing room so she could focus on them; the way they chatted and her interest in the fledgling art student's work, these are memories that Michael holds dear to this day. 'We would talk and I felt special one-to-one.'[44] Rita Malyon echoes those sentiments: 'She put herself out to be friendly and made you feel important. There wasn't a difference in the way she treated people.'[45] I first met Malyon at the V&A on 5 November 2013, the centenary of Leigh's birth. While doing an interview with curator Keith Lodwick for a web piece about the recent acquisition of Leigh's papers, we noticed a small, elderly woman and her friend observing the newly installed Vivien Leigh display case in the Theatre and Performance Galleries. When we approached, Malyon reached into her handbag and pulled out a bundle of letters written by Leigh. Several were addressed to Malyon's friends, Iris Stanley and Joyce Huddart, two names I had come across previously in my years of researching Leigh's life. I knew they were fans who had communicated with Leigh, but did not realise the wider significance of their association.

Fans often find joy in being part of wider communities where they can meet and talk with other people who share the same interests. Malyon was in her early 20s when she took an interest in Leigh's career. She had admired some of her films but it was only in 1954, when she saw Leigh and Olivier on stage at the Phoenix Theatre in the Terence Rattigan comedy *The Sleeping Prince,* that she became a full-fledged fan. 'The atmosphere of the play' captured her imagination. 'Their personalities shone on stage. They were very charismatic, and very good looking.'[46] Malyon met Rosemary Antrobus outside the Shakespeare Memorial Theatre in Stratford-upon-Avon in 1955 and became the fourth member of a group of friends who would wait by stage doors for Leigh and Olivier to appear. Letters were exchanged and they were invited backstage several times (Figure 7.4). After the Oliviers divorced in 1960, Malyon, Huddart, Stanley and Antrobus remained loyal to Leigh. Her kindness left a lasting impression; it was an aspect of Leigh's persona that rarely made it into the press. 'She had a soft spot for ill people,' Malyon says. Iris Stanley had been diagnosed with multiple sclerosis and by the mid 1960s was too ill to take part in group activities. When Leigh learned of Stanley's situation, she sent flowers. It was a gesture that meant a great deal to a young woman who had found so much pleasure in Leigh's work.[47]

Following Leigh's death in 1967, Antrobus got married and Stanley's health deteriorated. But Malyon and Huddart continued their posthumous dedication to their favourite actress. Fed up with press stories focusing on Leigh's personal issues rather than her achievements as an actress, they endeavoured to do something about it. Out of this frustration emerged the Vivien Leigh Circle. It was a memorial club rather than a typical fan club – they wanted to leave a lasting contribution. With Huddart as the Chairman and Malyon as Secretary, they advertised for members and contributions in newspapers like the *Daily Telegraph*. The original goal of the Circle was to have a theatre in the UK named after Leigh. When it became evident that this was not feasible, they turned their attention to dedicating an antique clock in Leigh's name to the actors' nursing home Denville Hall in West London.[48] A host of Leigh's famous friends – including Lady Diana

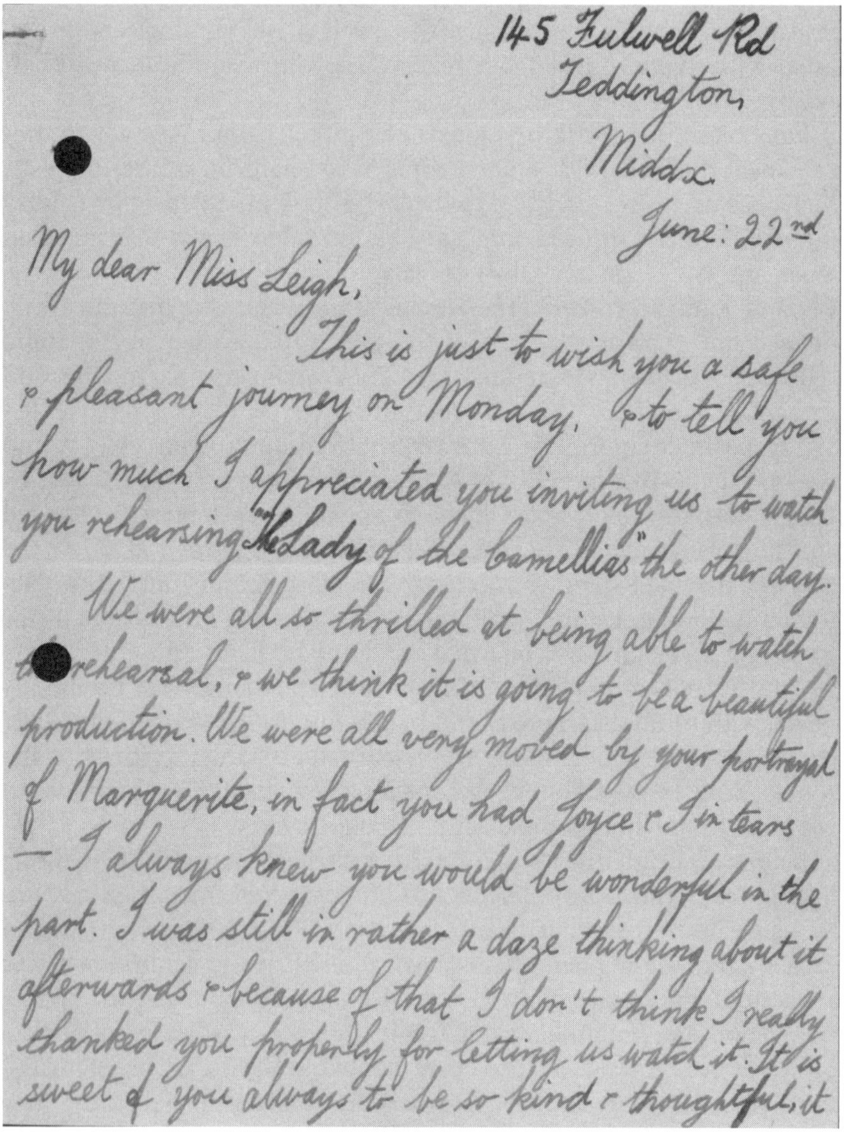

145 Fulwell Rd
Teddington,
Middx.
June: 22nd

My dear Miss Leigh,

This is just to wish you a safe
& pleasant journey on Monday, & to tell you
how much I appreciated you inviting us to watch
you rehearsing "Lady of the Camellias" the other day.
We were all so thrilled at being able to watch
the rehearsal, & we think it is going to be a beautiful
production. We were all very moved by your portrayal
of Marguerite, in fact you had Joyce & I in tears
— I always knew you would be wonderful in the
part. I was still in rather a daze thinking about it
afterwards & because of that I don't think I really
thanked you properly for letting us watch it. It is
sweet of you always to be so kind & thoughtful, it

Figure 7.4   Letter from Rita Malyon to Vivien Leigh.

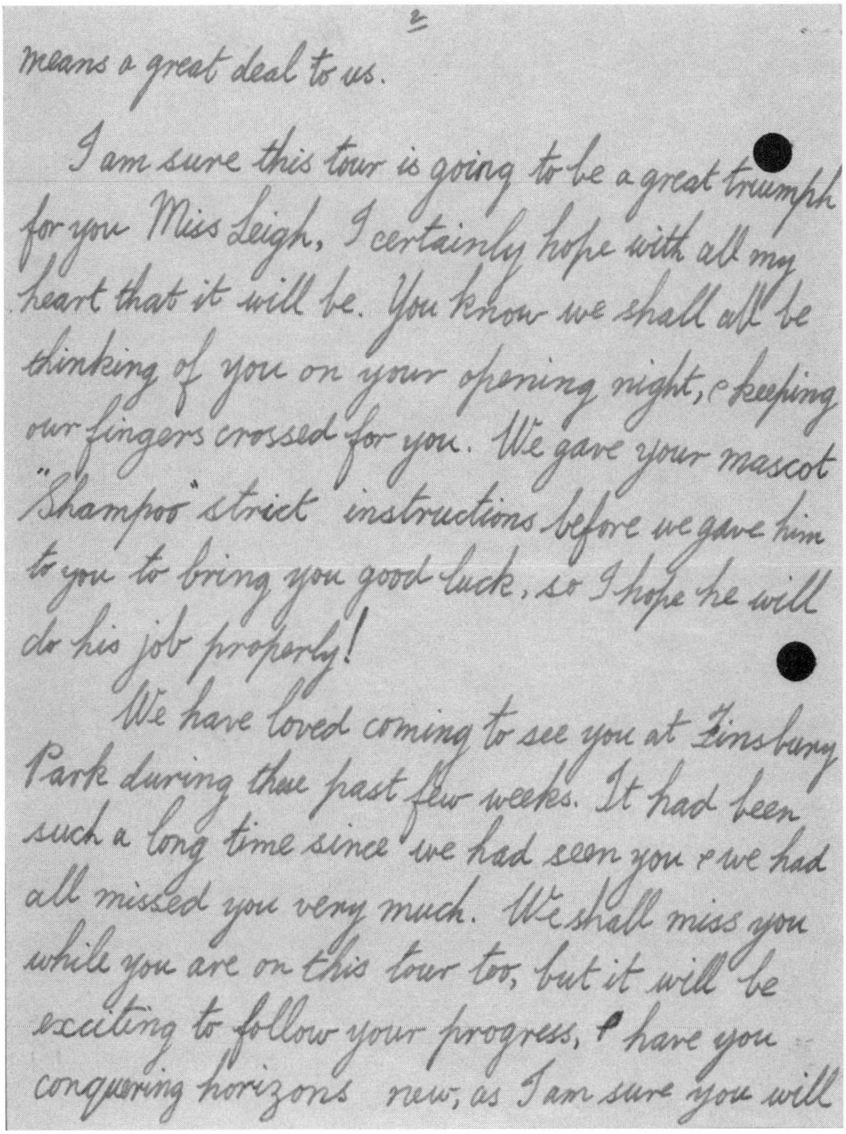

means a great deal to us.

I am sure this tour is going to be a great triumph for you Miss Leigh, I certainly hope with all my heart that it will be. You know we shall all be thinking of you on your opening night, & keeping our fingers crossed for you. We gave your mascot "Shampoo" strict instructions before we gave him to you to bring you good luck, so I hope he will do his job properly!

We have loved coming to see you at Finsbury Park during these past few weeks. It had been such a long time since we had seen you & we had all missed you very much. We shall miss you while you are on this tour too, but it will be exciting to follow your progress, & have you conquering horizons new, as I am sure you will

Figure 7.4   (Continued)

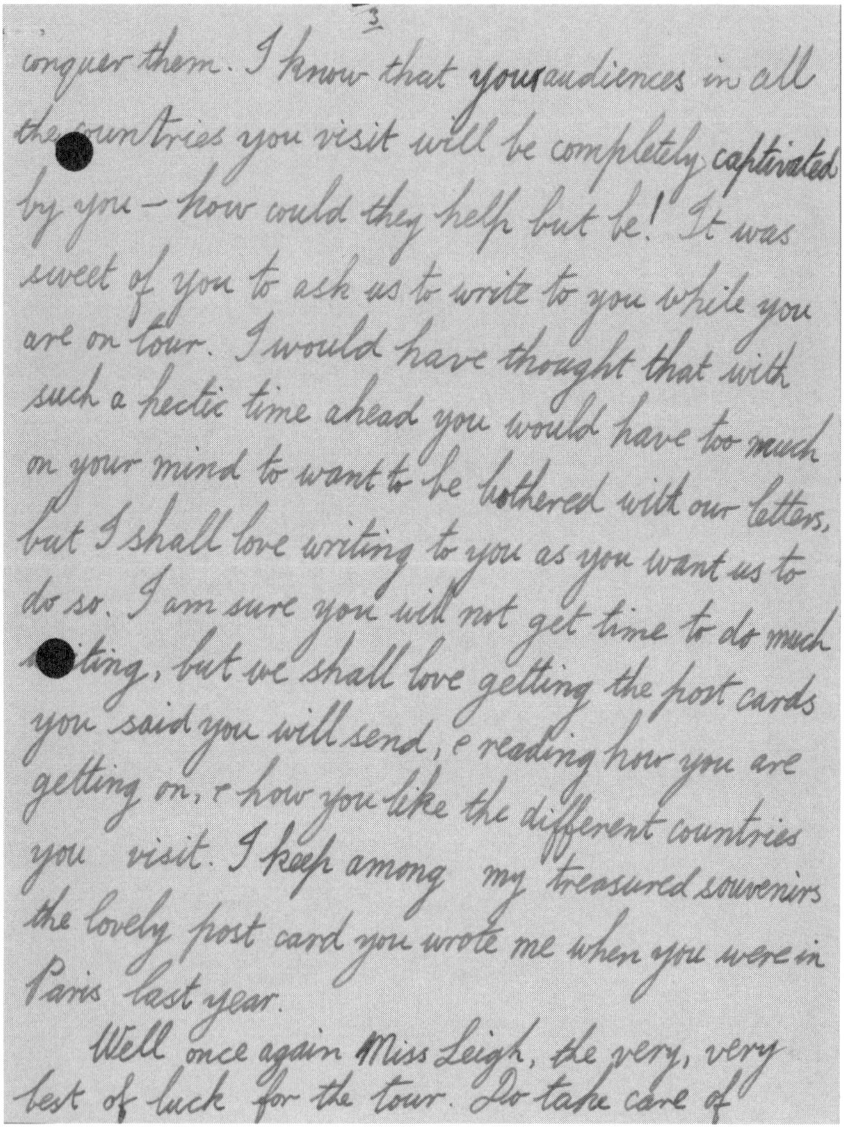

conquer them. I know that your audiences in all the countries you visit will be completely captivated by you – how could they help but be! It was sweet of you to ask us to write to you while you are on tour. I would have thought that with such a hectic time ahead you would have too much on your mind to want to be bothered with our letters, but I shall love writing to you as you want us to do so. I am sure you will not get time to do much writing, but we shall love getting the post cards you said you will send, e reading how you are getting on, e how you like the different countries you visit. I keep among my treasured souvenirs the lovely post card you wrote me when you were in Paris last year.

Well once again Miss Leigh, the very, very best of luck for the tour. Do take care of

Figure 7.4 (Continued)

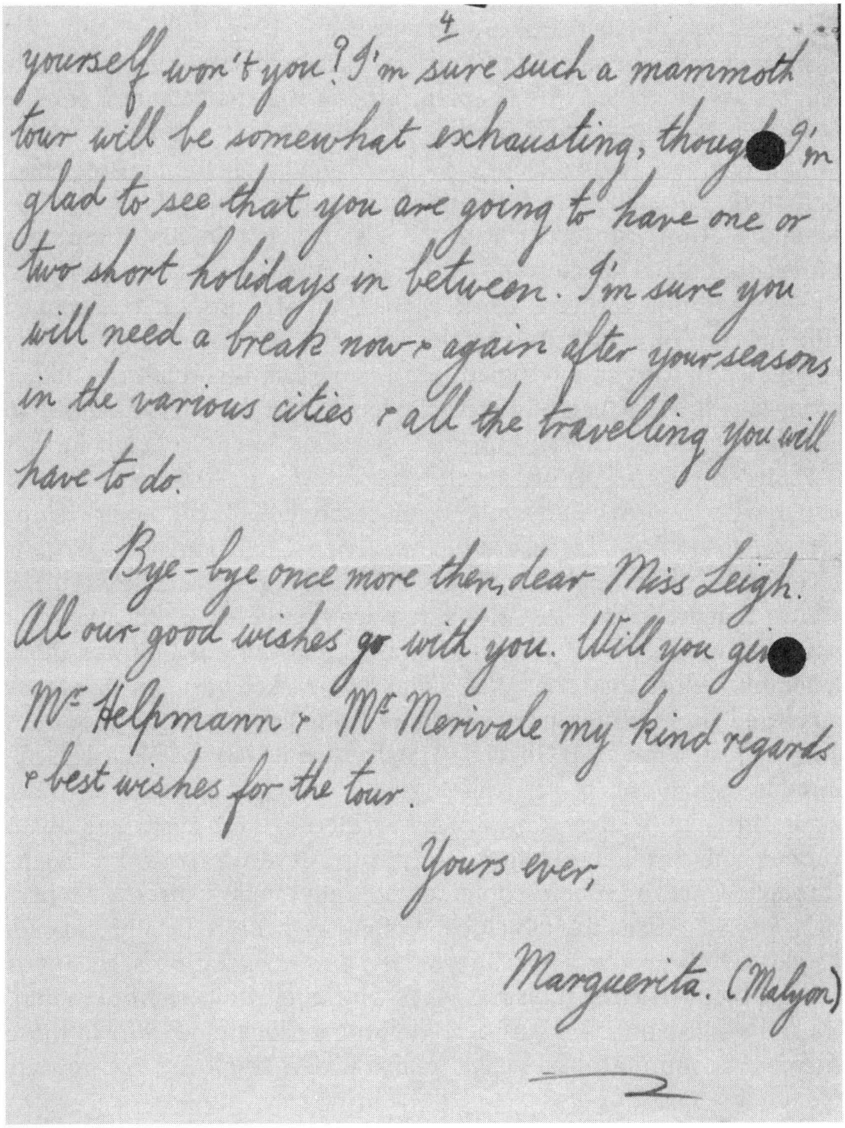

yourself won't you? I'm sure such a mammoth tour will be somewhat exhausting, though I'm glad to see that you are going to have one or two short holidays in between. I'm sure you will need a break now & again after your seasons in the various cities & all the travelling you will have to do.

Bye-bye once more then, dear Miss Leigh. All our good wishes go with you. Will you give Mr Helpmann & Mr Merivale my kind regards & best wishes for the tour.

Yours ever,

Marguerita. (Malyon)

Figure 7.4   (Continued)

Cooper, Alan Dent, Emlyn Williams, Dame Peggy Ashcroft, Rex Harrison and Fleur Cowles – agreed to come on board as Founders and Patrons.[49] The dedication ceremony took place in March 1972, presided over by the critic Alan Dent and actor Michael Denison. Leigh's mother Gertrude Hartley and daughter Suzanne Farrington were also in attendance, as was the local Harrow newspaper.

Malyon has kept all of the Circle's associated documents and kindly let me use them for this chapter. Among the many letters sent to Malyon from fellow Circle members during the 1970s are two from a fan in New York named Don McCulty. McCulty was then acting President of the American fan club, the Vivien Leigh Society. He suggested he and Malyon join forces, with the Vivien Leigh Society continuing on as a traditional fan club and the Circle acting as its 'charity bureau'.[50] The fan club merger never came to pass, but McCulty's letters opened up a new line of inquiry into Leigh's fan base. The Vivien Leigh Society originated in 1963 as the Vivien Leigh Fan Club. It is unclear whether other fan clubs for Leigh existed previously, but the Vivien Leigh Fan Club's original president, Eugene Schuessler, wrote to Leigh for her blessing in creating an official club in her honour. 'It is most kind of you to wish to form a Fan Club,' Leigh responded. 'I will be very happy for you to do so.'[51] Members of the Vivien Leigh Fan Club/Society received news of Leigh's activities on stage and screen through the Club's fanzine – *Curtain Call* – a handcrafted yearly publication that was truly a work of art (Figures 7.5 and 7.6). *Curtain Call* was a collaborative effort that contained hand-drawn sketches; fan questions answered by Leigh; excerpts of letters from honorary club members such as Joan Crawford, Olivia de Havilland and Gertrude Hartley; collectable candid and portrait photographs of Leigh; features on other actors in Leigh's circle, and articles written by club members about various topics relating to film and theatre. It also provided a means through which members could contact one another directly as pen-pals, and advertised the fan clubs of other stars. Both the Vivien Leigh Circle and Vivien Leigh fan Club/Society ceased operation in the 1970s but not before leaving their members with interesting archival materials and a sense of being part of something worthwhile. Some of those members continue to be active in the Vivien Leigh fan community today.

Contemporary fans

In many respects, the nature of fandom has not changed since Leigh's time. The methods by which we connect with other fans has evolved – social media and blogging have replaced the traditional fan club

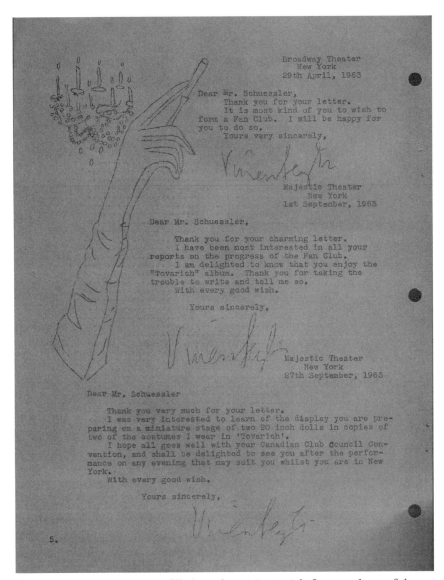

Figure 7.5 Questionnaire filled out by Vivien Leigh for members of the Vivien Leigh Fan Club. Published in *Curtain Call*, November 1963.

and handcrafted newsletters – but fan communities still exist. For example, the Vivien Leigh Circle was recently reinstated by a group of younger fans with Rita Malyon acting as honorary President. They base their operation on Facebook and Instagram. My own Facebook page dedicated to Leigh and Olivier is nearing 40,000 followers at the time of writing. The Internet has made connecting with like minds much easier and allows people from all over the world to come together with

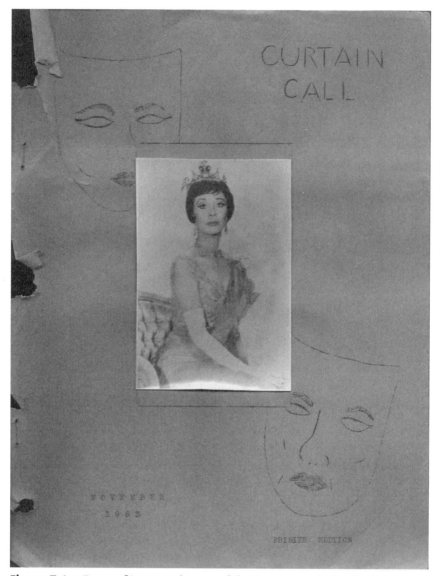

Figure 7.6 Cover of inaugural issue of the Vivien Leigh Fan Club publication, *Curtain Call*, November, 1963.

the common goal of celebrating Leigh's work and her life. In the past decade or so, there have been a handful of fan-made websites dedicated to Leigh's memory, most of which have long since ceased to exist, although they can still be accessed in archaeological form through the Internet Archive. All of these sites, no matter how short-lived, were their creators' way of sharing a passion and educating others. My own efforts in this area have fallen along the same lines. The launch of VivAndLarry.com in 2007 led to the formation of a wider network of fans, and eventually to the publication of articles and an illustrated biography about Leigh's life. Through these means, I hope to make a lasting contribution to Leigh's legacy. Wanting to learn more about how other fans relate to Leigh today, I created an online questionnaire at VivAndLarry.com. The questions were straightforward: How did they discover Leigh? What is it about her or her work that continues to inspire? Do they have any special memories revolving around Leigh or her films? Responses came in from nearly one hundred and fifty fans ranging from under 20 to over 65 years old, in twenty-two different countries – proving that Leigh continues to have international appeal and to interest new fans with each passing generation.

While a few people wrote in saying they first encountered Leigh through films such as *A Streetcar Named Desire* or *Waterloo Bridge*, *Gone With The Wind* appears to remain the prominent point of discovery for new fans, likely due to its wide accessibility. It is one of a select group of iconic films from Hollywood's 'golden age' that has been given multiple cinematic re-releases and DVD restorations by its current parent company, Warner Bros. (others include *The Wizard of Oz*, 1939 and *Casablanca*, 1942). And it is Leigh's performance as Scarlett that continues to draw fans in.

As we move further into the digital age, Leigh's work and details of her life are ever more accessible at the touch of a button. Information and photographs that were once inaccessible without special permission are increasingly being digitised by archives and museums. What I found most intriguing about the questionnaire responses is that much more is known about Leigh's life today than when she was alive; the carefully constructed and maintained star façade has been pulled down, revealing a woman who had her own demons and insecurities and did things that people found uncomfortable and even unmentionable during her lifetime. And yet some of the more difficult aspects of Leigh's life – particularly her struggle with mental illness – have, for a growing number of fans, gone from being taboo to being a source of inspiration and admiration.

Kenneth R. from California discovered Leigh in his teens and admires many facets of her acting and personality, including her perseverance against mental health issues. He eloquently explained how he connects with Leigh through his own struggle with depression: 'Her tenacity and perseverance are admirable, especially following the split from Olivier, to whom she was inextricably bound. I'm drawn to something elusive and ineffable, something beyond the screen. Courage, compassion, love for the written word, the art of friendship. An intimate knowledge of personal and public horror, and the resultant desire to seize every scintilla of beauty within grasp – and the struggle to reach for more ...'.[52] Giulia G., a student in New York, wrote in with a similar, touching story:

> I have had depression for a few years now, but since discovering Vivien, my depression has been much more manageable. I am so inspired by Vivien's strength, determination, and kind heart. She suffered with a mental health disorder, as well as tuberculosis, yet she accomplished so much in her life. She always thought of others before herself, and was always considerate of her friends. I find it endearing, yet also very sad, that such a beautiful person (inside and out) couldn't see her own beauty. I feel a closeness to every character Vivien has played because I feel that every character was a tiny piece of who Vivien was. Vivien said she thought Scarlett had more courage than she would ever have, but I completely disagree. I think Vivien is one of the strongest people I have ever read about.[53]

Other fans mentioned living with obsessive-compulsive disorder, bipolar disorder and other manifestations of mental illness. Leigh never talked about her uphill battle with manic depression in public; it was seen as shameful, a career-breaker (see Maggie B. Gale's Chapter 3). Stigma remains an unfortunate issue today, yet learning about Leigh's experience appears to help some fans come to terms with their own.

Determined, inspiring, strong, intelligent, style, presence, timeless, beauty, ambition – these are some of the words that fans around the world associate with Vivien Leigh. She has been, and continues to be, admired for both her talents and personality. As long as her films survive, and information about her life and work is made available, she will doubtless continue to draw interest from future generations.

Notes

1 John Hufcoop, to Vivien Leigh, 14 June 1951. Laurence Olivier Archive, Add MS 80632.

2 Though they divorced in 1960 and went on to have other partners, the amount of Vivien Leigh material in Olivier's archive and *vice versa* suggests that the documents accumulated during their twenty-five-year relationship were never separated properly by their respective estates.

3 David Lewin, 'Vivien Tells', *Daily Express*, 17 August 1960.

4 Camilla Koch, to Vivien Leigh, 13 March 1951. Vivien Leigh Archive, THM/433/2/11.

5 Hedda Hopper, 'Hedda Hopper's Hollywood', *Los Angeles Times*, 16 January 1939, p. 10.

6 Clinton Chamberlin, to Vivien Leigh, 2 June 1961. Named Correspondence, C2: Vivien Leigh Archive, THM/433/2/3.

7 Ibid.

8 Glen Byam Shaw, to Vivien Leigh, 14 October 1952. Vivien Leigh Archive, THM/433/2/2.

9 Oxford University Dramatic Society. The play was co-directed by John Gielgud.

10 Glen Byam Shaw, to Vivien Leigh, 14 October 1952. Vivien Leigh Archive. Named Correspondence B 2, THM/433/2/2.

11 Yvette Curran, to Vivien Leigh, 19 August 1963. Vivien Leigh Archive. Named Correspondence C 2: THM/433/2/3.

12 Yvette Curran, to Vivien Leigh, 4 August 1963. Vivien Leigh Archive. Named Correspondence C 2: THM/433/2/3.

13 Yvette Curran, to Vivien Leigh, 30 October 1964. Vivien Leigh Archive. Named Correspondence C2: THM/433/2/3.

14 Ibid.

15 In order to avoid a 'C' or 'condemned' rating from the Legion, which would have hurt the film's box office chances, Kazan cut from the film several crucial minutes that were deemed morally indecent by 1950s standards. The cuts were later restored for a 1993 director's version video release.

16 Vivien Leigh, 'Who's Right About "A Streetcar"? Vivien Leigh's Point of View', *The Stage*, 27 October 1949, pp. 1–8.

17 Ibid. p. 8

18 Vivien Leigh, handwritten notes for Elia Kazan, undated. A Streetcar Named Desire. Vivien Leigh Archive THM/433/4/3 11.

19 Yvette Curran, to Vivien Leigh, 30 October 1964. Named Correspondence: C 2, Vivien Leigh Archive, 3.THM/433/2/3.

20 Joyce Atwood, to Vivien Leigh, 24 July 1961. Vivien Leigh Archive, 1. THM/433/2/1.

21 Kenji Honda, to Vivien Leigh, 27 May 1952. Fan letters to Vivien Leigh, Laurence Olivier Archive, Add MS 80635.

22 M. Soejima, to Vivien Leigh, 18 December 1963. Fan letters to Vivien Leigh, Laurence Olivier Archive, Add MS 80635.

23 Toshitake Fukumoto, to Vivien Leigh, 19 December 1950. Fan letters to Vivien Leigh, Laurence Olivier Archive, Add MS 80635.

24 Jeanne de Casalis, to Vivien Leigh, 1937. Vivien Leigh Archive, THM/433/2/4.

25 Lorn Loraine, to Vivien Leigh, 29 August 1955. Named Correspondence L2, Vivien Leigh Archive, THM/4332/12.

26 Alexander Knox, to Vivien Leigh, 1946. Named Correspondence: K 2, Vivien Leigh Archive THM/433/2/11.

27 Leigh was on mandatory bed rest while she recovered from tuberculosis.

28 Roy Boulting, to Vivien Leigh, 12 December 1945. Named Correspondence B2: Vivien Leigh Archive, THM/433/2/2.

29 Harold Acton, to Vivien Leigh, 16 November 1965. Named Correspondence, A2: Vivien Leigh Archive, THM/433/2/1.

30 Alfred Kingsley Lawrence, to Vivien Leigh, 25 August 1951. Named Correspondence, L2: Vivien Leigh Archive, THM/433/2/12.

31 Alfred Kingsley Lawrence, to Vivien Leigh, 4 September 1951. Named Correspondence, L2: Vivien Leigh Archive, THM/433/2/12.

32 Helen Keller, to Vivien Leigh, 31 March 1952. Named Correspondence, K2: Vivien Leigh Archive, THM/433/2/11.
33 Jennifer Arnott, Interview with Kendra Bean, 6 April 2016.
34 Ibid.
35 Leigh describes meeting Keller in a letter to Meriel (Mu) Richardson, Ralph Richardson Archive, Add MS 82044.
36 Nancy Abraham and Helene Sender, to Vivien Leigh, n.d. Named Correspondence, A2: Vivien Leigh Archive, THM/433/2/1.
37 Ibid.
38 Ibid.
39 Nancy Abraham and Helene Sender, to Vivien Leigh, 16 October 1963. Named Correspondence, A2: Vivien Leigh Archive, THM/433/2/1.
40 Ibid.
41 Ibid.
42 *'Great Performances' Laurence Olivier: A Life*. England: Nick Elliott, Nick Evans, Robert Bee, 1983. Video.
43 Maxine Audley, to Vivien Leigh, June 1955. Named Correspondence, A2: Vivien Leigh Archive, THM/433/2/1.
44 Michael Kerr, Interview with Kendra Bean, 4 January 2016.
45 Rita Malyon, Interview with Kendra Bean, 9 March 2016.
46 Ibid.
47 Ibid.
48 Ibid.
49 Rita Malyon, *Vivien Leigh Circle Newsletter*, Spring 1971. Private collection.
50 Don McCulty, *Letter to Rita Malyon*, 1 December 1972. Private collection.
51 Eugene Schuessler (ed.), *Curtain Call, November*. Vivien Leigh Fan Club Newsletter, 1963, p. 5.
52 K. Ringler, *The Vivien Leigh Fan Survey*, 2015 [Email].
53 G. Gionta, *The Vivien Leigh Fan Survey*, 2015 [Email].

References and bibliography

Bean, Kendra (2013) *Vivien Leigh: An Intimate Portrait*, Philadelphia: Running Press.
Denison, Michael (1985) *Double Act*, London: Michael Joseph.
Dent, Alan (1969) *Vivien Leigh: A Bouquet*, London: Hamish Hamilton.
Vickers, Hugo (1988) *Vivien Leigh: A Biography*, New York: Little Brown and Company.

8

Dressing the part: costume and character
Keith Lodwick

Vivien Leigh recognised that a costume designer is central to an actor's transformation. She understood early in her career how their contribution to theatre and filmmaking practice enabled her to create each new character, and it is fitting that her archive is now in the Victoria & Albert Museum with its emphasis on exploring and celebrating the place of design in practice. Using Leigh's own archive, the British Film Institute Special Collections and scrutinising her film performances, this chapter explores some of her creative collaborations: on stage, on film and in Leigh's role as a public figure and unofficial fashion ambassador. At the heart of Leigh's archive are annotated scripts, letters, telegrams and her written notes carefully describing the character-building process that would become central to her work as a stage and screen performer. The archive offers an account of this design process and Leigh's role as an active and creative participant in it. Among the papers in the *A Streetcar Named Desire* file is one unassuming handwritten note, scribbled while she was talking on the telephone to director Elia Kazan in 1950, about the costumes for Blanche DuBois. 'You do know that when I said I'm worried about the way I'll look, I didn't mean good I meant right.'[1]

Leigh had an enduring fascination with clothes and the role they played on and off stage. It is no coincidence that some of her closest friends were also her designers. Beatrice 'Bumble' Dawson was a life-long friend from her schooldays. Roger Furse designed many of the Oliviers' stage and film productions throughout the 1940s and 1950s. Oliver Messel created exquisite costumes for *A Midsummer Night's Dream* (1937) and *Caesar and Cleopatra* (Gabriel Pascal 1945). René Hubert was responsible for some her important early British film work. In Hollywood, Walter Plunkett's designs for *Gone With The*

Wind (Victor Fleming, 1939) remain some of the most inspired work in film history. Lucinda Ballard only designed one film for Leigh – *A Streetcar Named Desire* (Elia Kazan, 1951) – and she was credited by the actress in enabling her to win her second Oscar: 'I am so grateful to Cindy Ballard, who helped me, through the clothes, to bring Blanche to the screen.'[2]

Like her contemporaries, Marlene Dietrich and Katharine Hepburn, Leigh became a role model for mid-twentieth-century style, her wardrobe and performance costumes copied and reproduced in fashion and film magazines. With Laurence Olivier, she was one half of the most famous couple of the era and the public were steered by her taste and elegance; while Olivier endorsed cigarettes, Leigh endorsed the luxury shoe manufacturers Rayne. In film press packs and promotional material, her characters' costumes were marketed to an eager audience: 'clothes you can wear, copied from Vivien Leigh's, in her role of Lady Hamilton',[3] and the work of the costume designer became an inspiration for that season (see Figure 8.1). Her public image and her character's costumes became intertwined, Leigh viewed her public appearances as an extension of her stage roles; as couturier Hardy Amies commented for *Woman and Beauty* magazine in 1951, 'when she needs a fresh outfit, she explains the occasion for which it is intended. The best costume in the world fails in the wrong setting'.[4]

The rituals and order inculcated into Leigh during her early days at convent school had a lasting effect on her. After an idyllic early childhood in Darjeeling, India, she began her Roman Catholic education in 1920 and spent the next eight years at the Convent of the Sacred Heart in Roehampton just outside London. The school had a strict environment, children rose at 6.30am, and washed in tepid water before beginning their studies. Baths were taken wearing long, white shirts so that their nudity was never on display. Schoolfriend Maureen O'Sullivan (the future film star) took her clothes off, but Leigh never disobeyed 'although she detested the cold wet clothing on her body' (Edwards, 1977: 22). There was a nightly ritual of neatly folding underclothes and covering them with a white nightgown so that underwear was not exposed, with stockings then placed on top, folded into the shape of a cross. In her professional career, Leigh was fastidious about her costumes, and continued the ritual of placing a silk handkerchief over her folded clothes every night before she went to bed. At school, it was noted by her friends that Leigh was 'always the better dressed, wearing silk stockings and gold bracelets' (Vickers, 1988: 15).

Leigh left school in 1928 and completed her education in a series of finishing schools across Europe; the experience gave her a cosmopolitan outlook and she became fluent in French, German and Italian. She

Figure 8.1   Vivien Leigh on the film set of *Lady Hamilton* (1941).

later dubbed her own films for the European market, being one of the few actors of her generation to have this ability:

> Apart from the fact I learnt to speak several languages more or less fluently and had an opportunity of studying diction and the theatre in many countries, I met people of all types and nationalities. They gave me that flexibility of mind which is so necessary to an artist and taught me, I hope, understanding. Through knowing them I have always been able to recognize the characters I play and love them.[5]

It was in a French finishing school in Auteuil, outside Paris, that Leigh received coaching from Mademoiselle Antoine, an actress from the Comédie Française. She taught Leigh acting technique, elocution and 'how to wear period clothing on stage'.[6]

Leigh attended London's Royal Academy of Dramatic Art in 1932 and the training, along with her own interest in literature and culture, gave her a respect for text, language and character development. 'I learn lines easily and I've always had an ear for languages and accents.'[7] After graduation from RADA, she was keen to have as much exposure to casting agents as possible and sought good photographs of herself for inclusion in the industry casting 'bible', *Spotlight*. To earn extra money, she began modelling clothes. In an early photograph by Cecil Beaton (who would later design costumes for her) for *Vogue* magazine in 1935, Leigh wore a simple, floor-length gown of satin designed by Victor Stiebel, who would become a lifelong friend and who would create stage costumes for her in *Because We Must* (1937).

Even before her stage debut, Leigh managed to engineer for herself a high-profile public appearance. Her husband's cousin was married to Alwyn Boot, the daughter of Sir Jesse Boot, founder of Boots the Chemist, and it was this connection that enabled her to be presented at Court in 1934. The Lord Chamberlain issued the royal summons that stipulated strict full court dress had to be worn. This comprised a white evening dress and train with short sleeves (pink or ivory was permitted), worn with long white gloves; a veil with three ostrich feathers was attached to the hair. The ensemble was finished off with pearls. On 13 June, she was presented to King George V and Queen Mary. She was aware of the impact that her dress had to make: the full length taffeta gown crackled as she walked towards the monarch. In the grand salon of the Palace, it was her first high-profile appearance, watched by courtiers and the press. This was a moment that would have a profound effect on her development as a performer and in her role as public figure: 'I imagined myself as part of the Royal family, I walked as if on stage and knew all eyes were upon me.'[8]

Costumes for stage

An actress must be able to assume different dialects, accents, mannerisms and actions. When she walks out on the stage she must be equipped to transform herself. The clothes are essential to this. No matter how much she must change her personality she must always seem natural. When I stepped on stage, I felt every inch the character and the costume made by Nathan's helped me shape my performance.[9]

Figure 8.2   Vivien Leigh in *The Mask of Virtue* (1935).

Within a year, Vivien Leigh made her West-End debut in *The Mask of Virtue*: she noted, 'I was helped by the entire cast, with that wonderful generosity of the theatre world towards a newcomer' (see Figure 8.2).[10] Crediting her fellow actors, she was also acutely aware of the role that the designer played in completing her interpretation.

The play was a period piece set in the 1760s and Leigh's Act II wedding dress was designed and made at Nathan's, the oldest theatrical costumiers in London. Established in 1790, Nathan's had provided costumes to Charles Dickens for his amateur theatricals and had designed for the great Victorian and Edwardian performers, including Henry Irving, Ellen Terry and Lillie Langtry. Nathan's would often repurpose vintage clothing and adapt it into theatre costumes, especially for high-profile West End productions, giving delighted actors an opportunity to wear authentic period dress on stage. Wearing 'real' clothes altered their movement, stance and performance. Leigh would have a long association with Nathan's, which would continue to make costumes for her until her death in 1967.

Leigh's early stage characters (Queen Anne in *Richard II*, Jenny Mere in *The Happy Hypocrite*, Anne Boleyn in *Henry VIII*) strongly associated her with period plays, to the extent that when cast in Ingaret Giffard's contemporary play *Because We Must*, Harold Conway in *Theatre News* was provoked to announce that 'Vivien Leigh Forsakes Costume Drama'.[11] Offstage, her increasing public profile was built around her clothes. The *Daily Sketch* reported in 'What Women Wore at the Grand National': 'If I had to nominate the prettiest girl in the crowd it would be Vivien Leigh, who looked lovely in beige and brown with touches of yellow, she and Ivor Novello had come over from Southport, where they are playing in *The Happy Hypocrite*.'[12]

Leigh's exposure to designers and photographers made her aware of her own body image. As her film career progressed, she quickly became conscious of a number of perceived disadvantages: her neck was long and she was self-conscious about her hands, which she thought unfeminine. She often hid them in photographs and wore gloves in public. When she read Ellen Terry's autobiography *Memoirs* she felt an affinity with the great Victorian actress: Terry also thought she had large hands. For her own clothes, Leigh created a visual compromise: she simply lengthened the cuffs of her dresses and asked costume designers to do the same.

From the 1930s to the 1960s, Leigh worked with some of the leading theatre designers of the era. In 1937, she made her debut with the Old Vic company as Ophelia to Olivier's Hamlet at Elsinore. She became friends with designers Roger Furse, Oliver Messel and Doris Zinkeisen, who were all establishing their careers at that time. Messel was a designer, maker and painter, who worked across theatre, opera, ballet, film and interior design. His first collaboration with Leigh was Titania, at the Old Vic in 1937. *A Midsummer Night's Dream* was staged as a nineteenth-century extravaganza, balletic fairies flew in front of over-sized painted flowers, and Leigh's fairy queen was 'like an exquisite picture from some Victorian lady's keepsake'.[13] Oberon, played by ballet dancer Robert Helpmann, resembled a shimmering stag beetle. Messel's exquisite taste and expert knowledge of fabric was hugely appealing to Leigh. Her dress was made from organza, a material Messel enjoyed using, adorned with fairy wings and flowers. Margaret Furse (wife of Roger) created the costumes from Messel's designs. Titania's crown was made from cellophane, imitation pearls, coloured foil flower and sequins, all designed to catch the light, utterly magical in effect and entirely practical as it was very lightweight to wear. When the play ended its run, Messel kept the headdress and created a box to keep it secure, naming it Vivien.[14]

By the mid 1940s, Roger Furse was the unofficial designer in residence for the Oliviers and was appointed one of the directors of Laurence Olivier Productions in 1948. Furse, who was descended from the Kemble acting dynasty, trained as a painter in Paris and the Slade School in London and became known for his expert period recreations. Furse and Leigh had a long correspondence, and he would often sketch costume ideas onto letters for her input and approval. For Sabina in *The Skin of Our Teeth* (1945), Furse was given an opportunity to display Leigh's comic timing and versatility through a series of costumes that reflected the ambitious narrative of Thornton Wilder's epic play. Furse sourced Sabina's Air-Raid Warden jacket from Nathan's: 'I have found the perfect jacket for you, it will be far too big, but that's the point.'[15] The jacket was accessorised with a large leather belt at Leigh's suggestion. He commissioned Matilda Etches (who would later make clothes for Leigh) to make the Atlantic City Beauty Contest costume, and for the maid he designed a cheeky short black dress with a frilly white apron, accessorising with a feather duster. Leigh used the prop to comic effect, often improvising with it on stage. Furse's sketch for Sabina was a favourite of Leigh's and the design was framed and displayed on the wall in the Oliviers' home in Chelsea. It was Furse that suggested to the Oliviers that they should produce Shaw's *Caesar and Cleopatra* in repertory with Shakespeare's *Antony and Cleopatra* at St James' Theatre as part of the Festival of Britain. This would give a unique chance for the public to see Leigh in a role she'd already played on screen – in the 1945 production of Shaw's play. The costumes were designed by Audrey Cruddas, who had also originally trained as a painter and had worked as a land-girl during the Second World War.

Furse's design used the same set of pillars and a sphinx on a revolve for both productions, and Cruddas' costumes had to develop with the character as she aged from a teenager to a woman in her 30s. She used lightweight fabrics for the young Cleopatra, emphasising her youth and inexperience; as Cleopatra ages, Cruddas used thicker, heavily-weighted cotton, and accessorised with more beads and jewels. This helped disguise the re-use of costumes in the two plays, as Britain was still gripped by rationing and fabric was in short supply. However, this also gave the design coherence as Leigh wore the same coronation robes in both plays. When it transferred to Broadway, Cruddas won the Donaldson Award for Outstanding Achievement for Best Costume Design[16] (see Plate 2).

Costume for film

Swiss designer René Hubert was responsible for costuming Leigh's early screen roles. Silent film star Gloria Swanson had lured Hubert to Hollywood from Paris in 1925, where he had been designing for the stage. He worked with Swanson for ten years before working for

Alexander Korda in Britain in 1935, creating, among others, the futuristic designs for *Things to Come* (William Cameron Menzies, 1936), as well as four of Leigh's pre-*Gone With The Wind* films. When Hubert began his preparation for a film, he liked to sketch an actor in movement, so that period clothes would feel comfortable and look natural when the actors wore them.

In *Fire Over England* (William K. Howard, 1936), Leigh played lady-in-waiting Cynthia to Flora Robson's Queen Elizabeth. The film was in a series of prestigious, big-budget historical biopics produced by Korda, which followed on from the success of *The Private Life of Henry VIII* (1933). It was Leigh's first film appearance with Laurence Olivier (with whom she was now romantically involved). She challenged Hubert to address what she considered her 'flaws' – her long neck and large hands. Hubert used ruffs to disguise her neck and cleverly designed the costumes with elegant, sweeping collars which would set off her delicate features. Like his work with Swanson in Hollywood, his designs for the film ignited immediate interest from the fashion press who exclaimed 'Elizabethan fashions will be popular this season'.[17] The UK's most popular film magazine, *Picturegoer*, featured Leigh in her period costumes alongside 1930s evening gowns inspired by Hubert's design,

> I had a talk with Vivien in her dressing-room and René Hubert, the famous designer, came in and explained all the ins-and-outs of Elizabethan costumes. He told me that the tiny bows of gold tissue which Vivien wore instead of ear-rings were authentic and he also added that a certain lady of title, who had just seen Vivien on the set, had ordered a similar pair to be made for herself. Vivien confided with justifiable pride, that she was wearing her own hair, but those of you who still have long tresses can take heart and copy the Elizabethan style, with your hair curled high on top of your head.[18]

Hubert adapted one of his Elizabethan ruffs for Leigh in their next film together *Dark Journey* (Victor Saville, 1937). The ruff was repurposed into a collar for a black crepe dress with a low V-neck and accessorised with a jewelled brooch. In this convoluted spy-drama, Leigh had her first leading screen role, playing a double-agent masquerading as the owner of a boutique dress shop (codes are secretly sewn into clothing). This gave Hubert an opportunity to dress Leigh in sophisticated daywear and elegant evening gowns, all accessorised with a fur coat. Leigh commented that a period film cannot escape the era in which it's created, as she told a reporter from *Picturergoer*: 'It's about Stockholm in war-time, although my dress is, as you can see, very 1936. The men wear 1917 clothes, but the war-time fashions for women would make the film look like a museum piece.'[19]

Figure 8.3   Robert Taylor and Vivien Leigh in *A Yank at Oxford* (1938),
costume designer René Hubert.

Although Leigh's next screen role was smaller, the role of Elsa was
engineered to get her in the race for Scarlett O'Hara. *A Yank at Oxford*
(Jack Conway, 1938) was Metro-Goldwyn-Mayer's inaugural production in the UK, and Korda strategically loaned Leigh to MGM to give
her exposure in the American film market and, more importantly, to
stage an acting opportunity for an unofficial screen test for Scarlett.
The search for Scarlett had been masterminded by producer David O.
Selznick and had gripped the American public since the book's publication in 1936. Every major Hollywood actress was being considered
for the role – Norma Shearer, Bette Davis, Joan Crawford, etc. – and
the ensuing publicity kept the film alive in the audience's minds. *A
Yank at Oxford* is peppered with discreet references to the forthcoming
epic: when the 'Yank' of the title, Robert Taylor, is asked by his Oxford
tutor what he is reading, Taylor misunderstands and replies, 'I'm
about halfway through *Gone with the Wind*' (see Figure 8.3).

In Leigh's annotated script, she highlights the character description:
'Elsa, despite her air of deliberate innocence, is extremely well equipped
in the art of provoking attention from the floating male population.'[20]

If Elsa was seen as an English version of Scarlett O'Hara, then Hubert's costumes skilfully enhanced this. In her first appearance she wears a leopard-skin trimmed jacket, a short skirt, and flirts with Taylor in a bicycle repair shop. Leigh expertly brings Elsa to life with a series of scene-stealing double-entendres, 'I hope I'm not too fast for you!' Hubert's witty wardrobe combines large picture hats to artfully frame her features and short bolero jackets, emphasising her small waist and hips. Although Elsa's clothes look 'ladylike', she behaves in an extremely unladylike manner, which adds to the comedy as her character climbs out of windows or is caught in comprising positions with her various admirers. A contrast to Elsa is Maureen O'Sullivan's student Mollie, who is scholarly, demure and is costumed in old-fashioned pleated skirts.

After two glamorous screen roles, Leigh was finding herself typecast so relished the opportunity to play Libby, a pickpocket/busker in London's theatreland in *St. Martin's Lane* (Timothy Whelan, 1938, costume designer John Armstrong). She told *Picturegoer*: 'It's a relief to wear a shabby and grubby coat and skirt in which you can just squat down whenever you like, without worrying about the clothes.'[21]

Hubert's final work with Leigh was for the epic romance: *Lady Hamilton* (1941 – released as *That Hamilton Woman!* in America). He based his costumes on George Romney's portraits of Emma Hamilton. Romney had painted over forty portraits of her in a series of 'Attitudes' depicting allegorical and mythological figures and the paintings were Hubert's inspiration for charting Emma's rise and fall as one of the most famous women in Europe. The film's epic time frame (1790 to 1815) gave Hubert scope to design eighteen costume changes for Emma. In the prologue, Leigh is almost unrecognisable as the haggard Emma incarcerated in a Calais prison, arrested for stealing alcohol. She had no reservations about making herself look unattractive, aware that her beauty was hard to diminish on screen. 'I must look terrible, I'm in a cell, starving, drunk, I have to look like all the other street girls!'[22] It's a successful transformation, and the film's patriotic message appealed greatly to Winston Churchill, who apparently adored it and watched it repeatedly throughout the Second World War, befriending the Oliviers in the late 1940s. Like his previous work with Leigh, Hubert's designs for *Lady Hamilton* had a major impact on early 1940s fashions: 'Spring brought Regency fashions, graceful and beglamouring [sic]. Those Hamilton Clothes – on offer is an evening cape, like the one Lady Hamilton wore to board Nelson's ship, Regency frills, double collars and fichu-dresses will all be back in vogue.'[23]

Increasingly, the marketing and press campaigning for her films were modelled on Leigh's role as a fashion ambassador, and she continued to model clothes into the late 1950s. Even the film version of the contemporaneous play *The Deep Blue Sea* (1955) makes the most of Leigh looking glamorous. In its press campaign, 'Leigh models a stunning creation in heavy, sequin-embroidered silk satin which favorably compares with the famed actress' smooth performance'.[24] This is in spite of the downbeat nature of the play, which is set in a bedsit – although to escape the one-room theatre setting, screenwriter Terence Rattigan added a skiing sequence in Klosters and a flashback of Hester wearing evening gowns. The film was shot in colour and in Cinemascope, again at odds with the material. If Leigh wanted to escape her glamorous image by portraying a character Rattigan described as having 'no pretensions to great beauty', the film's producers had other ideas, pandering to the post-war taste for escapism (Rattigan, 1995: 14).

Gone With The Wind: the road to Scarlett

> Great balls of fire! They're my portieres now. I'm going to Atlanta for that three hundred dollars, and I've got to go looking like a queen. (Scarlett O'Hara)

When adjusted for inflation, *The Guinness Book of Records* names *Gone With The Wind* as the most successful film in history.[25] The story of how the film was made has been well documented in books, exhibitions and documentaries. Leigh was a rank outsider for the role and, in the mid 1930s, virtually unknown outside the UK. Securing one of the most coveted women's roles in history and being able to carry the film (she appears in almost every scene of the three hour, forty-six minute epic) displays her enormous versatility as a screen performer. Leigh adored the novel and was keen to play Scarlett when the film version was announced in 1937. She memorised passages of dialogue and styled her hair and eyebrows in a 'Scarlett' style. Leigh also arranged to have her photograph sent to film producer David O. Selznick in the hope she would be screen-tested for *Gone With The Wind*.

It has been suggested that the 'costumes [by Walter Plunkett] remain one of the glories of *Gone With The Wind* and these have often been cited as a main source of the audiences' pleasure' (Taylor, 2016: 42). Plunkett's masterpiece of characterisation began with sketches, and these had a considerable influence on the casting of all the principal characters. He had been working on the film for over a year, scrutinised by producer David O. Selznick, who maintained a sharp attention to detail over every aspect of the production: 'this picture in particular gives us the opportunity – as in Scarlett's costumes – to throw a violent dab of colour at the audience to sharply make a dramatic point' (Behlmer, 1972: 99). Plunkett's own attention to detail is evident in his careful renderings of the personalities of the various characters, and he attached Margaret Mitchell's character descriptions to the sketches. He travelled to Atlanta to begin research at his own expense, taking notes and interviewing Mitchell, later recalling that she was amused when he pointed out to her that she had described nearly all of Scarlett's dresses as green. Plunkett received the author's approval to expand the colour palette for Scarlett, and Mitchell arranged for him to meet the elderly dowagers of Atlanta society, some of whom had trunks full of clothing from the pre- and post-civil war period. He was delighted as he handled and sketched these museum pieces, and was even allowed to clip samples from the seams so that he could reproduce the material for the film. He wrote that 'one woman in Charleston even sent her children out to gather a box full of thorns from a tree native to that area. During the blockage days of the war, there were no metal pins and clothing was held together by these thorns.'[26] *Gone With The Wind* and Plunkett's work remains one of the supreme examples of film costume design, each costume reflecting a progression in Scarlett's journey.

The costumes clearly reflect the two different periods of Scarlett's narrative – first the petulant Southern belle and later the post-war woman who turns her back on her earlier life of picture-book elegance to face despair, poverty and bare necessity to survive. Mammy (Hattie McDaniel) transforms the green velvet curtains from Tara into a dress for Scarlett, as a means to secure the tax money to save her beloved plantation. The costume is one of the most widely recognised and influential costumes in cinema history. Appearing halfway through the film, it marks a pivot in the fortunes of Scarlett's narrative. The dress comes to symbolise hope and regeneration, but also humiliation. Scarlett's appeal to Rhett to lend her $300 dollars to pay the taxes fails and she is forced to entrap and marry her sister's boyfriend.

In part two of the film, Plunkett dresses Scarlett in a darker, richer colour palette as she reinvents herself as a successful businesswoman in post-war Atlanta. One memorable example is the low-cut, figure-enhancing burgundy dress which Rhett forces Scarlett to wear to Ashley's birthday party. Plunkett was instructed by Selznick to enhance Leigh's cleavage, 'more breastwork' (Behlmer, 1972), demanded Selznick, so Plunkett taped her breasts together, thrusting them upwards and forward despite Leigh's reservations and discomfort: 'it was difficult to wear for reasons that are obvious on screen, but it did help my entrance to the scene'[27] (see Figure 8.4).

Figure 8.4 Walter Plunkett supervising Vivien Leigh's costume fitting in *Gone With The Wind*.

Released in December 1939, the film became a significant global success, exceeding all expectations. Leigh became an international film star and made history by becoming the first British woman to win the Academy Award for Best Actress. *Gone With The Wind* had a huge influence on fashion.[28] Lillian Churchill wrote in the *New York Times*: 'It has created a great stir in the pool of fashion, the girdles, minute waistlines and ostrich-feather trimmings are sure to have an influence on the creations of Paris and New York. Dress patterns, hats, snoods, scarves and even wrist watches were marketed as inspired by the film.'[29]

In war-time Britain, the green 'curtain' dress was even more poignant, echoing the 'make do and mend' philosophy that would dominate millions of women's lives during the war years. As a publicity stunt, Selznick began to tour the costumes and designs around the United States to promote the film, showing them in each city for a single day. The 'costume caravan' was intended to be nationwide, but the tour was cancelled after the organisers realised the damage it was causing to the costumes. The green curtain dress had currency in other films after *Gone With The Wind*: Anna Lee wears the costume in the horror film *Bedlam* in 1946 (made in black and white so it was less recognisable to an audience), as repurposing costumes for other films was common practice in Hollywood. Eventually, this dress and four others were donated to the Harry Ransom Center in Austin, Texas, as part of the David O. Selznick archive. The costumes have since been conserved and have been displayed in a variety of exhibitions including at the V&A during the *Hollywood Costume* exhibition in 2012.

While preparing for the film version of George Bernard Shaw's play *Caesar and Cleopatra* (1945), Leigh wrote to Oliver Messel, 'I told Pascal [the director] that nobody in the world must do the costumes except you'.[30] Messel was on war duty designing camouflage but the temptation of a high-profile film in Technicolor was too strong. Leigh wanted to keep her familiar theatre troupe around her, and asked Messel to hire designer Margaret Furse to assist him with the huge task of costuming the lavish production.

In 1944, Britain was fatigued by five years of war and, for Messel, creating an Egyptian court with hundreds of extras was a Herculean task. Clothing and material were still under strict rationing and the usual costume-making staff were redeployed on war service. Messel drew on the stores of theatrical costumiers Berman's, Nathan's and B.J. Simmonds to create a working wardrobe. He then sourced and acquired Indian saris from Liberty & Co., and used the fabric to create shimmering, lightweight, diaphanous costumes. Messel designed nine costumes for Leigh's Cleopatra, mapping the character's journey from the inexperienced juvenile Queen hiding from Caesar's army in the paws of the Sphinx, to her encrusted and elaborate state robes. Relishing the opportunity to work on a colour film (which was scarce during the Second War World), he used shades of white, blue, purple and gold chiffon decorated with ornate jewels and lotus flowers. The

Figure 8.5   Vivien Leigh in *Caesar and Cleopatra* (1945), costume designer Oliver Messel.

fabric gives the characters an ethereal quality, but the actors shivered in the costumes in the long, damp summer of 1944 (Figure 8.5). Hugh Skillan, a former actor turned prop maker, made Leigh's headdresses, skilfully interpreting Messels' designs from papier-mâché, glass and cellophane. Beatrice Dawson, who created all the jewellery for the film, was managing a 'make do and mend' shop in London's Oxford Street, so came to the project well equipped to turn everyday objects into accessories for the Egyptian setting.

Messel's great friend and rival was Cecil Beaton. Leigh first worked with Beaton when he photographed her for *Vogue* magazine in 1935. By the mid 1940s, Beaton was a noted designer, royal and war photographer and diarist. He was known as a specialist in period costume design and nineteenth-century fabrics – essential for creating a high-quality *Anna Karenina* (1948) with Leigh in the title role. For Anna's first appearance, in a snow-covered train, Beaton designed a burgundy velvet dress trimmed with sable and worn with a sable hat, muff and cape. The luxurious ensemble was entrancing to post-war audiences still restricted to clothing rationing books and coupons. The press book is packed with references to Dior's 1947 New Look that revolutionised fashion after the war, and includes the observation,

> only a slight modification would bring these dresses and costumes right up to date. Indented waistlines, full skirts, flower trimming and shoulder capes seen in the film are almost identical with accepted current fashions.[31]

A *Streetcar Named Desire*: stage to screen

At Beaton's suggestion, and as part of her desire to expand her range, Leigh read Tennessee Williams' *A Streetcar Named Desire* and, like *Gone With The Wind* ten years earlier, became fascinated by the lead role. Post-war audiences hoping to see Scarlett O'Hara live on stage would witness a very different kind of Southern belle, and one that would cement Leigh's fame as an established stage and screen actress. The character of Blanche DuBois appealed to Leigh on a number of levels, not least the change of pace it offered from period costume drama. As in *Caesar and Cleopatra*, Leigh surrounded herself with a familiar team of collaborators. Olivier directed, and Dawson was employed to design the costumes. Dawson designed Blanche as a jaded figure, with a faded Southern grandeur, a juvenile Miss Havisham with a trunk of moth-eaten furs and fake rhinestones. Williams peppers the *Streetcar* text with references to colour, fabric and the shape of clothing, conjuring up Blanche's previous offstage life. Stanley roughly ransacks Blanche's wardrobe trunk but fails to see what it contains – dated dresses and costume jewellery.

Dawson liked to dress a character 'from the skin out as it were. So you can feel them becoming the character. Vivien was very keen that the underclothes were correct. The shoes were also essential, so she could get the walk. Vivien liked to break shoes in and would wear then in rehearsals.'[32] Rayne, a former theatrical costumier founded in 1899 that began making couture shoes in 1920s, provided the shoes for *Streetcar*. Leigh was a regular customer and Rayne took the opportunity to place an advertisement in the Aldwych Theatre programme.

Make-up and hair were an essential ingredient to Leigh's transformation into Blanche, and her most trusted wig maker was Stanley Hall who dressed virtually every leading performer of the day – including Margaret Lockwood and Edith Evans – and played a crucial role in Leigh's on- and offstage appearances.[33] McBean wrote that Leigh reportedly disliked her own hair: 'After Rudolph Steiner was commissioned to style Leigh's hair for a photographic session, Steiner reportedly told the actress that 'I just brush and it stays where I want it. You are lucky, you never have to spend money on hairdressers' (McBean,

1989: 14). From that moment, Vivien took against her own hair (ibid). From the early 1940s onwards she wore a wig or a hair piece to disguise the fact that her hair was greying.

To disguise Leigh further, Hall created a cendré (ash-blond) wig for Blanche.

> The texture of hair in a wig can be important and tells an immediate story about the character. In *A Streetcar Named Desire* I feel it was essential for Blanche to have impoverished, rather thin hair of no particular colour to point out her highly nervous worn out character. When she did the film, I made her bleached wigs, the idea was that Blanche had gone through life neglecting herself. Vivien used to send the wigs back from Hollywood by air mail, to be cleaned and redressed by me, she didn't trust the American hairdressers.[34]

Elia Kazan had directed the original Broadway production and was reluctant to direct the film, not wanting to repeat what he had already created. Initially, he was hesitant about casting Leigh, believing she was too beautiful to play the role. Kazan wanted to plot the film from Blanche's perspective and added a scene of her arriving at New Orleans main railway terminus, establishing her displacement from the start. Perhaps aware of Leigh's fragile mental state, Kazan wanted her to feel as comfortable as possible and considered using the London stage costumes for the film, but when he saw the photographs, he didn't agree with the design. Concerned, he wrote to studio head, Jack Warner.

> I am worried about her costumes. I had thought for a while that we might be able to use the clothes she wore on stage. I changed my mind when I saw the pictures. They were 'English', I mean stuffy, dull and ultra-conservative. They have to be completely redesigned. As you know, I want Lucinda Ballard. All I can say about her is that she is the best. (Behlmer, 1985: 325)

Kazan liked to get to know his actors before filming and, with Leigh living in England, he started a long correspondence with her discussing all aspects of the production. In 1950 he wrote:

> The impression should be of a woman who is not equipped or prepared to withstand the violence and the noise, the harsh winds and the brutal contacts of modern US urban life. About the clothes, I'm not of a clear mind yet, I have a feeling now that there could be something more fragile, what Williams calls 'moth-like', a little delicate and flowering about them all, a lushness, the characteristic flower there is a magnolia.[35]

Leigh responds to the letter outlining her thoughts on the censored screenplay and the approach to playing the role on film:

> You probably know that playing Blanche is not exactly a rest cure so if I have said anything particularly stupid, I hope you forgive me and put it

down to temporary fatigue ... You do know that when I said over the phone I'm worried about the way I'll look, I didn't mean good I meant right. It is all very fine with the dear footlights to help one, but one can't pile on so much make-up with the camera.[36]

In June 1950, Kazan sent Ballard, who had designed the original Broadway production of *Streetcar*, to England to spend time with Leigh at Notley Abbey. Ballard arrived with her sketches prepared and a firm understanding of the character and the environment that Blanche inhabits. Ballard told Leigh:

> Tennessee Williams does terrible descriptions of clothes. He had Blanche arriving in a white linen suit with a big white linen hat. Now, linen is a kind of crisp material, which is wrong for Blanche. The effect of her clothes should be a terrible daintiness. She should have forget-me-nots from the ten-cent store sewed on her clothes. (Staggs, 2006: 189)

> Absolutely no white or a red satin wrapper, a prostitute she is not! I said the key to Blanche was her always feeling guilt about what had happened to her husband – his suicide. She was always cleansing herself mentally and physically, always fearful of dirt settling on her. (Walker, 1987: 200)

Ballard created a visual distinction between Blanche, her sister Stella, and the other characters in the film. Fabric choices played a crucial point in establishing Blanche as being out of place in the damp, rotting, suffocating apartment. Throughout the film, she wears light, ethereal fabrics, such as long-sleeved chiffon, in contrast to Stella in robust, practical cotton house-dresses. 'The first costume I later made for her [Blanche] had a collar of starched chiffon – several collars were cut and changed during shooting, for they always had to look fresh and give Vivien's face a look of fragility'(ibid: 200). (See Plate 3.)

Ballard designed the stage production and film with first-hand experience; she was from the South, and knew the characters that Williams was describing in his text, 'There's a certain kind of dress that, when I was young, women in the South always had a bath and changed in the afternoon and put on a freshly ironed thin dress. By four o'clock somebody might come over for tea or something like that, you'd be bathed, cleaned and fixed up' (Staggs 2006: 189). Kazan continued to play a crucial role in the design of the film. 'I asked Lucinda to make Blanche's dress for the rape scene of a light diaphanous material, the same color as the very light window curtains of the bedroom where Stanley corners her.'[37] Ballard's final costume is stripped of frills and lace anticipating Blanche's uncertain future. 'Vivien was very anxious about how she would look when madness overwhelmed her Blanche. I'd figured out a way of making a strait-jacket out of soft material that would wrap around Blanche but not imprison her' (Walker, 1987: 200).

Ballard's work was acknowledged with an Academy Award nomination for Best Costume Design in a Black and White Film.

'Vivien Leigh's Wardrobe: The Lady Who Leads'[38]

Throughout her career, Leigh's high-profile films, international stage appearances and glamorous private life were an ideal recipe for audience consumption. In 1935, Leigh was proclaimed by the press as 'the fame in a night girl', a role she inhabited with ease, and she then made the transition to film star, business woman, society host and establishment figure. Her relationship with designers enabled her to understand what looked good on her body, how to disguise perceived imperfections and project an image of herself which was sometimes at odds with her own personal life. Leigh maintained throughout her career that clothes and costumes were integral to a woman's persona. When asked by *Woman's World* in 1949, 'Does the modern girl spend too much on dress?', the actress replied 'No, clothes are part of her self-expression.'[39] In press interviews and magazine articles, Leigh's own irritation about her appearance becomes evident: 'to be truthful, I do not admire my own appearance. I consider the two greatest beauties of our age, Lady Diana Cooper and Greta Garbo. People think that if you look fairly reasonable, you can't possibly act, and as I only care about acting, I think beauty can be a great handicap.'[40]

From her early modelling days for *Vogue*, Leigh was attracted to high-end, luxury labels. When she became Lady Olivier, she adopted the role of unofficial ambassador for the emerging European luxury goods market. Both parties benefited from the arrangement: Leigh would wear designer labels on tour, on stage and on film; the exposure this gave to a designer's work, reputation and credibility was incalculable. Leigh was credited with bringing Dior's New Look to the Antipodes in 1948, when she toured with the Old Vic Theatre Company. Her wardrobe was closely scrutinised in every city where the company performed: 'Lady Olivier is not much over five feet in height, but her slight figure showed off the new look suit she wore. Her pleated skirt was the fashionable length of twelve inches off the ground.'[41] Throughout the tour, Leigh promoted the work of the couturier and her opinions were widely quoted: 'I love my clothes and wear them a long time. I'm partial to jersey in both wool and silk and I adore furs. From the English designers I prefer Victor Stiebel, John Cavanagh and Hardy Amies. Among French designers I prefer Balmain, Lanvin and Christian Dior.'[42]

In 1957, it was announced that Christian Dior would be designing the London production of *Duel of Angels*, which had been a success in

Paris in 1953. Dior died before the London production was realised and it was Yves Saint Laurent (who took over the house of Dior) who faithfully recreated Dior's costumes for Leigh and her co-star, Claire Bloom. They retained all the hallmarks of the New Look: tightly fitted and boned jackets, emphasising the waist, and full voluminous skirts.

Leigh requested that Pierre Balmain design the costumes for *The Roman Spring of Mrs Stone* (1961), her penultimate film. Here Balmain created a series of classic designs, cool and elegant, reflecting the jaded, wealthy widow adrift in modern Rome. Leigh's transformative hairstyle halfway through the film, although depicted on screen as being a result of a visit to Elizabeth Arden's Beauty Salon, was actually created by her regular wig-maker Stanley Hall, once again in cendré.

Leigh maintained a fastidious order to her wardrobe and she recycled and reused clothes and kept costumes she had worn on film. One of her favourite screen roles was Myra in *Waterloo Bridge* (1940), which gave her the opportunity to work with Adrian, the brilliant costume designer for MGM, who had been central to the film careers of Greta Garbo, Norma Shearer and Joan Crawford. Leigh adored the costumes and had managed to keep one of her coats (MGM were notoriously strict about keeping clothes after a film was finished), which she wore throughout the 1940s. Rosemary Geddes, Leigh's secretary in the late 1950s, offers us a unique insight into how Leigh organised her wardrobe, a routine which had been established from her formative days at school:

> She was well organised about her clothes. Apart from couture dresses, she used a dressmaker, Mrs. Wannamaker, who lived nearby. She never wore slacks, except in the country. She preferred suits for town-wear. Sometimes, she would send me to Harrods to bring back half-a-dozen summer dresses. She was very fond of bluish-mauve – she'd keep one or two she liked. She had loads of scarves and always wore them. She had about a dozen pairs of gloves, short and long, white and beige. She wore fairly plain court shoes from Rayne's mostly. She changed her handbags every year. She remained faithful to her favourite scent, Joy by Patou. She would have her hair straightened by Elizabeth Arden. Every so often she'd say, I think it's time to give the wardrobe a turning-out and I'd take the clothes to a high quality second shop called Pandora, near Sloane Square. (Walker, 1987)

Since her death in 1967, Leigh's costumes and characters have continued to have an imprint on popular culture. In 1981, the popular Tom Tierney Paper Dolls series featured Leigh, with 'twenty eight characters for you to cut out and dress'.[43] Bloggers, vintage clothing and film appreciation fan sites across the Internet reference Leigh's film roles. Auction sales of costumes worn by Leigh, especially in *Gone With The*

Wind, have attracted high prices. In 2012, one of Leigh's hats from the film sold for $55,000. In the same year, the V&A staged a major exhibition exploring 100 years of costume design for film. *Hollywood Costume* exhibited 130 characters and examined the designer's process of creating fictional people from the pages of the script to the screen. Two costumes elicited the most excitement: both from films made in 1939. One was Dorothy Gale's gingham dress and ruby slippers from *The Wizard of Oz*. The other was Scarlett O'Hara's green velvet 'curtain' dress from *Gone With The Wind* (Plate 4). Scarlett/Leigh's costume featured prominently in the media's extensive response to the exhibition. *The Sunday Times* exclusive led with 'Scarlett's dress, Superman's pants and Dorothy's shoes to garland V&A', of which 'the curtain dress was the centerpiece'.[44] *Gone With The Wind*'s costume designer Walter Plunkett's realisation of Scarlett, and Leigh's interpretation of the role, have become part of twenty-first-century popular culture, and an enduring inspiration to costume designers, film fans and dress historians. Experiencing the costume in close proximity (the costume was on open display) invited one visitor to comment, 'it was like being in the room with Scarlett, as if she was transported from the scene in the film, I was overwhelmed'.[45]

Costume design has played a central role in the persistent images of Leigh, strongly influencing the public perception of her achievements. Leigh as Scarlett or Blanche or Lady Olivier have become default positions on her legacy as a mother, actress, celebrity figure and more. Her legacy endures: in 1985, Angus McBean's photograph of her dressed in her Serena Blandish costume was used on a commemorative series of stamps to celebrate British Film Year (Leigh was the only woman featured). In 2013, a portrait by the photographer Sasha of Leigh in character in the play *Because We Must* (costume designed by Victor Stiebel) was used on a stamp commemorating the centenary of her birth. She is the only actress to be featured on a UK stamp twice. That these enduring images of Leigh are actually of her playing someone else shows how – through costume – the characters she played have become the images through which she is identified.

Notes

1 Vivien Leigh, to Elia Kazan, 16 June 1950, Vivien Leigh Archive THM/433/4/3/11.
2 Anon, 'Streecar Wins', 1952, Scrapbook, Vivien Leigh Archive THM/433/4/2/2.
3 Anon, 'Those Hamilton Clothes', 1941, American *Vogue*, Scrapbook Vivien Leigh Archive THM/433/4/2/8.
4 Ruth Jordan, 'The Lady Who Leads', *Women and Beauty Magazine* 1951, Vivien Leigh Archive, THM/433/9/1.

5 Anon, 'What Success Has Taught Me', 1951, Scrapbook, Vivien Leigh Archive THM/433/4/2/11.
6 Press interview, n.d., Vivien Leigh Archive THM/433/9/1-6.
7 Anon, 'What Success Has Taught Me', 1951, Vivien Leigh Archive THM/433/4/2/11.
8 Press interview, n.d., Vivien Leigh Archive THM/433/9/1-6.
9 Ibid.
10 Anon, 'What Success Has Taught Me', 1951, Vivien Leigh Archive THM/433/4/2/11.
11 Harold Conway, 'Vivien Leigh Forsakes Costume Drama', *Theatre Herald*, 1937. Scrapbook Vivien Leigh Archive THM/433/4/2/8.
12 'What Women Wore at the Grand National', *Daily Sketch*, 28 March 1936.
13 A.E. Wilson, review for *A Midsummer Night's Dream* (1937), Old Vic Theatre, Vivien Leigh Archive, THM/433/4/2/1.
14 Both headdresses are now in the V&A, Oliver Messel Archive, Theatre & Performance Collections, V&A Museum, London. Museum numbers S.507-2006 and S.491-2006.
15 Roger Furse to Vivien Leigh, 1945, Vivien Leigh Archive, THM/433/4/2/6.
16 This costume is now housed in the Theatre & Performance costume collection, V&A Museum, London. Museum number S.942-1982.
17 Betty Hand, 'It's an Olde English Fashion', *Fire Over England* article, personal collection.
18 Ibid.
19 Frank Evans, 'Vivien Leigh's Sudden Leap to Fame', 1936, Scrapbook, Vivien Leigh Archive THM/433/4/2/7.
20 *A Yank at Oxford* (1939), Vivien Leigh Archive THM/433/4/3.
21 Anon, 'Life on St. Martin's Lane', *Picturegoer*, 1938, personal collection.
22 Anon, 'The Making of Lady Hamilton', *Modern Screen*, 1941, scrapbook, Vivien Leigh Archive THM/433/4/2/2.
23 Anon, 'Those Hamilton Clothes', American *Vogue*, 1941, scrapbook, Vivien Leigh Archive THM/433/4/2/8.
24 Press book, *The Deep Blue Sea* (1955), personal collection.
25 Guinnessworldrecords.com.
26 Walter Plunkett, 'Dressing Right for *Gone With the Wind*', *American Screen Classic*, September/October 1982, p. 20, scrapbook, Vivien Leigh Archive THM/433/4/2/8.
27 Anon, *Gone With The Wind* article, 1940, author's personal collection.
28 Despite the film's global box office success and record Academy Award wins, Plunkett's work was never honoured except in film history books, as an Academy Award for Best Costume did not exist in 1939. Leigh enjoyed wearing Plunkett's costumes, keeping one of her nightgowns after the film was finished and later donating it to a museum in Topsham, Devon, where it is still on permanent display in the 'Vivien Leigh' room. Leigh's first husband's sister, Dorothy, gifted her house to the community in 1967 and it was converted into a museum.
29 Lillian Churchill, 'Hollywood Paints the Fashion Picture', 1940, Vivien Leigh Archive THM/433/4/2/1.
30 Vivien Leigh to Oliver Messel, 1943, Oliver Messel Archive, University of Bristol Theatre Collection.

31 BFI Special Collections, Press book for *Anna Karenina* (1948), London Film Production files, C/091.

32 'Dressing for the Part', undated clipping from Beatrice Dawson Biographical File, V&A.

33 Hall began his career under contract to Alexander Korda, based at Denham studios. He established *Wig Creations* in 1945 and served the theatre and film world for the next thirty years.

34 Stanley Hall Biographical File, V&A.

35 Elia Kazan, to Vivien Leigh, 1950, Vivien Leigh Archive THM/433/4/3/11.

36 Vivien Leigh, to Elia Kazan, 1950, Vivien Leigh Archive THM/433/4/3/11.

37 Kazan (1988: 384).

38 Ruth Jordan, 'The Lady Who Leads', *Women and Beauty Magazine* 1951, Vivien Leigh Archive THM/433/9/1.

39 Anon, press interview, *Woman's World*, 1949, Vivien Leigh Archive THM/433/4/2/9.

40 Ibid.

41 Jack Atkinson, 'An Interview with Vivien Leigh', 1948, *Sun Herald*, Sydney, Vivien Leigh Archive THM/433/4/2/9.

42 Ibid.

43 Tierney (1981).

44 Richard Brooks, 'Scarlett's Dress, Superman's Pants and Dorothy's Shoes to Garland V&A', *The Sunday Times*, 8 January 2012.

45 Visitor Profile Report, *Hollywood Costume*, V&A (2013).

References and bibliography

Behlmer, Rudy (ed.) (1972) *Memo from David O. Selznick*, New York: Viking Press.

———— (ed.) (1985) *Inside Warner Bros., 1935–1951*, New York: Weidenfeld and Nicolson.

Edwards, Anne (1977) *Vivien Leigh: A Biography*, New York: Simon and Schuster.

Kazan, Elia (1988) *Elia Kazan: A Life*, New York: Alfred A. Knopf.

McBean, Angus (1989) *Vivien Leigh: A Love Affair in Camera*, London: Phaidon.

Rattigan, Terence (1995) *Plays Two: The Deep Blue Sea; Separate Tables; In Praise of Love; Before Dawn*, London: Methuen.

Staggs, Sam (2006) *When Blanche Met Brando*, New York: St Martin's Griffin.

Taylor, Helen (2016) *Gone With the Wind*, London: BFI Classics/Palgrave Publishing.

Tierney, Tom (1981) *Vivien Leigh Paper Dolls in Full Color*, New York: Dover.

Vickers, Hugo (1988) *Vivien Leigh*, New York: Little Brown & Co.

Walker, Alexander (1987) *Vivien: The Life of Vivien Leigh*, London: Weidenfeld and Nicolson.

9

Leigh through the lens: photographic collaborators

Susanna Brown

'An artist-photographer's dream.'

(Vivienne, 1956: 35)

Vivien Leigh formed creative alliances with the twentieth century's leading portrait and stage photographers and became one of the most photographed women of her generation (Winchell 1950, cited in Vickers 1990: 214). This chapter explores the differing approaches of photographers including Sir Cecil Beaton, Angus McBean, Horst P. Horst, Florence Vivienne Entwistle and John Vickers, and investigates Leigh's active participation in the crafting of her public image – the tight control she retained over the editing, reproduction and dissemination of photographs. It also touches on those pictures not intended for public consumption: the personal snapshots that she and John Merivale took from the 1950s until 1967, which capture their 'off-duty' lives, with close friends at home and abroad. The research draws on material from four collections: the Vivien Leigh Archive at the Victoria & Albert Museum (V&A), the University of Bristol Theatre Collection, the papers of Sir Cecil Beaton at St John's College Library, Cambridge, and the photographic collection of the National Portrait Gallery, London, as well as published accounts by photographers and biographers.

The creation of a portrait is a collaborative process that hinges primarily on the rapport between photographer and sitter, their mutual trust and shared vision for the final image. A successful portrait is not only aesthetically appealing, well composed and lit, but also projects an atmosphere and something of the sitter's personality or attitude. It could be suggested that performers make the ideal photographic subjects, practised at conveying thoughts and feelings through facial expression and gesture. However, the confidence of even the most experienced performer can waver when he or she is not inhabiting a specific role, as Florence Vivienne Entwistle (known professionally as 'Vivienne') recalled: 'One would not expect Sir Laurence Olivier to be a most unhappy and reluctant sitter. He looked it when he came in and remained saturnine as I photographed him. I realised that, like some other great artists, he could best relax as a character, playing a part' (Vivienne, 1956: 36). Leigh suffered none of her husband's reluctance and was able to project a breadth of emotions when collaborating with a photographer. It was a talent attested to by *Gone With The Wind* author Margaret Mitchell, who wrote about the actress in a letter to the film's producer David O. Selznick: 'I am impressed by the remarkable number of different faces she has. In the stills you have been good enough to send me, she looks like a different person every time she is shown in a different mood' (Mitchell letter 13 March 1939, cited in Vickers, 1990: 117).

Professional photographs of Leigh served numerous purposes. In the movie industry, publicity stills were central to a film's promotion, and were usually created by the studios' in-house photographers, such as Clarence Sinclair Bull and Laszlo Willinger at MGM (Figure 9.1). Stills were reproduced in Hollywood fan magazines, including *Modern Screen* and *Picture Play* in the US, and *Picturegoer* and *The Screen Pictorial* in Britain (Plate 5). In the realm of theatre, carefully posed photographs were taken during a photo-call to be displayed at a large scale on the theatre façade and printed in popular magazines. The photo-call centred on the key moments of the play, performed without an audience and often rearranged by the photographer to achieve the most eye-catching compositions. Portraits of Leigh were also sold as collectable picture postcards; inexpensive and widely circulated, they were cherished by fans, in particular those she personally inscribed.[1]

Whether in magazines or newspapers, reviews and articles about Leigh almost always commented on her photogenic features in rapturous and romantic prose. In the article 'The Legendary Miss Leigh', writer Lesley Blanch praised her 'delicately tilted eyes, exquisitely flared nostrils and pointed chin.'[2] In her book *They Came to My Studio: Famous People of Our Time*, Vivienne described Leigh as 'an artist-photographer's dream and the fairest of the fair', and detailed the characteristics that made her so: 'Analyse her features – the proportion, the relationship of one to another, the harmony, the line. It is hard to fault them' (Vivienne, 1956: 35). In the early years of her career, Leigh capitalised on her photogenic qualities by working as a fashion model for several women's magazines, the most prominent of which was *Vogue*. Cecil Beaton, one of *Vogue*'s major contributors, praised Leigh

Figure 9.1   Vivien Leigh by Laszlo Willinger, 1940.

in the press, writing: 'That tiny waist, those wonderful shoulders ... Vivien Leigh gives clothes terrific piquancy.'[3] A short, undated description of Leigh by Beaton exists among the many 'pen portraits' in his personal papers at St John's College Library. In the text he listed the attributes so widely celebrated: 'The nut brown hair, the lilac-mauve eyes, the perfect, slightly retroussé nose, the delicious lips and the elongated neck created an effect of dazzling prettiness.' But Beaton ended with an ambiguous sentence, hinting that he viewed Leigh's beauty as less than authentic: 'Perhaps we were blinded by such a dazzling vision into believing that here was true beauty.'[4]

A self-proclaimed 'rabid aesthete', Beaton was one of *Vogue*'s most prominent photographers, and in a career spanning the late 1920s to the 1970s the fashion auteur contributed percipient articles, elegant illustrations and thousands of photographs to the magazine. He also designed sets and costumes for several productions starring Leigh: the film *Anna Karenina* (1948, directed by Julien Duvivier), *The School for Scandal* (1949, directed by Olivier) and Noël Coward's *Look after Lulu* (1959). He was the official photographer on *Caesar and Cleopatra*

(Gabriel Pascal, 1945) with costumes by Oliver Messel. Beaton and Leigh both had fierce professional ambitions and shared a preference for theatre over film (Beaton diary 24 November 1941, cited in Vickers, 1990: 149). In the surviving correspondence from the 1940s, the cama-raderie between Beaton and the Oliviers is evident: a letter from Olivier to Beaton dated 15 October 1948 ends 'All our love to you, dear boy. Longing to see you.'[5] It seems that Leigh had Beaton to thank, in part, for one of her most widely acclaimed roles: in 1947, he wrote to Olivier from the New York Plaza: 'It has been quite a dull season on Broadway and the only sensation is "A Streetcar Named Desire" which has quite a wonderful part for Vivian [sic] if she ever wanted to play it.'[6] The play had opened on Broadway on 3 December with Jessica Tandy in the role of Blanche, the part that Leigh would later make her own. Olivier replied on 30 December 1947: 'My dear Cecil, Thank you so much for your adorable letter,' and ended with thanks, 'for the news about "Street Car Named Desire" which Vivien has taken with her to the Studios to read today. All our love, dearest fellow, for the New Year.'[7]

The Vogue studio

In the 1930s, the modelling profession was still in its infancy and young actresses, dancers and debutantes were frequently photographed for *Vogue* wearing the latest designs. One of Leigh's early appearances was a double-page spread by photographer Shaw Wildman for the British edition of the magazine, published in 24 July 1935. Shaw's pictures were accompanied by the following text:

> New portraits of Miss Vivien Leigh whose very sensitive performance in the St. James's comedy *The Mask of Virtue* has aroused such whole-hearted admiration. She has chosen (for the occasion) one of the early models from the Matita autumn collection – one of those extremely smart yet practical affairs designed with an eye to the moors and the coming season's many outdoor events.[8]

The text emphasises Leigh's recent success on stage, and also makes evident her collaborative role in the shoot: she selected the outfit herself. The following year a picture of Leigh by Horst P. Horst was published as part a *Vogue* fashion feature entitled *London Lines*, for which Horst had photographed numerous subjects in fashions by London design-ers, juxtaposed with 'mysterious objets d'arts' (Brown, 2014: 100 and see Figure 9.2). The picture includes a model of a suit of armour and the accompanying caption details 'a double file of steel buttons to suggest a waistcoat on a black braid-edged town suit with hand tucked organdie blouse' from the designer Dilkusha at Lansdowne House.

Figure 9.2   Vivien Leigh by Horst P. Horst, 1936.

The strength of the image lies not in the garments, but in Horst's masterful lighting and the strong diagonal composition, an upward thrust from bottom left to top right, emphasised by the pointed feather in Leigh's hat.

Horst had joined the staff of French *Vogue* in the early 1930s and his images soon began appearing in all three editions of the magazine – French, British and American. Early examples such as this display his love of classical sculpture, form and proportion, and his skill with studio lights. Mysterious and dramatic shadows became central elements of Horst's photographs and he was known to spend up to two days arranging the lights for a single sitting. The fierce heat of the studio lights combined with the slow shutter speeds of large plate cameras made working with *Vogue* photographers something of an endurance test for Leigh. Horst explained the complex process of photographing with the cumbersome studio equipment.

> First you posed the model. Then you put a black cloth on your head, and focused the eight-by-ten camera, which was mounted on wheels. Then you tightened the camera extension. You folded back the black cloth to prevent it covering the lens. Then you took the film holder from its carriage and put it into the camera. You pulled out the slide, and put it away. Then you told the model to 'hold it,' and clicked the camera. Since there were no light meters, you had to guess the correct exposure, generally two to three seconds, and time it with the help of an alarm clock that stood on the box containing the film holders. In other words, you had to watch the clock and watch the model at the same time. Of course throughout this entire cumbrous operation, the model had to hold her pose. In fact, she might as well have been part of a still life. (Lawford, 1984: 63)

The resulting negatives measured eight by ten inches and possessed clarity and detail unparalleled by smaller cameras. Horst's 1936 photograph of Leigh would reappear in *Vogue* several years later, to mark her Oscar-winning performance in *Gone With The Wind*, alongside a study showing her in a white Cellophane and taffeta dress by leading London couturier Victor Stiebel.

Leigh wore a sumptuous magenta and turquoise gown by Stiebel for a *Vogue* study by John Rawlings in 1936 (Figure 9.3). The image is the epitome of seductive 1930s glamour. Lounging in a dark interior, Leigh reclines against an ornately carved studio prop with the vast skirt of the dress spread out in the foreground, a luxuriant mass of fine fabric. She gazes over her shoulder directly into the camera; her slightly arched eyebrow and posture form an image of supreme confidence. *Vogue* commented on Stiebel's inventiveness and innate understanding of women's sartorial desires: '[He] has taken the lives and hearts and aspirations of Englishwomen and transmuted them into clothes, adding that touch of the artist, something that is rich and strange and exciting' (Shephard, 2010: 127).

For *Vogue* sittings, Leigh often favoured dresses by Stiebel; he became her close friend and would send her new designs created especially for her.[9] Although it was not always stated in the magazine, it seems likely that Leigh selected the outfits she wore in *Vogue* herself, rather than leaving the decision to the magazine's fashion editors. This supposition is informed by evidence of the meticulous control Leigh exercised over theatrical photo-calls and costumes. Letters from 1947–1948 between

Figure 9.3   Vivien Leigh by John Rawlings, dress by Victor Stiebel, 1936.
British *Vogue*.

Cecil Beaton, Martin Battersby and Laurence Olivier discuss the costumes that Beaton designed for *The School for Scandal* at the Old Vic,
and reveal Leigh's strong opinions on the subject. At that time, Beaton
was working in New York and appointed Battersby to oversee the exe-
cution of his designs. In one letter to Beaton, Battersby complains of
Leigh's uncompromising stance regarding the pearl buttons intended
for her dress: 'A hard glint came into Miss Leigh's eye, a hard tone in

her voice and a very hard line in her jaw. "We won't bother about that and I <u>don't</u> want buttons"."[10] *Vogue* photographers' accounts of working with Leigh's contemporaries reveal that other actresses had similarly directorial attitudes. Marlene Dietrich, for example, instructed Horst to use her favoured dramatic lighting when she posed for him in *Vogue's* New York studio in 1942: he recalled, 'She came in with this terrible hat and said in that voice, "Remember the von Sternberg lighting"' (Lawford, 1984: 236).

Among the several thousand photographs in the Leigh archive at the V&A is a handsome gelatin silver print, mounted on card and signed by Beaton in a flourish of red paint (Figure 9.4). Leigh stands in a pale satin dress by Stiebel and huge floral corsage, her gaze cast down-wards, hands held in front of her, composed and demure. Next to her are two ornate chairs and a marble bust bearing a resemblance to Queen Victoria, a draped lace curtain behind. The picture is quintes-sential Beaton – a romantic theatre set created within the photographic studio, exhibiting his love of antiques and rich textures. Beaton was well aware that his approach was contrary to that of his peers across the ocean at American *Vogue*. He saw his photographs as a counter-point to Edward Steichen's harder-edged aesthetic, which chimed with the geometry of Art Deco design: 'Steichen's pictures were taken with an uncompromising frankness of viewpoint, against a plain back-ground, perhaps half-black, half-white, my sitters were more likely to be somewhat hazily discovered in a bower or grotto of silvery blossom or in some Hades of polka dots' (Beaton, 1951: 53). A variant version of the portrait, minus the marble bust, was published as a full page in British *Vogue* in July 1935 with the caption: 'Stiebel's slipper satin has sculptured lines that echo Vivien Leigh's own serenity and grace.'[11]

Leigh wore another Stiebel gown, in chartreuse green, to pose for Beaton in a scene resembling the backstage of a theatre (Figure 9.5). The rolls of paper, heavy chains hanging from above, and thick cables trailing across the floor convey the mechanics behind the glamour of the theatre. These functional materials strike a contrast with the ele-gantly dressed Leigh in the centre of the frame, her faraway gaze and posture reminiscent of a classical sculpture. This sense of discord, combined with the eerie shadow on the white wall, produces a less harmonious image than others by Beaton. In the winter of 1941, Beaton was in Edinburgh taking photographs to illustrate an article about the city and had the opportunity to watch her perform in Shaw's *The Doc-tor's Dilemma*. He noted in his diary: 'Vivien in dark purple velvet costume & black hat, with sables of last act looked so beautiful and beguiled us by being so completely unspoilt' (Beaton diary 24 Novem-ber 1941, cited in Vickers, 1990: 149). He photographed her at her

Figure 9.4   Vivien Leigh by Cecil Beaton, dress by Victor Stiebel, 1935. British *Vogue*.

dressing table and afterwards took her out for supper. They returned to the hotel and continued talking long into the night. Beaton described the evening in his diary, summing up her simultaneous feelings of joy and exhaustion in his typically perceptive manner:

> Vivien was as sweet as ever and as lovely – though older and more tired. She said that she liked to arrive early at the theatre so as to be in her

Figure 9.5   Vivien Leigh by Cecil Beaton, dress by Victor Stiebel, 1936.

dressing-room as much as possible. She loved talking to people in her dressing-room [...] receiving messages and letters. She loved the life of the theatre so much that she could never stop realizing how happy and lucky she was [...] We gossiped about the theatre until after 3 o'clock in the morning. One by one the other tables emptied and the lights were turned down until we had to move. We went back to the lounge of the hotel and here we sat for further hours while the night porter hoovered ... more lights out until we sat in the light of one overhead lamp – Vivien looked tired and drawn – and said how exhausting the theatre is – everyone prematurely old and each time they assemble at the station for the next journey they look smaller and tireder than before.

Vivien is almost incredibly lovely. Hollywood is at her feet [...] The adulation of her beauty leaves her cold – she loves talking late into the night and here she found someone intrigued and stimulated to continue even until she was tired. (Beaton 24 November 1941, cited in Vickers, 1990: 149–150)

Beaton moved away from his lavish studio sets during the war years, when materials were scarce and *Vogue* promoted utilitarian fashions. Instead, he created intriguing, surreal-infused pictures using minimal props. One striking example, from 1945, shows Leigh's upper body protruding through a hole cut in a white paper backdrop (Figure 9.6). The area behind her head and shoulder is very light, allowing her profile to be seen clearly. The effect was probably achieved by placing a 1,000-watt bulb directly behind the sitter, which would bleach out part of the backdrop, allowing the face to stand out clearly against the pale area behind. It was a technique Beaton would often employ for his portraits of Elizabeth II and the British royal family.

Figure 9.6   Vivien Leigh by Cecil Beaton, 1945.

Photo-calls and character portraits

Beaton once described his contemporary, Angus McBean, as 'the best photographer in England' (Wilson, 2009: xi). McBean had become interested in photography as a boy and bought a 2.5-by-3.5-inch Autographic Kodak camera. In the mid 1920s he began work as a restorer in the antiques department at Liberty, London's eclectic luxury store. In his spare time he made masks and took photographs; when his creations were exhibited at a London teashop they caught the eye of the leading Society photographer Hugh Cecil. McBean became his studio assistant and over the course of a year he mastered the large reflex camera, which produced half-plate negatives that could be retouched by drawing directly onto them with a pencil.

McBean left Hugh Cecil's employment to launch his own studio in Belgrave Road, Victoria. For the next twenty years, McBean's favoured camera was a half-plate Soho Tropical reflex camera with Zeiss lenses and Kodak Panchromatic black-and-white glass negatives, which measured approximately 6 by 4 inches. A breakthrough came when, in 1936, he was invited to design masks for *The Happy Hypocrite* starring Ivor Novello as Lord George Hell and Leigh as the young dancer Jenny Mere. Novello asked McBean to take the publicity pictures, which were a triumph: 'McBean's startlingly chiaroscuro, intensely black, dramatic prints were utterly unlike the flat photographs taken by the Stage Photo Company, which then photographed nearly every West End show' (Wilson, 2009: x). Rather than relying on the existing stage lighting, McBean brought atmosphere and depth to his pictures through the manipulation of his own auxiliary lights, and a style indebted to films of the 1920s – the expressive black and white close-ups of Hollywood stars he admired in his youth, such as Lillian and Dorothy Gish and Mae Marsh (Woodhouse, 2006: 18). McBean's primary audience was not the readership of *Vogue*, but the crowds on city streets who would stop to admire his large-scale prints on theatre façades, and would perhaps be inspired to buy a ticket to the play.

The Happy Hypocrite opened on 8 April 1936 at His Majesty's Theatre, and McBean's photographs, measuring up to 24 by 20 inches, were displayed outside (ibid: 87). Three weeks later, all five of the British magazines that devoted pages to the theatre (*The Sketch*, *The Tatler*, *The Bystander*, *The Illustrated London News* and *Britannia and Eve*), featured a McBean photograph as a frontispiece (ibid: 87). As well as launching McBean's career as a theatre photographer, the play marked the beginning of his thirty-year connection with Leigh. He became her trusted photographic collaborator and she became his muse.

Leigh visited McBean's Belgrave Road studio in 1938, while appearing at the Gate Theatre in the title role in *Serena Blandish*. Soon after McBean had taken the production pictures at the theatre, she telephoned to arrange for him to take some publicity shots for her own use (ibid: 146). He charged his standard fee of six guineas for eight portraits and captured her beneath a spray of blossom, in the wide-brimmed hat that she wore for the play (Figure 9.7). The photographs were part of a group sent by her agent John Gliddon to producer David O. Selznick in Hollywood, when Leigh was pursuing the part of Scarlett O'Hara in *Gone With The Wind* (Vickers, 1990: 83). Before the photographs were sent, Gliddon had suggested to Selznick that Leigh might be suitable for the role, but Selznick cabled his New York office stating his lack of interest: 'I have no enthusiasm for Vivien Leigh. Maybe I will have, but as yet have never even seen a photograph of her. Will be seeing *Fire Over England* shortly, at which time will of course see Leigh' (Selznick memo 3. February 1937, cited in Vickers, 1990: 83). McBean noted that other photographs by Harlip (the Bond Street studio run by Dr Gregory Harlip, and after his death in 1945, by

Figure 9.7 Vivien Leigh by Angus McBean, 1938.

his widow Madame Monte Harlip) were sent along with his own (Woodhouse, 2006: 149), but he does not describe Harlip's pictures and no record has been found of the precise images. Leigh's collection of photographs at the V&A includes a youthful portrait by Harlip (Figure 9.8) in which her skin appears luminescent against a dark backdrop and deep shadows are cast by her eyelashes, cheekbones and lips. Her eyes are closed, head tilted back, to produce an image of striking sensuality and reverie. This portrait is a counterpoint to McBean's bright, floral confection, and it might logically be deduced that a copy of this particular photograph was sent to Hollywood along with McBean's, in order to show Leigh's versatility – the 'different faces' that would later impress Margaret Mitchell (Mitchell letter 13 March 1939, cited in Vickers, 1990: 117).

A single portrait often has multiple uses. The photograph beneath the blossom was also printed as a frontispiece in *The Bystander* on 19 October 1938 (Woodhouse, 2006: 149), and, decades later, in 1985, it was used by the Royal Mail on the 31-pence stamp to celebrate British Film Year.[12] Perhaps because the portrait helped Leigh win that most

Figure 9.8   Vivien Leigh by Harlip, 1930s.

coveted of film roles, it became one of her favourites and she continued to give prints of it to her fans until at least 1951 (Woodhouse, 2006: 149). McBean's photographs were also used as reference material to inform film productions. According to McBean, several of the camera angles used in Elia Kazan's *A Streetcar Named Desire* were close copies of the poses McBean had instructed the actors to take during the photo-call for the play at the Aldwych Theatre, many months before the film was made. The poses arranged by McBean, and subsequently recreated for the film, included Blanche DuBois' fight with Stanley Kowalski, in which she leans back over the table, Blanche at the dressing table and on the telephone (Woodhouse, 2006: 237). In another example of the instructive use of McBean's stage photographs, the pictures he took in 1953 of Leigh as Elsie Marina in *The Sleeping Prince* at London's Phoenix Theatre were requested for Marilyn Monroe during the filming of the screen adaptation, *The Prince and the Showgirl* (1957): 'Monroe's press agent had rung up and ordered, at vast cost, two copies of every one of the sixty-three shots that Angus had taken of the original *The Sleeping Prince* which showed Vivien, so that Monroe might study them for her role' (ibid: 274).

One of McBean's best-known collaborations with Leigh is a surreal composition titled *Aurora, Goddess of Dawn* (Figure 9.9). It was published in *The Sketch* on 6 April 1938, one of a quartet of McBean photographs of actresses, commissioned for a special beauty issue. The inspiration for the picture of Leigh floating through clouds in a Grecian-style dress was derived from several sources. The technique of using quick-drying plaster and flannelette to create the dress was an idea McBean had perfected in an earlier portrait of Diana Wynyard, and the forms of the cotton-wool clouds are reminiscent of *A couple with their heads full of clouds* (1936) by Salvador Dalí, one of the Surrealist artists that McBean admired. It also calls to mind the series of *Goddess* portraits by Yevonde Middleton (known professionally as Madame Yevonde), for which she captured society figures dressed as subjects from mythology. First exhibited at her premises in Berkeley Square in 1935, and also featured in *The Sketch* (Woodhouse 2006: 126), Yevonde's inventive series of photographs was made using the Vivex Carbro colour process, an early colour technique involving three negatives.

While McBean eschewed colour, Yevonde embraced it. She was a pioneer of the medium and her photograph of Leigh in 1936 flaunts the ability of the Vivex process to capture jewel-like reds and greens: a red backdrop matches Leigh's lipstick perfectly, and the green shirt complements the colour of her eyes (Plate 6). Yevonde first experimented with colour in the early 1930s and in her bold address to the Royal Photographic Society in 1932 titled *Why Colour?* she proclaimed:

Figure 9.9   Vivien Leigh as *Aurora, Goddess of Dawn*, by Angus McBean 1938.

'If we are going to have colour photographs, for heaven's sake let's have a riot of colour, none of your wishy-washy hand-tinted effects.'[13] Advances in colour photographic technologies ran parallel with advances in colour movie film, but one major drawback was cost. Colour film was expensive and colour pictures cost a great deal to print in magazines, so had to be used sparingly. In the late 1930s, the cost of each page of *Vogue's* colour editorial 'was subsidised by a corresponding page of colour advertising' (Brown, 2014: 155), but many other magazines of the period reserved colour for the cover alone.

Professional courses or colleges teaching photography barely existed in the first half of the twentieth century. Most photographers learnt by assisting an established practitioner, or by joining the family business. Vivienne was not the only member of her family who possessed a talent for portraiture. While she was still working as a miniature painter, and her husband was running a school for fashion drawing, their enterprising son, Antony Roger, set up a portrait studio in a spare room of his parents' house (Vickers, 1990: 59). Working under the name Antony Beauchamp, he had his first success aged only 16 – Leigh was one of his early sitters, shortly before she found fame in *The Mask of Virtue*. McBean's assistant, John Vickers, went on to launch his own successful studio and, like McBean before him, became the favoured photographer of the London Old Vic, photographing over 1,000 theatre productions. Today his archive is cared for by the University of Bristol Theatre Collection and comprises some 21,000 photographs, 16,500 glass plate negatives, 20,000 film negatives and 1,800 slides, as well as boxes of manuscript material, and handwritten appointment books. One such notebook records that a sitting with Leigh took place on 10 November 1943. The corresponding portraits (Figure 9.10) show attractive, if conventional, studies of the actress both standing and seated in a heavily embellished puff-sleeved gown. Vickers adopted a much less conventional approach for an undated but startlingly modern profile portrait, which depicts Leigh's dark silhouette against a white backdrop (Figure 9.11).

The idealised image

One reason that photographers favoured black and white over colour was because colour photographs were much harder to retouch (Wilson, 2009: vii). Today, the computer is the dominant means of modifying photographs, but in earlier decades, painstaking manual retouching was carried out on negatives and prints using a variety of materials including specially formulated paints, fine sable brushes, graphite powder and soft pencils. Retouching was a vital stage in the creation of any celebrity portrait. At the height of his career, McBean employed two retouchers, or 'finishers', to assist in 'erasing the awkward wig joins, the forehead lines, the unglamorous wrinkles and unattractive facial marks' (ibid: xii). Pictures for *Vogue* were likewise carefully retouched before being reproduced. Horst's friend Simone Eyrard in Paris, and Beaton's assistants Miss Bell and Wendy Saunders in

Figure 9.10   Vivien Leigh by John Vickers, 1943.

Figure 9.11   Vivien Leigh by John Vickers, 1940s.

London, would work under the photographers' instructions to slim waistlines, remove blemishes and carefully accentuate eyelashes and lips, to craft *Vogue*'s ideal version of beauty.

While photographers and retouchers removed some unwanted details, Leigh disguised others herself. She believed her mouth was too small and compensated by lengthening the lower lip with make-up. Biographer Hugo Vickers suggests she made no secret of the trick: 'She knew that this was an artifice and never minded friends watching her apply make-up' (Vickers, 1990: 59). McBean's recollections indicate that Leigh's opinions regarding make-up were as strong as her views on costumes, and during the photo-call for Shakespeare's *Antony and Cleopatra*, in 1951 (in Manchester, prior to opening at St James's Theatre, London), McBean learnt never to criticise her make-up. Ultimately, Leigh was so thrilled with the photographs of herself as the Egyptian queen that she allowed one to be used to advertise Max Factor's theatre make-up (Woodhouse, 2006: 255, see Figure 9.12).

Leigh was insecure about her hair, the size of her hands and the length of her neck.[14] She often chose to wear a wig or a hat to hide her hair. In 1945, for a sitting with Vivienne, she requested to be photographed in a 'little head-hugging black hat' (Vivienne, 1956: 35), which obscured most of her hair. An image from the shoot was used on the cover of French magazine *L'Ecran*, in August 1947. In her recollection of the sitting a decade later, Vivienne made it evident that Leigh was an active collaborator, but also trusted the skills of the photographer: 'Vivien Leigh's first sitting was during the rehearsals for her most exacting role in *The Skin of Our Teeth* and I knew the nervous tension that that involved. But any idea that soothing balm would be necessary was groundless. She was completely relaxed, amenable to any pose and even allowed me to rearrange her hair' (Vivienne, 1956: 35). Although the photographer asserts that this was the first sitting with Leigh, a portrait credited to Vivienne appeared in *The Tatler* on 7 February 1940, five years before *The Skin of Our Teeth*[15] (Figure 9.13). Even on the magazine page, the retouching is immediately evident – individual upper and lower eyelashes were painted on, and the irises more clearly defined to draw attention to her eyes.

By the late 1940s, Leigh was worrying about ageing: costume designer Emma Selby-Walker recalled that 'Vivien did not like the special photographs of her in her *School for Scandal* costumes for the front of the house, and replaced them with more youthful versions taken from the Cyril Maude readings in 1942' (Vickers, 1990: 202). Beaton also wrote on the subject of ageing; while working on *Anna Karenina*, he noted in his diary of Leigh's appearance: 'It is not at all what she would like. It has deteriorated and appals her. Each photograph shown to her is further confirmation of her fears. She is always

Figure 9.12 Vivien Leigh in Shakespeare's *Antony and Cleopatra*, by Angus McBean, 1951.

seeking to be in a dark light – muffled up in veils and furs' (Beaton diary May 1947, cited in Vickers, 1990: 190). She disliked the appearance of her hands, considering them to be unfeminine, an assumption that Beaton did nothing to dispel when, during filming at Shepperton Studios, Leigh complained to him that he had made her gloves too small, to which he somewhat cruelly replied that her hands were too large (ibid: 191). A 1964 sketch of Leigh by Don Bachardy accentuates her mascara-ed eyelashes, lined lips and left hand, looming large in the foreground. Bachardy sent a photograph of the sketch to the actress, with a letter stating 'I would be delighted if you still want to use it on

Figure 9.13   Vivien Leigh by Vivienne. Published in *The Tatler*, 7 February 1940.

your Christmas card."[16] Her desire to use this image – which clearly emphasises her hand and the artifice of her make-up – suggests that by her 50s Leigh had overcome her worries about the physical traits she had previously viewed as flaws.

Control and conflict

Although photographers' recollections of Leigh tend to emphasise mutual admiration and a sense of harmonious collaboration, some accounts reveal how strictly the actress supervised the editing and publishing of images. After a photo-call or portrait session, it was customary for Leigh to examine the prints and select the ones she deemed suitable for reproduction. Those she disliked would be torn at the edge, and the corresponding negative taped so that it could not be printed (Woodhouse, 2006: 236). McBean recalled Leigh's eagerness to see the results of her first portrait session at his studio: she summoned him to Durham Cottage at 10 o'clock on a Saturday night, and 'we lay on the green carpet in front of the gas fire in the sitting room, looking at the pictures' (ibid: 148). *LIFE* magazine contributor Philippe Halsman experienced a similar impatience following a sitting in New York in 1946: 'The telephone rang. It was Vivien, who was worried about her pictures and wanted to see them. Whenever I photograph for a magazine my rule is never to show a picture to the sitter before publication. But how could I say no to an angel, who without complaining left her sick bed to pose for me a second time?' Halsman took his favourite photographs from the sitting to Leigh at the Waldorf Astoria, where she was resting upon doctors' orders. Rather than sharing his delight, she was appalled: 'Instead of an angel I saw a wounded tigress. "These pictures are terrible," she said, "and I forbid you to show them to the magazine. I know your boss, Mr. Luce, personally; if you disobey me, I will destroy you."'[17]

Nobody else was present to corroborate Halsman's story, but there exist similar reports of Leigh's wrathful reaction to bad photographs. Even her trusted portraitist McBean 'was told he had betrayed her and would never work again' (Woodhouse, 2006: 236) following the photo-call for *A Streetcar Named Desire*. Leigh had insisted that he share the photo-call with several other photographers, which made the event more difficult than usual for McBean, but upon seeing his pictures, she rejected just one. However, the offending photograph soon appeared, uncredited, on the cover of *Picture Post*. On close examination, McBean realised that that picture was very slightly different to his own, and must have been taken by *Picture Post* photographer Kurt Hutton, who had been positioned behind McBean during the photo-call. After he was able to explain what had happened to Leigh, she apologised profusely. The debacle led to Leigh banning public photo-calls for her theatrical performances, another example of the authority she held over the work of photographers (ibid: 237). Other anecdotes indicate she could be jealous and competitive when sharing the limelight with another photogenic star: 'The results of the photo-call for *Duel of Angels* (Christopher Fry's version of Jean Giraudoux's last play) at the Apollo Theatre in April 1958 would result in anguish for McBean and the producers. Of the seventy shots taken by McBean and then refinished by his staff, only twenty-five were approved by the two stars. Claire Bloom had vetoed all the photos in which Vivien Leigh looked more beautiful, and vice-versa' (Wilson, 2009: xiii).

A personal album

In the 1950s, Leigh purchased a 35-mm Stereo-Realist slide camera, a device that became popular with Hollywood stars and was endorsed by Fred Astaire. One magazine advertisement from 1950 claimed it to be 'the camera that puts real third dimension in your pictures ... actual depth and proportion in glorious natural color!' The camera used Kodachrome, a colour slide film produced by the company Kodak, and took a pair of half-frame images which, when mounted in cardboard slides and placed in a handheld simple viewer, produced a bright, 3D picture. The technology for creating 3D photographs was far from new: the craze for collecting and viewing mass-produced professional stereographs had reached a peak in the late nineteenth century. Those small black and white (and sometimes hand-tinted) images were produced by professional photographers, but the Stereo-Realist camera allowed amateurs to create their own 3D pictures. The 1,500 stereoscopic slides now in the V&A collection indicate that the Stereo-Realist camera was used occasionally by Leigh, but was taken up enthusiastically by John Merivale, who became the chief documenter of Leigh's latter years, including American tours, holidays abroad and life at Tickerage Mill in Sussex (Figure 9.14). The slides capture a side of Leigh's existence that few professional photographers were granted access to. A request from Italian photographer Gino Begotti to photograph Leigh at home for a magazine in 1964 was met with a brief reply stating Leigh 'sincerely regrets that time does not permit'.[18]

Figure 9.14   Vivien Leigh on the set of *The Roman Spring of Mrs Stone*, by John Merivale, 1961.

Collectively, Leigh's stereoscopic slides have a strongly autobiographical character, recording the life she lived after her divorce from Olivier. Many of them show groups of friends gathered for a meal or a party: New Year celebrations with Robert Helpmann, Warren Beatty, Joan Collins and others; lunch with John Gielgud, Alan Dent, Sir Kenneth and Lady Jane Clark; relaxing with Noël Coward and Leigh's beloved cat, Poo Jones. After years of collaborating with professional photographers, Leigh had mastered posing for the camera and had surely gleaned something of the professional's approach to lighting and composition.

One of the most fascinating photographs by Merivale shows the actress preparing for *Duel of Angels* in 1960, the year Leigh and Olivier officially divorced (Plate 7). She is pictured applying her make-up in the mirror of her dressing room at the Huntington Hartford Theatre in Hollywood. Merivale is partially reflected in the mirror too, and around its frame are positioned postcards and photographs, including an image of Leigh presenting at the 1960 Tony Awards in New York. Arranged on the dressing table, among the vases of red and yellow flowers, perfume bottles, make-up and trinkets, are framed photographs of Olivier and a newspaper clipping about him. The portraits of Olivier seem dated – their black and white tones mark them out as mementoes of a bygone era, in stark contrast to the vibrant colours of the 1960s space. What appears to be at first glance an amateurish snapshot becomes, on closer looking, a multi-layered composition that comments on love, the passage of time, and the ritual and artifice of the theatre. Above all, it shows Leigh as herself, preparing for her work.

Notes

1 Since the invention of the *carte de visite* (a small photograph mounted on a piece of thick card) in the 1850s, portraits of stars have been widely collected. Later in the nineteenth century, this format gave way to the larger cabinet card and picture postcard.

2 Undated press cutting, University of Bristol Theatre Collection: MM/REF/PE/AC/1168.

3 Unknown author, Vivien Leigh: Dressed and Photographed by Cecil Beaton, *Illustrated*, 26 July 1947, University of Bristol Theatre Collection: MM/REF/PE/AC/1168.

4 Beaton, undated, St John's College Library: Papers of Sir Cecil Beaton D/2/1/0.

5 Vivien Leigh Archive, THM/433/2/2.

6 Cecil Beaton, to Laurence Olivier, 16 December 1947, Vivien Leigh Archive. THM/433/2/2.

7 Laurence Olivier, to Cecil Beaton, n.d., Vivien Leigh Archive. THM/433/2/2

8 British *Vogue*, 24 July 1935.

9 The V&A's Fashion and Textiles collection includes a wool coat trimmed with fur and leather, donated by Vivien Leigh, and designed in 1955 by Victor Stiebel for Jacqmar: V&A Museum number: T.449-1967. Stiebel also turned his hand to theatre costumes, working on productions including the musical *Music in the Air* (1934). Stiebel's press cuttings books are housed in the V&A Archive of Art & Design: AAD/1994/1.

10 Martin Battersby to Cecil Beaton, 9 December 1947, St John's College Library, Cambridge, Papers of Sir Cecil Beaton A1/36/3.

11 British *Vogue*, 24 July 1935, p. 52.

12 The other stamps featured Peter Sellers by Bill Brandt, David Niven by Cornel Lucas, Charlie Chaplin by Snowdon and Alfred Hitchcock by Howard Coster.

13 Yevonde 1932, cited www.madameyevonde.com.

14 Wilson 2009: xii: 'Vivien Leigh always hated her own hair, and had a large selection of wigs at her disposal' Vickers 1988: 59; 'Vivien was very worried when James Agate wrote that her neck was like a tulip, and added that Vivien's hands were her major flaw. She thought them clumsy and ungainly effect.'

15 *The Tatler*, 7 February 1940, p. 169, University of Bristol Theatre Collection. MM/REF/PE/AC/1168.

16 Don Bachardy, to Vivien Leigh, 18 September 1964, Vivien Leigh Archive, THM/433/2/2.

17 Halsman 1972, cited http://vivandlarry.com/vivien-leigh/cover-story-vivien-leigh-by-philippe-halsman.

18 Letter from Gino Begotti, to Vivien Leigh, 20 February 1964. Response from C.R. Darnell, 4 March 1964. Vivien Leigh Archive, THM/433/2/2.

References and bibliography

Beaton, Cecil (1951) *Photobiography*, London: Odhams Press.

Brown, Susanna (2014) *Horst: Photographer of Style*, London: Victoria and Albert Museum.

Halsman, Phillipe (1972) *Sight and Insight*, New York: Doubleday.

Lawford, Valentine (1984) *Horst: His Work and his World*. New York: Alfred A. Knopf.

Shephard, Sue (2010) *The Surprising Life of Constance Spry*, London: Pan Macmillan.

Unknown author (1947) Vivien Leigh: Dressed and Photographed by Cecil Beaton, *Illustrated*, 26 July 1947. Unpaginated. University of Bristol Theatre Collection MM/REF/PE/AC/1168.

Vickers, Hugo (1986) *Cecil Beaton*, London: Weidenfeld & Nicholson.

———— (1988), 'Lady At A Loose End', *Sunday Times*, 2 October 1988, pp. 73–77. University of Bristol Theatre Collection: MM/REF/PE/AC/1168.

———— (1990) *Vivien Leigh*, London: Pan.

Vivienne (1956) *They Came to my Studio: Famous People of our Time*, edited by A. George Hall, London: Hall Publications.

Wilson, Frederic Woodbridge (2009) *The Photographs of Angus McBean: From the Stage to the Surreal*, London: Thames and Hudson.

Woodhouse, Adrian (2006) *Angus McBean: Face-maker*, London: Alma Books.

10

'A living set': at home with Vivien Leigh

Hollie Price

A striking image from the stereoscopic slide collection held in the Vivien Leigh Archive at the Victoria & Albert Museum shows Leigh at home in Eaton Square, Belgravia in 1961 (Plate 8). Leigh peers from the left-hand side of the frame, with her painted fingernails, cigarette in hand and the debris of a party on the floor just visible. She leans in to examine Carl Toms' set model for *The Lady of the Camellias*, the play in which she appeared as central character Marguerite Gauthier during the UK and world tour of the Old Vic production in 1961–1962. When viewed in 3D, Leigh appears to take the position of spectator and the miniature set stretches into the distance, offering a view of the different layers of the set and the props on the stage. The photograph also provides a glimpse of her living room in Eaton Square: in the foreground, there is an elaborate arrangement of white lilies and other pink, white and yellow flowers in a huge vase, while heavy lavender velvet curtains with pastel-coloured upholstered furniture are pictured in the background. Albeit strewn with the debris from the party, the decoration of the flat is visibly glamorous, comfortable and elegant.

Throughout Leigh's career, she ensured her homes were meticulously decorated and furnished. These interior design schemes were often described in the British popular press in comparison with designs for the stage, and referencing her and Olivier's public careers as performers. In 1958, for instance, *House and Garden* featured an article titled 'The Oliviers Off Stage'. The feature explores the décor of their Eaton Square flat as part of the magazine's section on furnishing and interior decoration, pronouncing that 'here [...] is a flat that is theatrical as a set by Mr Cecil Beaton is theatrical: a living set' (Anon a, 1958: 66). To illustrate this, the article features photographs of the interiors designed by Sybil Colefax and John Fowler. Photographs of Olivier's study and Leigh's bedroom in vibrant colour, and black-and-white images of other rooms, are accompanied by vividly detailed descriptions of 'the resplendent Chinese Chippendale mirror' in the hall, the 'library steps covered in lime-green leather', floor-to-ceiling mirrors, the Degas above the fireplace and 'windows [...] elaborately, even voluminously, swagged and draped' in the drawing room (ibid: 62–67). The text emphasises that 'the visitor is surprised and delighted to find that this elegant manner is quickened, coloured and made wholly personal to its owners by several magnificently theatrical touches. Indeed, there is throughout – not in the circumstances, surprising – a pervasive feeling of the theatre' (ibid: 63).

In order to convey this 'feeling of the theatre', the article emphasises the connection between the interiors in Eaton Square and the stars' public roles on stage and screen: 'there is a sense of spaciousness, emphasized perhaps by the fact that each room is so complete in itself, and such a direct contrast to its neighbour. How easy to imagine, sitting in any of the rooms, that one is awaiting the turn of a revolving stage for the next scene to come into the limelight!'(ibid). In this style, the experience of the interior is detailed using comparisons with the stage and the material surroundings of the theatre: the archway from the hall into the dining room is 'draped with theatrically-minded curtains' with 'window curtains of maroon velvet silk heavily swagged with deeper coloured velvet hang dramatically against the walls of burnt vermilion red' (ibid: 66). Indeed, the interiors are explored in close connection with Leigh and Olivier's careers as actors. No explicit connection is made to their contemporary appearances respectively in *Duel of Angels* and *The Entertainer* but photographs of Leigh and Olivier in costume throughout their careers provide a border at the top of the article. These include photographs of Leigh as Scarlett O'Hara, Anna Karenina and Blanche DuBois, and Olivier as Henry V, King Lear and Hamlet, as well as images of the pair on stage together. With this border of photographs, the couple's transformative performances on stage are presented in close proximity to the dramatic, carefully composed interiors of Eaton Square (ibid 64–65 (Figure 10.1).

Film historians have acknowledged the role of private life – and the function of the home, more specifically – in the publicity surrounding stardom.[1] For instance, Simon Dixon describes the Hollywood star's home as a 'domestic mise-en-scène', in which 'the star's domestic décor is everywhere marked by his or her screen role' and as a key form of film publicity in *Architectural Digest* magazine (Dixon, 2003: 82). The home thus serves as an extension of a star's public roles, offering an insight, however constructed, into their private life. The representation of Leigh and Olivier's home in *House and Garden*

Figure 10.1   'The Oliviers Off Stage', *House and Garden* (May 1958).

does precisely this and, notably, characterises their home itself as a performance.

Using evidence from Leigh's notes, correspondences, receipts and inventories, and the accounts of other historians, the first part of this chapter examines the settings, and the sense of theatre, that Leigh created in her homes. The second part suggests that, by portraying their home as a 'living set', magazines did more than merely emphasise the composition and performance of Leigh's interior designs; they also used these interiors to promote a particular vision of domestic modernity (ibid: 66). Through an exploration of magazines which investigated Leigh's homes from the 1930s to the 1950s, I indicate that the 'pervasive feeling of the theatre' in her homes throughout the period negotiated broader contemporary issues of domestic femininity, national identity and consumerism (ibid: 63). In doing so, I contend that the 'living sets' evoked by Leigh's homes not only convey a sense of theatre that combines her public star image with her private life, but that they also embody 'living' parts of a British middlebrow culture preoccupied with shifting ideas of home and modernity (ibid: 66).

At home with Vivien Leigh

Numerous historians and biographers have noted Leigh's interests in interior design, often citing the influence of her first husband, Leigh

Holman, on the development of her connoisseurship and taste for antiques in the 1930s. Thomas Kiernan describes how their 'house, at 6 Little Stanhope Street in Mayfair's quaint, ancient Shepherd Market, needed much in the way of decoration and furnishing. Antique furniture was a subject that interested Leigh Holman, and together he and Vivian devoted their energies and imaginations to outfitting their new home' (Kiernan, 1981: 141). According to Hugo Vickers, the 'final details were [...] co-ordinated by Miss Browne of the General Trading Company' but Leigh was evidently developing a highly imaginative approach to furnishing their home (Vickers, 1988: 40). On an often-noted trip to the shops, Leigh had been given £50 and instructed to return with a refrigerator, but purchased a 'small, exquisite' painting by Eugène Boudin instead (Walker, 1994: 75). This is an indication of her impulsive, characterful and individual way of fashioning her home as a setting characterised by beauty (and one in which her growing collection of paintings would often later provide focal points).[2] At Durham Cottage, the eighteenth-century gamekeeper's cottage she moved to with Olivier in 1937, this flair for interior decoration was developed with an increasingly bold, highly individual sense of character and 'discriminating eye' (Lasky Jr and Silver, 1978: 52). Leigh experimented with furnishings, decorations, light fittings and colours in the upholstery, wallpapers and carpets. On one of his visits, Angus McBean describes the bold (and somewhat intoxicating) effects of Leigh's efforts, which included 'wall-to-wall apple-green carpet up to the knees everywhere, which was very new at the time', 'the biggest double bed I had ever seen and a bathroom rather bigger with two of everything and everything green' (McBean, 1989: 15).

Leigh's close attention to the detail and composition of her domestic surroundings was demonstrated on a much larger scale with the refurbishment of Notley Abbey, the twelfth-century abbey in Buckinghamshire the Oliviers bought in 1945. Complete with grand hall, three reception rooms, five principal bedrooms and four bathrooms – as well as an orchard, spinney, meadows and gardens – this was an extensive project.[3] She was frequently advised by Lady Sibyl Colefax and John Fowler, with regular appointments scheduled in her diaries in the late 1940s.[4] Colefax and Fowler's elaborate schemes of chintz, colours, swagged curtains and 'sophisticated Regency furniture' complemented and emboldened Leigh's eye for composition and made for even more theatrical schemes (perhaps influenced by Fowler's experiences designing theatre sets) (Jones, 2000: 17). In *House and Garden* magazine in 1938, Fowler stated that he liked 'the decoration of a room to be [...] comfortable, stimulating, even provocative, and finally to be nameless of period – a "fantaisie" expressing the personality of its owner' (Cornforth, 1985: 153–154). Leigh's bills and letters from antiques dealers still show her personal involvement in choosing furnishings and her connoisseurship in selecting items – which in 1945 included an eighteenth-century satinwood table, a little pink morning tea service, a William and Mary period walnut table and matching wing chair with cabriole legs and scroll feet c. 1690.[5] Indeed, one letter from an antiques dealer is marked with pencil ticks and crosses on a list of items – including a small blue china bell, pink floral design vases and a decorated satinwood bow front cabinet – which further shows her enthusiasm, thoroughness and active role in picking furnishing and decorations.[6] The rooms at Notley were testament to this enthusiasm and Leigh's connoisseurship for carefully cultivating her surroundings using her accumulated treasures. In the dining room, items included a vast collection of china and glass – including Rockingham scalloped-border leaf-shaped dishes, antique wine glasses and goblets, a Spode Ware dessert service with an apple green border and paintings by Jan Brueghel de Velours and Walter Sickert.[7] The principal bedroom exhibited: a Georgian mahogany wine bin, a Queen Anne oyster walnut and satin banded chest, and a scroll-back easy chair covered in green and floral brocade; an array of ornaments such as an old pink lustre ware jug and a green and gilt tortoiseshell box; vibrant blue, violet striped, pink and canary yellow lampshades and upholstery; fleece and leopard skin rugs and oval wall mirrors in black and gilt frames; and miniature oil paintings by Francesco Guardi and a portrait of Leigh by Sickert.[8]

   In many of the rooms at Notley, the look of an elegant manor house – evocative of the national past – was created. The hall featured luxurious Colefax and Fowler designed Primavères ('a large-scale flower and leaf-design') wallpaper, an oak framed chair with carved scroll rail and stuffed seat covered in green floral pattern woolwork, an Old English barometer and thermometer, an engraving of Notley from 1730 and a small coloured print of a 'Knight in Armour' (Jones, 2000: 100).[9] A note from Leigh on the early 'shaping' of Notley instructs that the 'tapestry <u>must</u> go over stairs and the Aubusson would go <u>so well</u> not only furnishing the great room but also with the Georgian mantelpiece'.[10] Suggested by Leigh with an eye on its visual appeal, this was clearly a carefully staged composition, offering a spectacle for Notley's visitors. However, with its antique furnishings and nods to medieval history, it is also a setting which exhibited Leigh's 'taste for an "atmosphere" '(Walker, 1994: 59). The drawing room – with its 'massive open fireplace recess' and 'linen-panelled door [which led] to a Priests' hiding place' – similarly offered this feeling of immersive adventure.[11] This was complemented and reinforced by the comfortable miscellany of objects and furnishings in the room, which included antique oak and leather bellows, an ivory conductor's baton, an Aubusson rug with a rose and leaf pattern, a pair of Old English black and gilt frame open armchairs, an oblong stool covered in ruby colour velvet, French lyre shaped wall mirrors and a tapestry panel (Figure 10.2).[12] The 'atmosphere' offered by the room (and Notley in general) – that of romantic escape from the everyday into an idyllic English past – was almost theatrical in its construction, and certainly in line with the Oliviers' growing status as 'the theatre royals of the postwar world' (Walker, 1994: 59; Robyns, 1968: 106). Gwen Robyns notes how 'with all the drive, imagination and sincere make-believe of the theatre Sir Laurence and Lady Olivier made their new estate Notley Abbey into the ancestral home they never had'(ibid). This combination of escape, history and theatre was reinforced by theatrical memorabilia – including numerous reminders of historical performances (such as a coloured engraving of Edmund Kean as Richard III in the early 1800s).[13] In the same vein, the history of Leigh and Olivier's own careers was also in evidence, with portraits of Olivier as Romeo (by Harold Knight, 1936) in the dining room and as Richard III in one of the guest bedrooms, as well as a number of watercolour sketches by friend and set designer, Roger Furse.[14] The frequent rounds of redecoration at Notley and at Durham Cottage also contributed to this feeling of escapism and theatre in their often transformed surroundings. In the 1950s, the

Figure 10.2 The 'Handsome Drawing Room' at Notley.

continuing development of Notley's interiors evidenced an increasing emphasis on status, grandeur and luxury. Kenneth Clark, who had praised Leigh's intelligence, 'sense of style' and her ambitious redecorating scheme at Notley, was somewhat critical of the house in its later stages and its increasing similarity to a stately home, especially in the drawing room (Clark, 1977: 59–60). In his autobiography, Clark explains that the 'big drawing room felt too big for me and made me feel I was staying at Petworth, a resemblance accentuated by the after-dinner games', with the insinuation that Notley's interiors had become too grand, and – for him – therefore less personal and less comfortable (ibid: 60). Leigh also continued to work on Durham Cottage in 1950, making a huge number of purchases from a host of antiques dealers and furniture shops, as well as Colefax and Fowler, who continued to give guidance. Alongside the continual additions made to Leigh's collection of paintings, acquisitions included furnishings and ornaments – such as a white opaline lamp with Greek key design in gold, white spun-silk lampshades, 'old glass candlesticks' and crystal wall brackets for the dining room – which were indicative of an ever-developing sense of luxury at Durham Cottage.[15] A list of queries and requests for samples of chintz for the landing and cornicing designs for the dining room, which Leigh put to Alex Waugh at Piccadilly Fabrics and Furnishings (who was helping with the design and refitting of the cottage), shows her heightened level of involvement in the practicalities of the new design, as well as her overwhelming desire for 'delectable' prettiness in the schemes. Besides requesting 'really pretty' curtains for the kitchen, her thoughts on the bedroom were as follows.[16]

> The more I think about it the more I would like a white varnish-able wallpaper for my bedroom with large soft pink & rose coloured roses on it – something like existing curtains. All paintwork white & ceiling unless you think wallpaper would be pretty up there too [...] I LOATHE our present bedroom, it was always a crass mistake and was painted quite wrong, also having a wallpaper which cannot be varnished is an obvious mistake. I wouldn't mind a new wallpaper but it's difficult to do this at a long range unless you know of a delectable paper and can send a sample of it.[17]

In the 1950s, Leigh's highly dramatic bedroom featured swathes of curtains, a long dressing table along the broad window on one side of the room, cornicing around the room and another level of wallpaper stretching onto the ceiling. Like *House and Garden*'s later acknowledgement of the 'pervasive feeling of the theatre', with the archways and 'theatrically-minded curtains' in maroon silk at Eaton Square, these rooms invoked the material architecture of the theatre and further established Durham Cottage as a setting of outlandishly escapist and sumptuous, expensive luxury (Anon, 1958 a: 62–67).

From her bold and luxurious sense of style, to her creation of escapist and often nostalgic settings, Leigh's homes exhibited her captivation with performance. They provided stages: in all of her homes, Leigh's eye for composition showed a sense of the rooms as a spectacle to be looked at in the same way as a stage in a theatre would be constructed to be viewed by an audience. These interiors were sets: they created a feeling of escape and 'atmosphere' which mimicked her experience as a performer, of moving through a set, inhabiting a role and escaping into a fictional milieu. A number of visitors to Notley Abbey noted that Leigh's homes served as extensions of her public role as a performer. Anthony Havelock-Allan suggested:

> She was an actress in person. When you went to Notley she played the perfect hostess. She had wonderful manners, she was very considerate, she talked very interestingly, brought people out, but it was a performance, she was performing the ideal, gracious, great lady, great personality entertaining, and being very friendly and warm and nice but it was a performance.[18]

Similarly, Joan Plowright, Olivier's wife following his divorce from Leigh, suggested that 'You just felt it wasn't a home. It was a place for show' (quoted in Coleman, 2005: 308). Both accounts indicate that Notley's role as a 'performance' and 'a place for show' meant that it departed from conventional definitions of domestic comfort and homeliness. However, the remainder of this chapter proceeds to take a more nuanced view of the relationship between domesticity and performance in Leigh's homes. With reference to a selection of representations of her homes published in magazines between the 1930s and the late 1950s, I suggest that this sense of performance – and specifically the elements of style, escapist romance and extravagant luxury identified as part of this thus far – engaged with shifting domestic ideals of practicality, Englishness and historical tradition which were inherent in British middlebrow culture.

Style and practicality

Following Leigh's promising star turn with her 'fame in a night' performance in *The Mask of Virtue* (1935), her home life – along with interests in interior design – was a subject of some interest in the British press.[19] In an article titled 'Return To Elegance', one monthly home magazine described the interiors of the Queen Anne house at Little Stanhope Street she shared with her first husband Holman and baby Suzanne. Exploring the home from top to bottom with fascination, the glamorous

Moderne style is evidenced by streamlined furniture; use of greens, blues and silvers; and luxurious fabrics including 'satin, velvet, brocade and even quilted shantung' used predominantly in Leigh's bedroom, the drawing room and the spare room.[20] The couple's shared interest in antiques was also documented, particularly in the dining room, with its 'walls panelled half-way up, with round-backed chairs, a heavy oak chest [...] and wrought-iron candle-brackets fixed to the walls'.[21] Leigh's home in the 1930s was therefore presented as a glamorous setting befitting a new star. Yet, as contemporary monthly magazines including *Ideal Home* and furniture catalogues often featured this combination of designs – the streamlined Moderne style evoking Hollywood glamour and the antique furniture and fittings more typical of the English country cottage – it also embodied a nuanced, suburban idea of modern style, which was promoted in the wider culture of the mid 1930s.

Leigh's home is also explored with an eye on this kind of modernity through the emphasis on her considered composition of the interiors with reference to the careful connoisseurship of fabrics, colours and furnishings, but particularly on the clever arrangement of space, lighting and the use of mirrors. In the description of Little Stanhope Street's interiors, the drawing-room is described as 'an illuminating example of how to treat a comparatively small room': with 'strip lighting inserted behind the woodwork' of the open cupboards on either side of the mantelpiece and 'In the one dark corner a lining of mirror glass [...] used to reflect the light from the room, and a vase of very tall, bright flowers placed beneath on a small shelf'.[22] Likewise, contemporary editions of *Ideal Home* magazine promoted the construction of Leigh's home through close attention to 'room planning', 'good lighting arrangements' and 'glass in decoration' with mirrors, dressing-table surfaces and plate-glass shelves.[23] While conveying the modern glamour of her home, this account of the careful composition of the décor also draws attention to the practicality of her schemes and the organisation of her household. It emphasises that her highly decorative furnishing choices are part of rational and carefully planned space-saving solutions. This fitted in with a wider culture that stressed the technological and scientific prowess of the modern housekeeper. Cultural historian Judy Giles describes how 'the home was becoming increasingly subject to the forces of scientific rationalism' (Giles, 2004: 21). As in one article by Amelia Clough B.Sc., 'For the Beginner in Housekeeping', the role of housewife and mother began to be described (often by such architectural, design and domestic science 'experts') with an emphasis on a semi-professional, scientific 'organisation of work, management of staff, purchase of foodstuffs, household equipment and quantities'.[24] Although this often focused on new labour-saving devices such as washing machines, refrigerators and vacuum cleaners, and new methods of domestic upkeep, Leigh's careful spatial planning, and particularly the emphasis on her work with lighting schemes in the home – while somewhat more decorative – similarly nod to this new scientific economy of home-making (ibid: 486). This sense of practicality is even linked with Leigh's role as a mother: the article mentions her provisions for Suzanne and it is explained that 'Suzanne has her own chairs, bookshelves and cupboards made to her dimensions'.[25] Although the article makes reference to the provisions for a nanny, its note that 'the double-guarded fire is a precaution worth copying' makes some attempt to connect Leigh's glamorous home with a concern for providing safe, modern nurseries and practical advice specifically aimed at mothers.[26]

The article clearly focuses on Leigh's central role in arranging these schemes. Indeed, the first page of the article features a photograph of her in costume (for her role in *The Mask of Virtue*), as if leaning and looking down into the drawing room below. Her star image as a successful actress in the theatre is shown in tandem with the careful crafting and composition of her elegant home (Figure 10.3). A number of contemporary reviews praised her abilities on stage at the same time as stressing her domestic responsibilities. *The Bystander* – a tabloid concerned mostly with society gossip and film and theatre news – announced that 'though launched in domesticity, yet she found time to continue her stage career'.[27] In the *Bulletin* review announcing her 'fame in a night' in *The Mask of Virtue* and 'her new £50,000 film contract' in 1935, she was also pictured holding baby Suzanne and in the *Daily Mail*, she was described as a 'young suburban [...] lady', who has 'learnt the trick of combining marriage with a strenuous career' (Margaret Lane quoted in Robyns, 1968: 40).[28] Rather than demonstrating Leigh's adherence to old-fashioned, 'traditional' roles of housewife and mother, the treatment of her domestic life alongside her theatrical career can be understood as part of a new discussion of the inter-war 'modern young woman' (Bingham, 2004: 84). Historian Adrian Bingham's study of gender and modernity in the British press of this period stresses that: 'While the press continued to celebrate [...] traditional roles [of housewife and mother], performed by the majority of women, there was a widespread recognition that domestic life needed to be reformed to make it more suitable for modern conditions and acceptable to the new generation of seemingly assertive women' (ibid: 19). Bingham establishes that 'it is clear that the dichotomies between "flapper" and "housewife", or the "modern" and the "traditional", were by no means absolute', thus allowing Leigh to stand for a 'modern young woman' who could take on a theatrical career

Figure 10.3 'Return to Elegance', Unidentified magazine.

alongside domestic responsibilities (ibid: 84). As such, the focus on her home's style, composition and practicality in the magazine article on Little Stanhope Street is an instance of this 'reformed' model of domestic life and modern femininity (ibid: 19).

Romance and domestic Englishness

With Leigh's starring role in *Gone With The Wind* (dir. Victor Fleming, 1939) and her propulsion to transatlantic stardom, and her highly publicised relationship with Olivier, the depiction of her domestic life had shifted by the 1940s. In March 1949, an article on Durham Cottage published in *Woman's Own* magazine – a hugely popular weekly publication aimed at lower-middle-class women – omitted these earlier stresses on Leigh's motherhood. Instead, in keeping with the magazine's post-war preoccupation with escapism, entertainment and romance, the article emphasises their home as an idyllic haven for the star couple (White, 1970: 129). This is established with a prominent photograph of a happy Leigh and Olivier on the doorstep, wearing a glamorous spotted ensemble and suit respectively, and an image of Leigh by the fireside surrounded by 'red damask ... rows of books ... enchanting pictures' (Anderson, 1949: 9 and see Figure 10.4). Elizabeth Anderson's somewhat quaint descriptions of the cottage make an implicit association between the real-life romance of the star couple, their careers inhabiting fictional worlds and roles, and their 'charming' home (ibid). First, the article's beginning – 'Halfway down a quiet street in Chelsea a bright primrose yellow door stands in a high, grey brick wall. This is the garden gate of Durham Cottage' – evokes a near-magical fairy tale style (ibid). Once inside, descriptions of the vivid colours, furnishings and ornaments in their home are extensions of this landscape. In the bedroom, this includes 'a pale-bluey grey spot design' wallpaper, a bedhead 'prettily curved and buttoned in shining plum-coloured stain', and 'exotic bottles of perfume' (ibid). Adding to a sense of the continuing magic and transformation of the surroundings, Anderson notes that: 'Neither the Oliviers nor their visitors can ever grumble about the *sameness* in the interior decorations and arrangements of Durham Cottage. Its delights never have time to grow stale [...] this dark blue stair carpet is coming up next week, I was told, and we are having an olive green one instead' (ibid). Leigh's penchant for redecoration is indicative of her sense of transformation. As such, the Oliviers' home appears to offer the kind of escape usually reserved for the fictional worlds of stage and screen – linking them with a highly romanticised, even otherworldly, milieu: an extravagant, brightly coloured one that was befitting their star status.[29]

The LAURENCE OLIVIERS' home

'Vivien Leigh in her drawing room . . . . red damask . . . rows of books . . . enchanting pictures'

ELIZABETH ANDERSON, 'Woman's Own' staff writer, takes you to visit the Chelsea home of Vivien Leigh and her husband Sir Laurence Olivier

"NOT," said Vivien Leigh rather sadly when I told her what I wanted to write about, "that we seem to be at home very often! A repertory of three plays seems to keep us pretty busy—but we do enjoy it when we are there." And that is just the impression that the Oliviers' charming littel house gives you—that it is the home of people who really enjoy home-making; people who study it and care about it.

Halfway down a quiet street in Chelsea a bright primrose yellow door stands in a high, grey brick wall. This is the garden gate of Durham Cottage. Once, I suppose, the coachman's lodging of a large town residence, and now the London home of two of the busiest and most brilliant stars of the theatre today.

Push open the garden gate, go up a paved garden path and there is their yellow front door, with a big welcoming brass-bound lamp swinging above it, and jasmine framing the window by the door. There is a feeling of friendliness, of home, about the entrance. Partly perhaps because the front door opens, informally, straight into the Oliviers' square, light dining room; but mostly, I think, because you only need to take one step across the threshold to know that somsone with an innate flair for furniture and furnishings and colour has been at work.

The walls are papered with an old-fashioned, chintzy, vine-leaf design, saffron yellow on white, the fitted carpet is of a plain mustard shade, and the curtains are yellow, and chair seats of a pale yellowy green are piped with deep cherry red. Behind the round dining table built-in shelves stretch from floor to ceiling, lit by concealed bulbs to display some lovely pieces of coloured glass: rich purples, dark Bristol blues and lustrous greens.

"We are both mad about pictures," said Vivien Leigh, and I found three of their favourites in the dining

room : two drawings by Augustus John and a painting by John Piper of the exterior of their country home, Notley Abbey in Buckinghamshire.

It is only a step through a curtained archway into their ivory-walled drawing-room, with its rich, red damask coverings and its rows of books flanking the fireplace. More enchanting pictures here too, among them one of Roger Furse's original costume drawings from *The Skin of Our Teeth*, in which Vivien Leigh played the lead.

NEITHER the Oliviers nor their visitors ca. ever grumble about the *sameness* in the interior decorations and arrangements of Durham Cottage. Its delights have no time to grow stale. Vivien Leigh is indefatigable in her search for improvements, always buying new pieces, turning them round, finding new treasures, substituting, altering and beginning again. For instance on the day I was there a small pie-crust table and a low Victorian fireside chair upholstered in brilliant cerise satin had just been delivered. Just two more things that Vivien Leigh had not been able to resist !

Another thing she cannot resist, in fact cannot live without, is flowers. Branches of fragrant white lilac filled the window, and on the writing desk mixed spring flowers were massed. And always her dressing room at the theatre is kept filled with fresh flowers at all seasons.

The foot of the twisting white staircase is by the archway between the two main downstairs rooms. Halfway up, cleverly placed so that it is eye-catching from the room below, hangs a glowing flower picture by Epstein. As I went upstairs (this dark blue stair carpet is coming up next week, I was told, and we are having an olive green one instead), I admired the lightness and airiness of the little house. I suspect that several new windows have been made at strategic points since its life as a coachman's lodging.

THE bedroom is a large, low-ceilinged spacious room filled with the teasing memory of a beautiful perfume. From the row of bottles on the dressing table I tried to put a name to it, could not, and deciding that it was some magical mixture of several of them, thought how right it seemed that the lovely Miss Leigh's room should be haunted by such a sweet fragrance.

The walls of the room are papered in a pale bluey-grey spot design and the paintwork is of a toning bluey-grey glossiness, while the bedhead is prettily curved and buttoned in a shining plum-coloured satin. (But then I wouldn't be surprised if, by the time you read this, Vivien Leigh hasn't had the idea of changing the colour scheme !)

However, I am sure that she won't have decided to change the beautiful simplicity of the unit which has been designed to fit right along one side of the room. A row of small windows draped with loops of fine white ninon runs along almost the entire length of this wall. At each end of the wall are roomy hanging cupboards and running beneath the windows is a luxurious built-in dressing table, glass topped for easy cleaning.

The space between the dressing table top and the floor is utilized with a series of smaller cupboards and curtained recesses. The whole effect is of great luxury, but the idea and the design is so essentially simple that

'The Oliviers at their yellow front door, opening straight into the dining room . . .'

any family with a handyman could take a look at the space available in their own home, and plan the same kind of fitment.

On Vivien Leigh's dressing table among the exotic bottles of perfume and the pretty pink jars stands the only photograph I noticed in the house—a close-up of Laurence Olivier. Another highlight in this room was the mirror over the mantelpiece—the signs of the Zodiac etched around the glass margin.

Last, but not least, in the Olivier household is an exquisite aristocrat of a cat—a Siamese called Boy. He is a beloved tyrant of a creature, and shares their life, travelling with them between town and country, house and theatre. At the New Theatre he is 'at home' in Vivien Leigh's dressing room, where a notice on the door warns the visitor to come in quickly and carefully so that Boy shall not slip out and disappear on one of his solitary tours of exploration.

whispered secret of strange, unfathomable beauty. She wanted to keep very still and protract the moment. Yet, through the wish, there spiralled the sensation she could not understand, but which always drove her to dispel such moments, the sensation that was wild and sweet and yet, oddly, reminded her of fear.

She was trying to sort this out when he said, "Loving you is like holding a rainbow. You change every minute."

"Not deep down," she insisted, "not deep down, but I like being a rainbow." She broke off, glancing ahead. "Oh, look at all the people coming. I knew they would on a day like this."

"We shan't notice them."

"What's the time ?"

"Almost twelve."

"We ought to get back by half past, so that you can have a go at the cooker."

"If I can't mend it," he said, "she *will* think I'm a mutt."

"No, she won't."

"I want to meet her."

"You'll love her. She's awfully pretty."

"I could guess that."

"No, you couldn't. We're not a bit alike." Again she broke off to repeat with disappointment, "Oh,

look at everybody, simply teeming in and going up our mountains, too, and into our wood."

"Never mind," he said, tenderly, "we've been lucky to keep them to ourselves so long. It was bound to happen with better weather."

Her face lightened. "I don't care really. They'll always be ours, won't they ?"

"Yes, always. We'll never forget them."

"Or the lake." She could not bear anything to be left out.

He nodded, and they began turning their steps towards home, linked arm in arm.

THEY reached the park gates and entered the wide and busy street. The pavements were so crowded with tired people seeking a few hours in the open that they had to cling tightly to one another, not to be jostled apart.

"I'm not much," he said, struggling to express his sense of inadequacy, "for anyone like you. It'll be a long time before I can give you real mountains and lakes, perhaps never."

She remembered the two little hammocks in the park and the small group of trees that they had called their mountains and their woods. "Silly," she said to him, "oh, silly. What a thing to think

about." She pressed his arm, and the dark look on his face lit with a wavering smile.

"But you don't *know*," he said, despairingly, "Fedora, supposing I don't get on."

"But you *will*," She was confident, and yet in the same moment the fretted faces of some of the women crowding by seemed suddenly, inexplicably close and clear to her. Look at us, they seemed to say, look at us. We were like you once. The sound of the traffic churned out a turbulent, discordant chorus to all the dragging steps. For a moment, she had a gasping sense of falling, a feeling of infinite weakness. Unconsciously she increased the pressure on his arm and looked upwards once more.

His smile held such a luminous humility that all her pride and joy in him came surging back. Her figure lifted with new strength. She was aware of nothing except her heart, and their love shining full within it. We aren't like anybody else, she thought, we'll never be. We'll stay just as we are now, forever. Her lips framed the words, "I love you," but she could not say them aloud.

People trudging by who saw the face of Fedora raised to her beloved, had a curious, fleeting sensation of recollecting something beautiful in which they used to believe, but could no longer clearly remember.

► THE END

9

Figure 10.4 'The Laurence Oliviers' Home', *Woman's Own* (25 March 1949).

However, there are two other characteristics at play in this celebration of the 'charming' romantic setting of Durham Cottage. First, there is an emphasis on a down-to-earth, ordinariness of the Oliviers' devotion to their home: the article begins by stressing that, despite their busy schedules in the theatre, the cottage 'is the home of people who really enjoy home-making, people who study it and care about it' (Anderson, 1949: 9). With this, there is an attempt 'to render the woman reader an "intimate personal service"' and to establish the tone of domestic advice shared by many of the other articles in *Woman's Own*, and which had been particularly evident in the inter-war and war years (White, 1970: 96). This tone serves to illuminate the Oliviers' home in a way which was in keeping with the everyday, domestic concerns of the community of readers. In fact, *Woman's Own* often featured British film stars in order to highlight family or relationship issues raised in advice columns (for instance, a photograph of David Farrar in the garden with his daughter illustrates an article titled 'British husbands share family life'); to demonstrate their home-making skills ('Anne Crawford's hobby is making lampshades from wine bottle labels'); or to model patterns for clothes (this includes the 'Jean Simmons blouse' and a 'Fashion note from Phyllis Calvert – an evening shawl for you to crochet').[30] The glamour of these screen stars is thus brought into line with the more ordinary self-fashioning and practical, homely concerns promoted by the magazine. Although the Oliviers undoubtedly belonged to a higher, more extraordinary and transatlantic strata of stardom than such British stars, there is similarly some attempt to show the practicality of the Oliviers' home, with explanations of the carefully planned units in the bedroom, which include 'a luxurious built-in dressing table, glass topped for easy cleaning'(Anderson, 1949: 9). It is even suggested that 'any family with a handyman could take a look at the space available in their own home, and plan the same kind of fitment' (ibid). (The article is closely followed by instructions of how to make a dressing table stool from a vegetable box.)

Second, further reinforcing this sense of domestic community established by the article, the cottage is furnished in a highly traditional, nostalgic style which evokes an image of idealised national community. The constant evocation of the cottage's rural imagery and colours instils a sense of it as part of a very English, pastoral landscape: with the 'old-fashioned, chintzy leaf design' wallpaper, 'chair seats of a pale yellowy-green are piped with deep cherry red' and a reminder of the Oliviers' close connection with this nostalgic Englishness with John Piper's painting of their country home, Notley Abbey (ibid). Furthermore, the description of Leigh's love of flowers evokes both her glamorous stardom – through their evocation of the gifts and dressing rooms of the stars – and this pastoral, national identity, with the 'branches of fragrant white lilac [filling] the window, and on the writing desk mixed spring flowers' (ibid).

These enduring elements of ordinariness, domesticity and Englishness owe a debt to the popular wartime depictions of the Oliviers and home. In British culture, the 'quiet, unassuming domestic side to British stardom constructed links to national identity, which became paramount in the promotion of popular British stars within the urgent wartime need for consensus' (Price, 2015: 29–30). With this in mind, on their return to London in January 1941, one column announced that 'Vivien Tries the Blitz', reporting the Oliviers' decision to move back to 'their little home in Chelsea' and Vivien's statement that 'We've got a glass roof in part of the house [...] but it's been alright so far'.[31] Around the same time, a photograph of 'The Oliviers at Home' featured on the front cover of *Picture Post* magazine, which offered documentary style photo-essays depicting British society and the war effort to contemporary readers.[32] In this realist style, Leigh and Olivier are pictured on their doorstep once more: fresh-faced, in a scarf and with hair pinned loosely, Leigh looks upwards as if in conversation, while Olivier cradles their cat. The bare bricks of their home visible in the background, the announcement 'Olivier is leaving shortly to join the Fleet Air Force' and a further banner stating 'in this issue: Torpedoed!' situates their home within a landscape characterised by wartime conditions.[33] Another magazine detailed how even though Durham Cottage had 'since been bombed to inhabitability', Leigh's adaption to wartime circumstances was to be commended.[34] One section details how:

> She has always liked to live simply, and now that that way of life is so necessary, she does not fret for orchids. She prefers the slow-moving dark brown cosiness of an English pub to all the chromium cocktail shakers of this bar or that. In their tiny London garden, she and her husband grew lettuces, spring onions, potatoes [...] Her preference is for very simple things [...] Above all, she is glad to be back among her own people, to be sharing with them the rough and the smooth; not hearing it reported by radio, as a far-away nightmare, but living it, a part of real life – her life as an Englishwoman.[35]

In contrast to symbols of Hollywood glamour – 'orchids' and 'cocktail shakers' – Leigh's femininity in the home is promoted as symbolic of 'a common femininity and shared hardship' cultivated by women's magazines in this period (Ferguson, 1985: 19). The association between the Oliviers' home and a 'real' English landscape, and the focus on the garden, is evocative of the communal war effort shared with the readership.[36]

Luxury and history

Alongside such suggestions of the ordinary, depictions of Durham Cottage maintained a sense of the luxury of the Oliviers' home. For instance, in 1941 Leigh's stoical statement that they were doing 'alright' at the cottage during air raids was accompanied by details of wartime upkeep and domestic maintenance such as: 'I never expected to have to cool the hot water in the frig because the cold water supply had broken down!'[37] While situated as an ordinary domestic bastion against the Blitz, the reference to the 'frig' makes clear that the cottage is also a home complete with modern appliances and consumer comforts. Indeed, by the late 1940s, 'The Laurence Oliviers' Home' article in *Woman's Own* illuminated Leigh's 'indefatigable [...] search for improvements, always buying new pieces, turning them round, finding new treasures, substituting, altering and beginning again' (Anderson, 1949: 9). Anderson details how 'on the day I was there a small pie-crust table and a low Victorian fireside chair upholstered in brilliant cerise satin had just been delivered. Just two more things that Vivien Leigh had not been able to resist!' (ibid). With this, the article celebrates Leigh's powers of consumption, her eye for purchasing new items for her home, but also makes clear her taste and careful selection of new furnishings. This negotiation of Leigh's refashioning of the cottage is situated as part of the post-war expansion of consumer culture and a new, conservative understanding of domestic modernity. Advertisements, monthly magazines such as *Ideal Home* and *Homes and Gardens* and the *Daily Mail* Ideal Home Exhibition promoted the possibilities of 'conspicuous consumption' for an audience of lower-middle and middle-class women, though with an emphasis on the 'acceptable', English and 'restrained' (Dolan, 2007: 48). Likewise, on one hand, Leigh's choices are characterised by extravagant luxury (particularly embodied by the 'brilliant cerise satin' here), which evoke the transformative possibilities of consumer culture. On the other hand, this contemporary emphasis on restraint and taste is made clear with the historical tradition – of the 'pie-crust table'; the 'low Victorian fireside chair', and also the antique tub armchair and dainty Victorian-style china ornaments decorating the mantel in the article's accompanying photograph of Leigh by the fire (Anderson, 1949: 9; see also Figure 10.5).

In 1949, this negotiation of consumer luxury and tradition in the Oliviers' home suggested ordinariness and Englishness – an enduring idea of wartime consensus and also elements of a post-war conservative modernity. However, in 'The Laurence Oliviers Off Stage', an article published in *House and Garden* magazine in 1958, the interplay of luxury and historical tradition had become outlandishly extravagant, and indicated dual narratives of optimism and 'cautious conservatism' in the consumer culture surrounding the home (Street, 2007: 133). A high-quality, monthly Condé Nast magazine aimed at affluent middle- to upper-class readers, *House and Garden* emphasised the 'bold', 'unusual' and highly luxurious décor at Eaton Square: with 'the wonderfully blackberry-purple wallpaper', 'acid green' carpet, 'curtains of heavy champagne-yellow water silk, full and pinch-pleated' and walnut Queen Anne bureau in Olivier's study; 'airy *trompe l'oeil* effect of having been draped with ruffled white organdie' on the wallpaper in the hall; and a settee 'covered in amethyst silk' and 'expanse of pale lime-green close-fitted carpet [...] relieved by a beautiful Aubusson in rose-pink and coral' in the drawing room (Anon a, 1958: 62–6). The flat often features French antiques and designs but, with its walls entirely hung with 'a white chintz bestrewn with old cabbage roses', 'canopied hangings [...] held back by chintz rosettes', soft pale green carpet, 'small sofa [...] covered in green silk' and 'painting of roses by Sir Winston Churchill', Leigh's bedroom particularly demonstrated an extravagant, nostalgic blend of luxury, history and Englishness (ibid: 66–67, and see Plate 9). On the one hand, this mix of bold colours, traditional designs with antique furnishings, ornaments and paintings was in keeping with the magazine's projection of a colourful, modern domesticity. Although Leigh often refused to be involved in commercial publicity, later in the same year an advertisement for Paul Kitchens even emphasised Leigh's personal endorsement and was illustrated by a photograph of her modern kitchen at Durham Cottage – featuring bright white units, red and white striped walls and a striking red carpet (October 1958 b: 179).[38] On the other hand, *House and Garden*'s exploration of Eaton Square presents a contrast to the emphasis on self-fashioning and the domesticity of British stars in *Woman's Own*, and a development of the restrained Englishness and historical tradition that had characterised the promotion of consumerism in 'The Laurence Oliviers at Home' a decade earlier.

In line with the concerns of its readership, *House and Garden*'s 'Oliviers Off Stage' article links the lavish design of the couple's home to their upper-class lifestyle, their roles as cultural figures – with an emphasis on the high culture of the stage rather than film in the text – and professional design. Whereas the earlier magazine articles discussed in this chapter often linked the highly distinctive interiors of Leigh's homes to more practical homemaking concerns (however successfully), *House and Garden* demonstrates Eaton Square's suitability for the 'heavy programme of entertaining' that accompanies the Oliviers' status: their 'unique place in international theatrical life' (Anon a, 1958: 65). The interior designs at Eaton Square are explicitly linked to their careers in the theatre and an upper-class lifestyle befitting figures associated with high culture. Whereas 1949 editions of *Woman's Own* had featured popular film stars such as Jean Simmons, Anna

Neagle and Dirk Bogarde, other articles in this later *House and Garden* series focused more frequently on the homes of elite figures including ballet dancer Boris Kochno, writer Somerset Maugham, architect Basil Spence and artist Derek Hill.[39] Colefax and Fowler's elaborate schemes at Eaton Square – showcased by the photographs of the empty rooms – shared the style of luxurious Georgian and Regency schemes pictured frequently at the time: in other articles on castles and country houses belonging to aristocratic figures, and in advertisements, particularly those for the designers and furniture shops of Sloane Square and South Kensington.[40] In contrast to starkly modern and mass-produced, Scandinavian-style designs available (as associated with the more democratic visions of domestic modernity offered mid century with the Festival of Britain), the association of the Oliviers' home with an upper-class lifestyle, high culture and wealthy locales indicated how their domestic life showcased an affluent and conservative aspect of consumerism by the end of the 1950s.

'A living set'

Alexander Walker suggests that, at Notley, 'Vivien's touch was visible everywhere' (Walker, 1994: 30). According to a 1947 fan publication, much like her homes, 'Her dressing-rooms invariably have an appearance all their own, which seems to owe little to actual furnishings. Always there are vases of fresh flowers, her own pictures on the walls, perfect order and harmony' (Burns, 1947). As we have seen, each of the magazine articles examined closely in this chapter similarly illuminates the sense of a style in Leigh's homes which was 'all their own': one which was undeniably influenced by her personality and her resounding influence on her homes. In the 1930s, the 'Return To Elegance' article on her home at Little Stanhope Street features a photograph of her leaning as if inspecting the photograph of her drawing-room and stresses that 'Miss Leigh has chosen soft, warm colours [...] a mole carpet, heavy brocade curtains in a lighter shade of the same colour, green and silver upholstery'.[41] In detailing a problem with space on the landing, the article notes how 'Vivien Leigh has solved it by having a bookcase made to fit the wall space, and filling the shelves with brightly covered books'.[42] The *Woman's Own* piece on 'The Laurence Oliviers' Home in 1949, with its vaguer, fairy tale quality, notes that 'someone with an infinite flair for furniture and furnishings and colour has been at work' in Durham Cottage, but also that 'Vivien Leigh [specifically] is indefatigable in her search for improvements, always buying new pieces' (Anderson, 1949: 9). By 1958,'The Oliviers' Offstage' article in *House and Garden* exhibits the highly unusual schemes and an 'elegant manner [...] quickened, coloured and made wholly personal to its owners': noting 'a painted Chinese silk panel, discovered by Lady Olivier in Warsaw' and the profusion of flowers throughout the home as an extension of Leigh's rose-covered bedroom (Anon, 1958 a: 63, 66).

In British middlebrow culture, Leigh's creation of character through her furnishing, decorating and redecorating was part of a popular performance of 'Vivien Leigh', actress and star. The houses in Little Stanhope Street and Chelsea, and the Eaton Square flat, were settings with which to explore variations of Leigh's public persona as it developed throughout her career: from her status as a domestic expert, mother and 'modern young woman' in the 1930s, and her place as an 'Englishwoman' and 'indefatigable' consumer in the 1940s, to her place as a consummate host and establishment figure by the 1950s (Bingham, 2004: 84; Anderson, 1949: 9).[43] *House and Garden* exclaims: 'How easy to imagine, sitting in any of the rooms, that one is awaiting the turn of a revolving stage for the next scene to come into the limelight!' (Anon, 1958 a: 63). This chapter has explored how Leigh's 'stages' at home 'revolved' throughout the mid-twentieth century in order to suit their context and climate (ibid). It is clear that, while these magazine articles explored an undoubted sense of theatre and her understanding of performance – with the sense of style, romance and luxury exhibited by Leigh's homes – they were also stages which highlighted different aspects of her homes and different roles for her within them. In doing so, they created performances which established connections with different audiences – ranging from addressing the concerns of middle-class audiences, to lower-middle-class housewives in *Woman's Own*, and to visions of affluence for the middle- to upper-class readers of *House and Garden*. They negotiated shifting ideas of practicality, Englishness and historical tradition, and thereby engaged with wider ideas of modern femininity in the 1930s, national consensus in wartime and immediate post-war years, and consumerism in the late 1940s and 1950s. Leigh's homes thus not only provided performances as an extension of her star image but, in a wider culture concerned with the home, also presented ever-'revolving stages' and 'living sets', which continually adapted to promote new ideals of domestic modernity (ibid: 63 and 66).

Notes

1 See deCordova (1991) and Dyer (1998.) Studies focusing on interior design, domesticity and stardom in a British context include: Kuhn (2009); Street (2000) and (2005).

2 By the time of Leigh's death, her extensive art collection included the work of impressionist and post-impressionist artists such as Walter Sickert, Edgar Degas, Édouard Veuillard, Pierre-Auguste Renoir, Berthe Morisot and Toulouse Lautrec. (As evidenced in Harbottle and Lewis Solicitors, 'List of Paintings in Vivien Leigh's will sent to Laurence Olivier', 12 February 1968. Laurence Olivier Archive, Add MS 80620. Her eye for paintings, but also their importance in her design schemes, was highlighted in 'The Oliviers Offstage' article in *House and Garden* in 1958. It describes how the 'mauves and greens of the small curving chimney-piece' in the drawing-room of Eaton Square are 'seen again, both in the wonderful Degas above the fire-place and in the early Sickert, a picture extraordinarily well suited to the room' (Anon, 1958 a: 65).

3 Messrs John Wood & Co., 'Brochure for Notley Abbey'. Vivien Leigh Archive, Notley Abbey, Correspondence, Deeds and Plans (3), THM/433/6/1.

4 Leigh's appointment diary for 1948. Vivien Leigh Archive, THM/433/7/15.

5 Letter from John Bell, Antiques & Works of Art, Aberdeen, to Mrs Olivier, 11 August 1945 and from J.H. Gillingham, Old English Furniture, South Kensington, 31 January 1945, Vivien Leigh Archive, Notley Abbey, Correspondence, Deeds and Plans (1), THM/433/6/1.

6 Letter from A. Fraser Ltd, Aberdeen, to Vivien Leigh, 11 August 1945. Vivien Leigh Archive, Notley Abbey, Correspondence, Deeds and Plans (1)THM/ 433/6/1.

7 Notley Abbey – Long Crendon, Bucks. An inventory of the furniture and effects, pictures, china, glass, silver, linen and outdoor effects – the property of Sir Laurence and Lady Olivier, Ralph Pay & Taylor, Valuers and Surveyors (April 1948) pp. 1–46. Vivien Leigh Archive, Notley Abbey, Correspondence, Deeds and Plans (3) p. 2-3THM/433/6/1.

8 Ibid., pp. 17–20 (although the Guardi paintings are noted as by 'G. Guardi' here).

9 Ibid., pp. 7–8.

10 Note to 'Wonder Lady, Wadham College Oxford'(c. 1945). Vivien Leigh Archive, Notley Abbey, Correspondence, Deeds and Plans (1), THM/433/6/1. Leigh took this same care over the planning of the gardens and her exacting ideas on the look of the flowerbeds. A hand-drawn diagram demonstrates her scheme for planting in the beds immediately outside Notley's backdoor, and accompanying correspondence on her search for *choisya ternata*, an evergreen shrub, at a number of nurseries in 1945. Vivien Leigh Archive, Correspondence, Deeds and Plans (1), THM/433/6/1 Notley Abbey.

11 Messrs John Wood & Co., 'Brochure for Notley Abbey'. Vivien Leigh Archive, Notley Abbey, Correspondence, Deeds and Plans (3), THM/433/6/1.

12 Notley Abbey – Long Crendon, Bucks. An inventory of the furniture and effects, pictures, china, glass, silver, linen and outdoor effects – the property of Sir Laurence and Lady Olivier, Ralph Pay & Taylor, Valuers and Surveyors (April 1948) pp. 1–46. Vivien Leigh Archive, Notley Abbey, Correspondence, Deeds and Plans (3), THM/433/6/1. pp. 9–14.

13 Ibid., p. 27.

14 Ibid., p. 3; p. 25.

15 Invoice Sibyl Colefax & John Fowler Ltd., Mayfair, to Vivien Leigh, 9 February 1950; Invoice from Mrs Shields Ltd – Decoration, Furniture, Upholstery,

Sloane Square, 24 May, 1950. Laurence Olivier Archive, Personal Papers, Domestic accounts, 1944–1953, Add MS 78940.

16 Leigh, quoted in letter to Cecil Tennant from Alex Waugh of Piccadilly Fabrics and Furnishings Ltd., Alex (16 September 1950). Laurence Olivier Archive, Personal Papers, General Correspondence relating to the Cheney Walk and Durham Cottage properties, Vol. LXXII, 1938-1956ADD 79837.

17 Ibid.

18 Anthony Havelock-Allan in interview with Charles Drazin c. 2000. Courtesy of Charles Drazin – private collection.

19 '"Fame-in-a-Night" Girl's £50,000 Film Contract – Stage and Screen Star at 19' Bulletin, 18 May 1935. Vivien Leigh Biographical File, V&A.

20 Kyle, Molly, 'Return To Elegance', Unidentified Magazine, p. 56.Vivien Leigh Archive, THM/433/4/2/7.

21 Ibid.

22 Ibid.

23 Denis Martineau, 'Suggestions for Room Planning and Good Lighting Arrangements', Ideal Home, July 1935, Odhams Press: London, pp. 6–7. Anon, 'Glass in Decoration', Ideal Home, May 1935, Odhams Press: London, p. 435.

24 Amelia Clough, 'For the Beginner in Housekeeping', Ideal Home, June 1935, Odhams Press: London.

25 Kyle, Molly, 'Return to Elegance', Unidentified Magazine, p. 56. Vivien Leigh Archive, THM/433/4/2/7.

26 Ibid.

27 'Vivien Leigh' The Bystander, 12 June 1935. London: Illustrated Newspapers. Vivien Leigh Biographical File, V&A.

28 '"Fame-in-a-Night" Girl's £50,000 Film Contract – Stage and Screen Star at 19' Bulletin, 18 May 1935. Vivien Leigh Biographical File, V&A.

29 The cottage interiors described in Anderson's article often evoke the material architecture of the theatre and her description of 'one of Roger Furse's original costume drawings from The Skin of Our Teeth, in which Vivien Leigh played the lead' explicitly draws connections between Leigh's roles on stage and her home (Anderson, 1949: 9).

30 These examples are from copies of Woman's Own (London: George Newnes Press) published between April and June 1949. (British Library collections.)

31 'The Compère – My Friends the Stars', Unidentified Publication. Vivien Leigh Archive, THM/433/4/2/7.

32 'The Oliviers at Home', Picture Post, 5 April 1941. London: Hulton Press, cover. Vivien Leigh Archive, THM/433/4/2/7.

33 Ibid.

34 'Vivien Leigh, Home from Hollywood's High-Lights Wears the Simplest Summer Wardrobe by Molyneux', Unidentified Publication, p. 35. Vivien Leigh Archive, THM/433/4/2/7.

35 Ibid.

36 Ibid.

37 'The Compère – My Friends the Stars', Unidentified Publication. Vivien Leigh Archive, THM/433/4/2/7.

38 Correspondence regarding Vivien Leigh's kitchen from Rex Publicity (January 1958). Laurence Olivier Archive, Papers and correspondence relating to requests to Vivien Leigh. Add MS 80624.

39 Articles on the homes of Boris Kochno, Somerset Maugham, Basil Spence, Derek Hill featured in *House and Garden* (London: Condé Nast) between March and August 1958. (British Library collections.)

40 Advertisements for West London Galleries and Charles Howard Decoration appeared in *House and Garden* (London: Condé Nast) in March and April 1958. (British Library collections.)

41 Kyle, Molly, 'Return To Elegance' Unidentified Publication, p. 56.Vivien Leigh Archive, THM/433/4/2/7.

42 Ibid.

43 'Vivien Leigh, Home from Hollywood's High-Lights Wears the Simplest Summer Wardrobe by Molyneux', Unidentified Publication, p. 35. Vivien Leigh Archive, THM/433/4/2/7.

References and bibliography

Anderson, Elizabeth (1949) 'The Laurence Oliviers' Home', *Woman's Own*, 25 March, George Newnes Press: London.

Anon (1958a) 'The Oliviers Off Stage', *House and Garden*, May, Condé Nast: London.

——— (1958b) PAUL Kitchens 'Vivien Leigh ... Chooses a Paul Guaranteed Kitchen', *Ideal Home*, October, Odhams Press: London.

Bingham, Adrian (2004) *Gender, Modernity, and the Popular Press in Inter-War Britain*, Oxford: Oxford University Press.

Burns, Richard (1947) MEET THE STARS No.1. Richard Burns introduces – Vivien Leigh and Laurence Olivier, Griffs: London.

Clark, Kenneth (1986 [1977]) *The Other Half: A Self-Portrait*, London: Hamish Hamilton.

Coleman, Terry (2005) *Olivier: The Authorised Biography*, London: Bloomsbury Publishing.

Cornforth, John (1985) *The Inspiration of the Past: Country House Taste in the Twentieth Century*, London: Viking in association with Country Life.

deCordova, Richard (1991) 'The Emergence of the Star System in America', in *Stardom: Industry of Desire*, ed. by Christine Gledhill, London: Routledge, pp. 17–29.

Dixon, Simon (2003) 'Ambiguous Ecologies: Stardom's Domestic Mise-en-Scène', *Cinema Journal*, 42 (2): 81–100.

Dolan, Josephine (2007) 'Post-war Englishness, *Maytime in Mayfair*, Utopian Visions and Consumer Culture', in *Englishness, Diversity, Differences and Identity: A Collection of Original Papers Exploring Notions of Englishness*, ed. by Chris Hart, Kingswinford: Midrash Publications, pp. 45–53.

Dyer, Richard (1998 [1979]) *Stars*, BFI Publishing: London.

Ferguson, Marjorie (1985 [1983]) *Forever Feminine: Women's Magazines and the Cult of Femininity*, Aldershot: Gower Publishing.

Giles, Judy (2004) *The Parlour and the Suburb: Domestic Identities, Class, Femininity and Modernity*, Oxford: Berg.

Jones, Chester (2000 [1989]) *Colefax & Fowler: The Best in English Interior Decoration*, London: Barrie & Jenkins.

Kiernan, Thomas (1981) *Olivier: The Life of Laurence Olivier*, London: Sidgwick & Jackson.

Kuhn, Annette (2009) 'Film Stars in 1930s Britain: A Case Study in Modernity and Femininity', in *Stellar Encounters: Stardom in Popular European Cinema* ed. by Tytti Soila, John Libbey Publishing, New Barnet, pp. 180–194.

Lasky Jr, Jesse and Pat Silver (1978) *Love Scene: The Story of Laurence Olivier and Vivien Leigh*, Brighton: Angus & Robertson.

McBean, Angus (1989) *Vivien: A Love Affair in Camera*, ed. By Adrian Woodhouse, Oxford: Phaidon Press.

Price, Hollie (2015) '"A Somewhat Homely" stardom: Michael Denison, Dulcie Gray and refurnishing domestic modernity in the postwar years', *Journal of British Cinema and Television*, 12 (1): 25–44.

Robyns, Gwen (1968) *Light of a Star*, London: Leslie Frewin.

Street, Sarah (2000) *British Cinema in Documents*, Routledge: London.

——— (2005) '"Got to Dance My Way to Heaven": Jessie Matthews, art deco and the British musical of the 1930s', *Studies in European Cinema*, 2, (1): 19–30.

——— (2007[1997]) *British National Cinema*, London: Routledge.

Vickers, Hugo (1988) *Vivien Leigh*, London: Hamish Hamilton.

Walker, Alexander (1994 [1987]) *Vivien*, London: Orion Books, reissued in 2001.

White, Cynthia L. (1970) *Women's Magazines 1693–1968*, London: Michael Joseph.

Index